switching careers

OTHER KIPLINGER BOOKS

Kiplinger's Practical Guide to Your Money
Kiplinger's Practical Guide to Investing
But Which Mutual Funds?
Making Money in Real Estate
Buying & Selling a Home
Financing College
Retire Worry-Free
Retire & Thrive
Dollars & Sense for Kids
Next Step: The Real World
Home•ology
Taming the Paper Tiger at Home
Know Your Legal Rights
The Consumer's Guide to Experts

KIPLINGER'S BUSINESS MANAGEMENT LIBRARY

Business 2010
Customer Once, Client Forever
Raising Capital
Taming the Paper Tiger at Work
Cash Rules
Hunting Heads
Parting Company
You Can't Fire Me, I'm Your Father

Kiplinger offers excerpts and tables of contents for
all of our books on our Web site (www.kiplinger.com)

For information about volume discounts contact:

Cindy Greene
Kiplinger Books & Tapes
1729 H Street, N.W.
Washington, DC 20006
e-mail: cgreene@kiplinger.com
202-887-6431
cgreene@kiplinger.com

switching careers

Career Changers
Tell How—and Why—
They Did It.
Learn How
You Can, Too.

Robert K. Otterbourg

KIPLINGER BOOKS
Washington, DC

Published by
The Kiplinger Washington Editors, Inc.
1729 H Street, N.W.
Washington, D.C. 20006

Library of Congress Cataloging-in-Publication Data

Otterbourg, Robert K.
    Switching careers : career changers tell how and why they did it : learn how you can too
/ Robert K. Otterbourg.
      p. cm.
    Includes index.
    ISBN 0-938721-86-0 (pbk.)
      1. Career changes--United States--Case studies. I. Title.

HF5384 .O874 2001
650.14--dc21   2001038034

This publication is intended to provide guidance in regard to the subject matter covered. It is
sold with the understanding that the author and publisher are not herein engaged in rendering
legal, accounting, tax or other professional services. If such services are required, professional
assistance should be sought.

First Edition. Printed in the United States of America.

9 8 7 6 5 4 3 2 1

Kiplinger publishes books and videos on a wide variety of personal-finance and
business-management subjects. Check our Web site (www.kiplinger.com) for a
complete list of titles, additional information and excerpts. Or write:
  Cindy Greene
  Kiplinger Books & Tapes
  1729 H Street, N.W.
  Washington, DC 20006
  e-mail: cgreene@kiplinger.com
To order, call 800-280-7165; for information about volume discounts, call 202-887-6431.

Dedication

To Susan, Laura, Katherine, Kenneth and Sam. Each helped me in their own way to focus on many of life's challenges.

Acknowledgements

C areer changing has hit home. Kathy, my daughter-in-law, after 15 years as a self-employed interior designer, has returned to college, the first step toward certification as a high school history teacher. *Switching Careers* was written for folks like Kathy who are planning to change careers.

Interviewing the folks profiled in this book was a delightful experience. What challenging stories they have to tell. I want to thank them for their candor in discussing their careers, past and present.

As you'll soon discover, no two career changers took the same route. You're in for a treat as they describe how they made their workplace and lifestyle journeys.

A few people were particularly helpful. As a Colgate University alumnus, I turn regularly to Jim Leach, assistant to the president of the university. Jim's a great guy who has an uncanny way of ferreting out the names of interesting folks to interview. Greg Duncan works here in Durham as director of admissions and student life at Duke Divinity School. I appreciate his forthrightness in describing the intricacies of a world I know little about—a divinity school education and the challenges facing ministers.

I am also grateful to the Durham County Public Library for stocking the books and magazines not available on the Internet. As I've noted in previous books, a library is a great place to do research when you're tired of staring at a computer screen.

Once again, I'd like to thank my literary agent, Edward Knappman of New England Publishing Associates. Among his many fortes, he moves a book project along and handles the numerous business and contractual arrangements.

This is my third book that Kiplinger Books has published in a relationship that dates back to 1993. It's time to give "gold stars" to David Harrison, publisher, and Patricia Mertz Esswein, managing editor. David has a flair in knowing how to work with authors in bringing books like *Switching Careers* to market. His involvement does not stop. David actively supports authors in the years after the first edition, first printing, hits the market. Once again, it has been a joy to work with Pat. She brings tact, skill and a personal touch to editing a manuscript, and she asks the questions, often humorously, that need to be asked so that the resulting book is both accurate and easy to read.

Thanks, also, to Priscilla Taylor, who smoothed the manuscript; to Allison Leopold, who proofed the pages; and to Heather Waugh, who created such an attractive cover and interior design for the book.

Lastly, thanks Susan. Did you know when we met more than 40 years ago that you would be listening to me years later drone on about the people I've interviewed and the things that I've learned?

ROBERT K. OTTERBOURG
Durham, North Carolina

Table of Contents

Introduction

When I was a kid back in the 1950s and early '60s, careers were forever.

The family breadwinners I knew (almost all of them fathers, with hardly an employed mom among them) all had a career, and it was the same occupation they started as young adults, right out of college or military service. And the odds were great that they would pursue this career for the rest of their lives.

There were exceptions, of course. There were fathers about whom it was whispered that "he can't hold a job," or "he's a restless sort," or "he doesn't know when he's well off." These men would change employers, or even occupations, every few years. Rather than admire their ambition, or at least respect their courage, we assumed something was wrong with them, and we felt sorry for their families—even if mom and the kids seemed otherwise "normal" and perfectly happy.

It was an era of relative economic stability. Workplace loyalty was strong, and it was a two-way street. Workers didn't change jobs very often, because people with a good, decent job considered themselves lucky. And employers rarely laid off employees who were doing satisfactory work, just because of a slump in the business. Sure, temporary layoffs and callbacks were always part of the blue-collar world of manufacturing, but "downsizing" and "restructuring" hadn't yet crept into the consciousness of white-collar managers.

But today, all of this is a long-ago memory. In the '60s and '70s Americans discovered "self-fulfillment" and "following your dream." After wrenching recessions in the late '70s and early '80s, the U.S. embarked on a nearly two-decade economic expansion that tightened labor markets and improved the employment prospects of restless career-changers. Back when workers were plentiful, an employer could easily pass over an applicant whose checkered résumé branded her as a "job jumper." But in a labor-tight world, job changes and career switches are no longer an automatic taint.

These days, career switching is as American as . . . fast food. I have to admit that I have no personal experience with it. I've spent my entire working life in one occupation, journalism, although I did work for three different news organizations in the 13 years before I came to Kiplinger in 1983.

But I count among my acquaintances many successful career changers, including a teacher who became a dealer in rare musical instruments, a nurse who is now a news photographer, a corporate lawyer who became a minister, and a businessman who now teaches high school calculus.

In his wonderful new book, *Switching Careers*, Bob Otterbourg will introduce you to many fascinating men and women who have pulled off successful career changes of their own. And he will give you lots of practical advice on how you can do the same—after plenty of planning, counseling and financial preparation.

Some folks profiled in this book made major financial sacrifices to pursue their dreams, while others dramatically boosted their earnings by following their gut instinct and changing careers. Either way, they all are happy they gave it a try. Perhaps you will be, too.

My best wishes to you as you contemplate—and perhaps embark on—a life-changing decision to hitch your wagon to a very different star.

Knight Kiplinger

Knight A. Kiplinger
Editor in Chief, *The Kiplinger Letter* and
Kiplinger's Personal Finance magazine

Preface

Ears prick up whenever I mention the subject of this book, career-changing, at a social gathering, and although I'm not a career counselor, my listeners pepper me with questions: Am I too old to change? How do you know that the new career is the right one? I wonder what my spouse, business associates and family members will say when I tell them?

I shouldn't be surprised that there is so much interest in career changing. Career changing is closely tied to workplace and lifestyle expectations. We expect to find meaning, challenge and satisfaction in our work lives, to be able to balance our work with our personal lives, and to earn enough income to support our varied goals. Career changing has few foes. Even career loyalists want to know if there is a more satisfying way to practice their trade.

At the heart of this book are profiles chronicling the experiences of nearly 70 career changers. For many people, deciding to switch careers begins with or proceeds from a series of casual conversations, like those I just described. They're sniffing out the possibilities. Reading this book is like attending a cocktail party with 70 career switchers who have accepted the invitation to share their stories with you.

All of the people I interviewed have changed careers within the past few years, although some are still in professional or graduate school on their way to their new careers. The profiles illustrate that a career change need not be some radical lifetime event. Through planning, making the change can appear to be a seamless transition. Other changeovers, like going to medical school at age 36, are more dramatic.

The profiles contain much more than an array of biographical information. From the profiles, readers can learn by "observing" how to plan a career change, how to pay for it and live while making it, how to anticipate the effects that career change will have on one's mate and children, how long it may take to get established in a new field, how old skills carry over to new careers, and, finally, how to fulfill the desire for greater control over one's life.

> **The older the career changer, the more deliberate the decision must be. Families, mortgages, and other obligations often temper risk.**

The profiles teach by example, but they also inspire and reassure. No two career changers have ever done it exactly the same way. They weigh their desires, skills and experiences, obligations and commitments, relationships, tolerance for risk and debt, and they devise their own recipe for success in a new career. The decision to change careers is sometimes all head, and absolutely rational; at other times it is all heart, and sometimes even divinely moved. The determination for some people was literally made overnight, while others mulled over it for several years.

I wrote *Switching Careers* for men and women who are old enough to have some career experience but young enough to have ample time to enjoy the fruits of their career changing for another 15 to 20 years—people ranging in age from just under age 30 to the early 50s. To some people the simple solution to career dissatisfaction is to retire in one's 50s and avoid the challenge of a career change. Others acknowledge this challenge in their 30s and 40s and switch careers. By age 65 they will have spent, say, the first 20 years of their work lives as a banker and an equal number of years teaching school.

Career changers under age 30 have the luxury of switching careers on a whim. Tired of teaching or writing advertising copy? Why stick it out? Nothing is really lost by going in a different direction, even if it means returning to college for another degree. Obligations are relatively few. But the older the career changer, the more deliberate the decision must be. Families, mortgages, and other obligations often temper risk.

That's why all the people I've profiled here are in their mid 30s to early 50s, except for Jerome Watson-Peters (profiled in chapter 2) who, now 60, relates his transition from overseas missionary priest to a life outside the church as a carpenter.

The people who are profiled had to pass an unofficial litmus test. I avoided celebrities and people who had made a killing in the stock market. What interested me were men and women who had had to make some personal or financial sacrifice to switch careers. The profiles sketch what their challenges were, and how they confronted them.

As this book points out, there is no simple way to describe career changing. The lawyer who leaves a law firm partnership to join a corporate legal staff or the teacher who switches from public- to private-school education are both career changers. They tweaked their careers with a simple U-turn. Other career changers are bolder, making a 180-degree career turnaround, often requiring years of additional education or entry into a risky venture. Whatever the strategy, most career changers adhere to one basic tenet: "Everything I've ever been, I still am."

Given their careers and interests, nearly all of the career changers presented in this book could easily have been profiled in two or more chapters.

Besides the profiles, each chapter in *Switching Careers* has two other key elements: (1) information on demographic trends in the market for the profession or set of skills being discussed and (2) tips for getting started in a particular line of employment, plus references to organizations, Web sites, and schools that might be helpful.

Although no index exists to describe the level of career changing today versus that of a decade ago, I sense that the tempo has picked up in recent years. Why? Thanks to diverse trends from downsizing to telecommuting, we are no longer a nation of "company men," dedicated to a single company or career for life. Our computer- and communications-driven society has opened up new lifestyle and workplace vistas hardly dreamed of a generation ago. The office, once a cubicle or suite in a corporate setting, is now as near as the spare bedroom down the hall. Even in the most formal offices, workers have shed formal or traditionally "corporate" attire in favor of an informal attire. Sportcoats once unheard of in a large law firm or commercial bank are considered acceptable attire. There's a sense of freedom and possibility in the air, fueled, too, by the so-called talent shortage. The advantage has been to the job seeker. What's more, we are impatient. We ask ourselves, Do we want to be lawyers, bankers, teachers, computer programmers, or chefs for the next 20 or 30 years? The answer "no" motivates many of us to switch careers.

Wherever possible, I've provided statistics to illustrate the possibilities and limitations of shifting careers. In some instances, I relied on data supplied by recognized industry or professional organizations. I also referenced two excellent U.S. government resources: the Department of Education's National Center for Education Statistics (www.nces.ed.gov) and the Labor Department's Bureau of Labor Statistics (www.bls.gov). Both agencies use real numbers that have been thoroughly researched.

Above all, my intention was to strike a balance so that how-to advice and statistics did not become overwhelming. The profiles provide the balance—showing real-life examples of men and women who switched careers in their late 20s to early 50s.

Finding the Career Changers

I feel at home writing about career changing. I switched careers in my mid 50s, when after decades in public relations, I decided once again to use my writing skills to write on subjects that interested me, the reason I had originally gone to journalism school.

Finding people to interview was never a problem. No need for me to prepare an Internet solicitation: "A writer needs names of people who have changed careers." I discussed my book with some close friends, who produced names, often their relatives. Through long-time New York friends, Dorothy and Larry Arnsten, I met Will Russell, their son-in-law (profiled in chapter 4), a computer technician who now owns an electronic recording studio. Deborah and Stanley Slom's son-in-law, Greg Vimont (profiled in chapter 5), a former commercial photographer, is a database modeler. From my college friend, Jack Travis, and his wife, Mary, I met Peter, their son (profiled in chapter 2), a litigation lawyer and law-firm partner, now an executive-search consultant. My wife and I play tennis with Tom and Marilyn Sawyer, whose son, Steven (profiled in chapter 7), a one time Navy helicopter pilot, practices corporate law. In fact, Peter Travis was exiting law about the same time that Steven Sawyer was graduating from law school.

The experiences of everyone that I've profiled, regardless of where they live, are illustrative of the challenges and rewards of career changing.

For other names, I didn't have to go much further for assistance than members of my family. My wife, Susan, suggested some students in one of her Duke continuing-education courses; daughter Laura came up with career changers in law, medicine, Web management, and computer programming; and son Ken and daughter-in-law Kathy led me to their current next-door neighbor, who went from sales engineer to owner of a graphics-design firm, and a former neighbor, a dress designer turned film curator.

When I interviewed Lucia Greene Connolly, she suggested that I call her career-changing sister, Stephanie Greene. Greene then recommended her husband, George Radwan, another career changer. Thus one family produced three profiles.

There's strong military representation in the profiles. Scott Maitland, Glenn Ruffenach, and John Shemwell are service-academy graduates (West Point or Annapolis). They left the service in their late 20s or early 30s to pursue careers in business, journalism and teaching respectively. Ramona Ramirez and Cora Straight were in the Army for 20 years. They took early retirement when in their early 40s and now teach school.

The part of North Carolina where I live, which has with three large universities and a number of smaller ones, proved to be a rich resource. It is also home to a flourishing community of artisans and craft potters. But almost half the people profiled are from 16 states, and the experiences of everyone that I've profiled, regardless of where they live, are illustrative of the challenges and rewards of career changing.

Because *Switching Careers* is meant to help readers prepare for a career change, I have included Web sites for most of the organizations that were cited. Ten years ago, I would have used an organization's mailing address, telephone number, and a toll-free number. For this book, I assumed that most wannabe career changers will use the Internet to do their basic research.

I believe that career changing is a natural occurrence in an age when we seek workplace challenges, a better lifestyle, and an ability to explore different occupational opportunities, while facing the possibility of being downsized from our present job. So, as the Boy Scout's motto says, "Be prepared."

switching careers

Leaving Behind 'A Foolish Consistency'

WHEN MANY OF US WERE CHILDREN, OUR PARENTS asked us, "What do you want to do when you grow up?" This was a serious question demanding an equally serious answer. It was assumed that the choice was binding, often for the next 40 years.

This attitude no longer prevails because the lifetime company employee is a vanishing breed. The stigma against career changing is declining, many workplace and lifestyle options considered radical a generation ago are becoming acceptable, and the financial risks are decreasing.

All types of estimates bounce around on the rate of career changing taking place in the U.S. At best, these figures are stabs in the dark. What is known, thanks to the outplacement firm of Drake Beam Moran, Inc.'s recordkeeping, is that job turnover is high—the average 32-year-old has held nine full- or part-time jobs since entering the workforce, and only one in three workers has held the same job for five years.

A willingness to switch careers harmonizes with what is occurring in other parts of our lives. We are peripatetic. We jet here and jet there. We begin college at one school and graduate from another. We dispose of products rather than repair them. We lease cars to avoid a long-term commitment, and, tragically, we sometimes even marry with the same attitude.

Even within the Roman Catholic church, an institution known for constancy and tradition, there are career changers. WEORC (an Old English word for work) is an association of former priests and nuns who moved from the full-time ministry to other work; its goal is to help these people make the transition to a civilian workplace. Its members include numerous social workers, teachers and even some lawyers and computer experts.

Writing in late 1999 in the *New York Times Magazine* before any signs of any economic slump, Michael Lewis said that ditching a job is today's secret for success—yet it runs contrary to the theme of persistence we were taught early in life, depicted in books like *The Little Engine That Could*. "Perseverance, like honesty, is one of those values that wind up being over-rated because no one likes to be seen making the case against them. But that case—the case for being a quitter—is, in the current economic boom, looking stronger every day...The taste for quitting is both cause and effect of the current boom, which is about people starting new things." Lewis's favorite quitters are Michael Dell and Bill Gates, both of whom left college before graduation to start, respectively, Dell Computer and Microsoft.

Bob McDonald and Don Hutcheson, career consultants and founders of the Highlands Program, a think-tank operation (www.highlandsprogram.com), consider 30 to be a pivotal age when an "I want it all—now" attitude starts to prevail. Donald and Hutcheson observe that turning points in adult working lives occur every seven to ten years, and with each turning point comes crisis—the feeling that everything in our lives is falling apart. During this period, people ask themselves some key questions: If my career keeps going in the same way it is moving now, where will I be in ten years? Why? What do I want to add to my life to make it fuller? What else should I be doing?

Reasons for Career Switching

The reasons for wanting to switch careers range from the practical to the idealistic. Most likely your list will include many of these factors:

- **You have a chance** to escape a fast-lane urban lifestyle.
- **Your job and career** no longer interest you; maybe they bore you.
- **The idea of 20 more years** in the same career has lost its appeal.
- **You would like to work** in a different part of the country.
- **You've been downsized,** fired, canned, pinked-slipped, or whatever you—and your former employer—want to call it.
- **You see little room** for future growth in your current career.
- **You feel a "calling"** to do something else in life.
- **You want to be** your own boss.
- **You want to convert** a hobby into a full-time occupation.
- **A "glass ceiling"** has frustrated your corporate-career plans.
- **You want to tap into** the more dynamic growth that is expected in other careers.
- **You don't want to work so hard.**
- **You want to blend** two or more careers into a single career, as Shawna Lemon (profiled in chapter 3) has done. Now working as a patent attorney with science-based clients, she has found a career that blends her doctorate in pharmacology with her law degree.
- **You realize** that you jumped into a first career without really thinking or were pushed into it by your parents.
- **You have inherited** or are about to inherit a tidy sum. Some economists predict that trillions of dollars will change hands from parent to child over the next 20 years. Along with this windfall will come the possibility of greater economic freedom and an ability to change careers without suffering a serious financial setback.
- **You want** to "make a difference." Regardless of the position or title they hold, many people feel that they are only cogs within their organizations, and they want to do work that they view as important—for their own sake and, often, for the sake of others.

Once you've made the decision, the next step is to do something proactive, said Lisa Schwartz, a career coach in Cary, N.C. The options are clear: Stay in the same job in the same organization, change jobs and companies, or switch careers.

Fewer Financial Consequences

Today we can take for granted that when we leave a job, we will take at least part of our retirement savings with us. Pension plans once were rather rigid. Changing jobs for any reason until being vested, which took seven or ten years, resulted in the loss of a pension. It might have been okay to change jobs once, but doing this every few years resulted in financial hardships in retirement because little had been placed in the pot to draw upon at age 65.

Along came a reduced vesting period. Now, depending on your company's plan, you can fully vest in five years, meaning you take 100% of your funds with you if you leave after five years (or sacrifice 100% if you leave before then), or in seven years, during which you gradually vest (you leave with nothing in years one and two of employment, and take 20%, 40%, 60%, 80%, and finally 100% if you leave in years three through seven respectively). Now, we also have defined-contribution pensions, such as 401(k)s (funded by your employer and you), individual retirement accounts, or IRAs (funded by you), and the hybrid cash-balance plan (fully funded by the employer, though the money is contributed to individual employee accounts). Although a vesting period is still required, when you leave your employer, you can take along any money that you have contributed and the vested portion of your employer's contributions. You can transfer the money to your new employer's plan, if the new employer accepts it, or transfer the funds to a rollover IRA and independently handle the investment in such a way that it avoids any governmental penalties, taxes and withholding.

In short, people have become free to change jobs or careers without totally sacrificing the retirement income they've earned. Yes, you would receive higher pension income in retirement— maybe 50% more—if you stayed with the same company and the same pension plan for 30 years than you would if you switched employers every five years throughout the same period. But the reality is that most people today won't stay with an employer that long, and with smart use of 401(k)s, IRAs and Keoghs (the 401(k) for the self-employed), you can achieve the retirement income you need and want. (For more on financial planning for your retirement, see *Retire Worry-Free* from Kiplinger Books.)

Debunking a Few Myths

MYTH: Most career changers know which direction they'll take.
FACT: It isn't a straight-line process, like getting a job. There's a lot to explore, and a variety of options to test before taking the plunge.

MYTH: A career change is a radical shift.
FACT: Who says it has to be a 180-degree shift? For some, it is a seamless transition, with a new career based on a previous one and little or no additional training required. To illustrate, the engineer who works as a sales engineer continues to use technical know-how.

MYTH: Success in changing careers requires youth.
FACT: It's relatively easy to change careers before age 30. Little is lost because so little time has been spent in the workplace. Age complicates things. Skilled workers in their 30s point out that they have too many personal and family responsibilities to consider switching. And workers age 40 to 49 often note that they're too old to learn a new skill. Consider this: Why delay changing careers at age 40 because you think you're too old? In four years, you'll be 44 whether you switch careers or not.

MYTH: Changing careers means starting with a clean slate.
FACT: Nothing is further from the truth. Like it or not, the work you've done in the past leaves indelible traces on a new career. Jennie Keatts (profiled in chapter 2) is a hotel and travel marketer turned jewelry designer. Her past marketing skills influence how she promotes her line of jewelry.

MYTH: The first step is to quit working, and then prepare for a career change.
FACT: Who says the transition needs to be so drastic? While medical schools typically require a full-time academic schedule, many professional and graduate schools and community colleges conduct evening and weekend classes. Hands-on skills as a chef or carpenter can be learned by moonlighting. There's little reason that co-workers or a boss need know that you're

considering a new career. This way you learn while you're still a paid employee.

MYTH: Career changes can be made within a company.
FACT: According to career coach Bill Stanley of Ridgewood, N.J., the concept of the corporate generalist is disappearing in larger organizations, and when it exists, only a relatively few up-and-comers are picked as intracompany career changers. We live in an age of specialization. Companies are not interested in turning marketing types into purchasing agents. They'd rather hire purchasing agents. As a result, companies that are downsizing employees in one sector are hiring workers for another part of the operation. There are two main exceptions to this phenomenon: In smaller companies, managers and professionals are still expected to handle multiple assignments, and the military continues to move personnel into different types of jobs and leadership positions as part of its officer-leadership training.

MYTH: Central corporate offices are passé.
FACT: In some ways work has become decentralized. It is being done at home by telecommuters, part-timers, and contract employees. Employees like the arrangement; they work on their own turf yet maintain corporate relationships and benefits. It's a cottage-industry environment with "Fortune 500" guidelines. As you consider changing careers or work arrangements, don't disparage the future of centralized offices, however. New and even larger corporate headquarters are being built both downtown and in suburbia. When climbing the management ladder is a career goal, telecommuters need to accept the idea that with new corporate responsibility comes an obligation to work in an office.

What About Downsizing?

Downsizing continues to be a fact of life throughout corporate America, in bad times and good. Just ask the thousands of employees who have been downsized by many of the leading Fortune 500 companies and those who have been part of massive layoffs at technology companies. Many will find comparable jobs; others will use the "opportunity" to shift gears and embark on new careers.

The American Management Association (www.amanet.org) has been monitoring downsizing trends since the mid 1980s. Past AMA surveys of layoff data from more than 1,400 midsize to large companies show that job elimination has continued to

PLANNING FOR A CHANGE

Planning a job jump soon? If so, start asking questions and gathering information about your current employer's pension plan and possible new homes for your money. Request investment and IRA information from banks, mutual funds and brokerage firms that are candidates for your rollover IRA business. You'll want answers to these questions about your retirement plan at work:

- **Must the payout** be in cash or can securities be rolled directly (without being liquidated) into an IRA or other qualified plan? If your employer is a major corporation, and you own company shares in your retirement account, you may want to hold on to that stock. Find out whether shares can be transferred with little or no cost. If taking your money means the stocks must be liquidated, however, you may want to stay put.
- **Can you leave the money** where it is? If your current investments are performing well, and the rules permit you to stay in the plan even

if you leave the company, that's an option you'll want to consider. Do some comparison shopping with similar types of investments offered elsewhere before you decide. If the money is in a growth-stock fund, for example, how are other growth-stock funds performing?
- **How long will it take** to complete the payout/transfer process?
- **What portion of the payout,** if any, represents voluntary after-tax contributions that you've made? This portion can't be rolled over into an IRA, but it won't be taxed when you withdraw it.
- **If your 401(k) money** is managed by one of the major fund families, such as T. Rowe Price or Fidelity, and you've been happy with your investments, you may be able to exit your company plan but stay within the fund family. Some fund firms will arrange an inside rollover—a quickie transfer from your 401(k) into a rollover IRA at the same firm.

be disproportionately higher among supervisory and managerial ranks, and among professional and technical employees. AMA notes that more than one-third of the companies surveyed in 2000 were eliminating employees in one sector of their operation while concurrently creating new jobs in another part of the organization.

The most vulnerable workers are those in middle management, who neither produce goods or services nor make top-management decisions.

As long as the urge to merge exists, the urge to purge will continue. Whatever the reason—financial, strategic, or marketing—companies will, on a selective or wholesale basis, prune their workforce. The most vulnerable workers are those in middle management, who neither produce goods or services nor make top-management decisions. Those employees who have portable skills, or skills that are needed in high-growth companies, have little difficulty in finding new jobs. Workers with outdated production, office, and managerial skills will no longer be in demand.

Outplacement consultants Challenger, Gray & Christmas (www.challengergray.com) contend that survivors of downsizing actually have an opportunity to move up a notch within the organization. "You are more than a mere survivor. You were chosen, selected, handpicked, whatever you want to call it, to help lead the company's future. The management of the company has clearly spoken that you meet the criteria of someone it wants to keep." There is considerable truth in the Challenger statement, with this exception: Today's downsizing survivor might become tomorrow's victim.

The Conference Board, a business research organization, (www.conference-board.org), has noted that downsizing foments employee stress and lower morale. "Surviving employees may worry that their jobs are next, mourn the loss of co-workers, and harbor anger toward the company. A decrease in productivity, less loyalty, more accidents, higher health care costs and higher personnel turnover follow in the wake of a round of layoffs."

While fear of downsizing may not be productive for the employer, it can be most productive for the employees. It shakes managers from their complacency and inertia by forcing them to look for either a new job or a new career, according to the outplacement consulting firm of Lee Hecht Harrison (www.lhh.com), which found that by the time the pink slips arrived, a majority of the surveyed managers were already preparing for what they assumed would be bad news.

Where Are the Jobs?

Anywhere in the high-tech sector looks like a good bet. Even with the demise of many dot-com companies, by 1999 the high-tech workforce had more than five million employees, having added about 1.2 million workers in six years. It's also the nation's best-paid industry, according to the AEA (previously the American Electronics Association; www.aeanet.org). In its 2000 salary survey, the AEA reported that the median starting pay for software and electronics engineers was approximately $46,000. Even with the economic downturn early in 2001, along with corporate downsizing, high-tech job openings still need to be filled.

For women in the technology job market, the news is mixed. According to current findings by the Bureau of Labor Statistics, women held only 28% of technical jobs, although the proportion of women in the workforce approached 50%. And that problem is not about to disappear, predicted Kimberly Jenkins, president of the Internet Policy Institute (www .internetpolicy.org). "Girls may be going into graphics design, but they are aren't going into computer programming or advanced computer science courses that will enable them to get high-level tech jobs." This is an anomaly, considering that the number of women attending medical, law, and divinity schools is nearly equal to, or in some instances higher than, the number of men.

Business-school graduates have plenty of reason to crow. The starting salaries for recent graduates from 11 top-tier business schools, such as Northwestern, Chicago, Michigan, Dartmouth, and Pennsylvania, jumped from $69,387 in 1996 to $86,540 in 2000. To top it off, nine out of ten of the surveyed graduates received a signing bonus that averaged $23,000. Consulting is the career preference for one-third of the graduates, followed by marketing and management, investment banking, and finance. A mere 3% of MBA students became entrepreneurs.

Of course, not everyone will want to switch into a high-tech career or obtain an MBA for a fast line into a successful business career. There will always be lists of the top-ten careers—paying the most or providing the greatest opportunities, and they're fun to consult. But, ultimately, you will have to pick the career that makes the most sense for you. Simply put, not everyone is cut out to get an MBA or a law degree, or to make more money, even when forecasters expect employment growth in these fields to continue. Throughout this book, people who have changed careers provide other reasons for their actions.

Multiple Career Changers

Some career changers are multiple career switchers. Over the last 30 years, Jane Hamborsky, now in her early 50s, has been a concert clarinetist, photographer, farmer, chef and restaurant proprietor, accountant, and financial manager.

"From an early age, I played the clarinet. I was trained as a classical musician, but I still wanted to be a jazz clarinetist like my uncle. My father was a lawyer who had a large music library of jazz; my mother played the flute and jazz piano. I really don't know how I became a classical musician."

After graduating from the University of Michigan in 1970 with a degree in music, Hamborsky earned a master's degree from the Manhattan School of Music. In 1974, at the age of 24, she made her debut at Carnegie Hall. Her life centered on the concert stage. She was one of the founders of the Orpheus Chamber Orchestra, taught clarinet at the Mannes School, and gave private lessons.

Then Hamborsky decided to concentrate on performing; she gave up teaching and most of her private music students. To pay her New York City living expenses, she put a long-time hobby, photography, to work in a photo lab at a photo shop. "I ran the darkroom for a few hours each morning. The owner paid me a percentage of the darkroom business. It gave me

POINTS TO REMEMBER

- **People want jobs** in which their work is a contribution that makes a difference to others.
- **Some career changers** want to escape the fast corporate lane.
- **Persevering** at something you don't care about can be a waste of time.
- **Greater retirement-savings** options are a boon to career changers.
- **Lifetime employment** with a single employer a thing of the past.
- **Inherited money** may accelerate the pace of changing career,
- **Downsizing** continues to permeate corporate life, providing an opportunity for workers to overcome career inertia.
- **Telecommuting** opportunities will continue to grow, but management-track opportunities for telecommuters may not. Someone will continue to "mind the store" at corporate headquarters, many of which are currently being built.
- **Don't become fixated** on "fast" and "slow" growth fields. These descriptions are just averages. Every field needs new, good, and inspired workers.

time to practice and take lessons.

"I didn't have a degree in business, but I have a good head for numbers. I left the photo store and started my own business doing portraits of musicians at $400 to $500 a photo session." Frequent traveling with the Orpheus Chamber Orchestra caused her to consider some other career options. She wanted to settle down. Visiting Chapel Hill on a concert tour, she decided to leave New York for North Carolina.

Back again she went to photography. She had three different photography-related jobs over six years at the Ackland Art Museum, the Art Department at the University of North Carolina, and the UNC photo lab, where she was production manager.

In the mid 1980s Hamborsky decided to branch out. She bought a 20-acre farm to do organic hydroponic farming, work she could do in conjunction with her job at the photo lab. It was a brief interlude. No sooner had she bought the necessary farming equipment than the concept was scuttled. She sold the property after her partner, Maggie, hurt her back.

Hamborsky's creative interests hadn't waned. She left her UNC job and started Maggie's Muffins, a coffee bar and bakery shop, a forerunner of today's coffeeshop craze. The business grew, expanding into deli products and along with the growth in business came a new name, Maggie's Café & Espresso Bar. Nine years later, in 1996, the difficulty of hiring and keeping good employees led Hamborsky to sell the restaurant.

> **Despite frequent career changes, Hamborsky saved money and invested it wisely. Money was not the issue in selecting her next line of work.**

Throughout this period and during her different careers, she played with several chamber music orchestras.

Despite frequent career changes, Hamborsky saved money and invested it wisely. Money was not the issue in selecting her next line of work. Already a parishioner, choir member, and volunteer at the Chapel of the Cross, an Episcopal Church in Chapel Hill, she was asked to work as its paid bookkeeper when severe financial irregularities were discovered. Hamborsky's work caught the attention of the Episcopal Diocese of North Carolina, which hired her as its interim business manager. Not wanting to commute 40 miles to Raleigh, she turned down a permanent job.

A proven financial manager, Hamborsky was hired as the Chapel Hill Tennis Club's accountant and was soon named club manager. "Even though I had never managed a membership club, I'm a fast learner. If someone had asked me 20 years ago what I would be doing at this time, the last thing on my list would be a tennis-club manager. It's a job where I can finally learn how to play tennis.

"There is a relationship between all the things I've done in the past. Handling financial matters for a church is very much like the manager's job at a tennis club. In both jobs you deal with members. My other jobs in restaurants, photography, and music taught me how to work with different people, and being a chamber musician gave me experience in filling different roles. Sometimes you're the soloist, and at other times you play a supportive role." With all her varied careers, one thing remains constant: She is still a classical clarinetist.

What's Ahead

As a youngster, I used to thrill at the predictions made by two 16th-century thinkers, Leonardo da Vinci and Nostradamus. How could they predict, I asked myself, the advent, centuries later, of airplanes, television, and other contemporary tools?

In a way this is the problem facing society today: How do we predict what products and services will be in demand in 20 years, and how the changes will affect careers? As recently as the early 1990s, only a few people other than some industry insiders could describe the workings of the Internet or artificial intelligence, or forecast growth patterns with any accuracy. In 1993, Colgate University's computer network served a constituency of approximately 3,500 students, faculty, and administrators and processed 15,000 e-mail messages a day. Who could have guessed that seven years later, e-mail communications would have mushroomed to 350,000 messages a day? What we do know is that technology will continue to create new career opportunities.

Planning Your Mission and Strategy

PETER TRAVIS, A CAREER PLANNER WHO IS PROFILED later in this chapter, describes his strategy this way: "I mulled over the concept of becoming a headhunter for about nine months before I decided to make the leap from law. I then began to get my financial world in order, scheduled a physical, went to the optometrist for new glasses and to the dentist. My wife Terrie did the same with our daughters so the benefits program at the law firm would pick up the costs. When I resigned, I gave the firm 30 days' notice, and I worked the full 30 days."

Of course, some hotshots don't understand the importance of planning. A few weeks after interviewing Travis, I conducted a continuing-education workshop at Duke University for potential career changers. One participant had just left a career in investment banking in search of something different to do, but she couldn't understand why planning was necessary. 'Just pick up and start something new' was her suggested tactic. As a single woman with strong savings to sustain her, she could afford to be something of a gunslinger.

For most career changers, such a cavalier attitude rarely works. Most of those described in this book had responsibilities—a spouse, children, and mortgages. Planning is a critical step in the career-changing cycle. It is particularly important if salary is cut or eliminated so that the career-changing family member can attend graduate or professional school, set up a business, or switch to a lower-paying, yet desired, career.

What's Your Mission?

If you're in your 30s or 40s, you probably can't afford another false start in your work life. Good research is a key to making the right choice. You'll probably begin with how-to books, such as this one, and data available on the Internet. But you'll be wasting your time if you haven't first asked yourself: What's my mission? Answering that question requires researching yourself.

Fay Krapf is a career coach (also profiled later in this chapter) who learned many of the basics as her job changed from potter to corporate organizational development manager and business school instructor to her current specialty. Like most other career coaches, Krapf helps her clients prepare an inventory of who they are and what they want from their lives. "I ask them to identify 25 achievements in their lives and careers. At first these clients find it difficult to do." The list helps them to evaluate different career-changing options.

Krapf also asks her clients, Do you want to go to school to learn new skills? What about your salary needs? Will you work for less money? She helps her clients understand the level of sacrifice they are willing to make. Why say you want to leave a $100,000-a-year job to become a social worker if you're not prepared to live on a $30,000 salary?

Marjorie Long, a counselor at Crystal-Barkley (www .careerlife.com), a career-counseling firm based in New York City, encourages the career changer to dream. "Allow yourself to play with your ideas until you are able to construct a statement of what you want to accomplish with your life. A portion of this can be the object of your work. Make that the mission statement of Me, Inc."

William Bridges, a career and job-transition specialist, developed his own checklist to help career changers focus on the key issues:

- **What do you want?**
- **How will you achieve it?**
- **Where do you want to go?**
- **What are your capabilities, realistically?**
- **What are your present and latent skills?**
- **How's your energy level?**
- **Do you have an ability to "sacrifice" to reach a goal?**

Take Some Tests

When John Selix (profiled in chapter 9) left his job as news director at a radio station in Eugene, Ore., he turned to the career-services office at his alma mater, the University of Oregon, for help. His goal was to teach school. A Myers-Briggs Type Indicator test showed that teaching was indeed one of Selix's strengths; the positive findings helped him confirm that he was moving in the right direction.

Myers-Briggs fits each test-taker into one of 16 different personality groupings, depending on where each falls on a scale between each of four opposing pairs of traits: extroverted versus introverted, sensing versus intuitive, thinking versus feeling, and perceiving versus judging. (For example, one such personality type is the ENTJ, which stands for extroverted, intuitive, thinking, and judging.) The use of Myers-Briggs and other personality tests helps each of us learn what motivates us.

There is no shortage of tests to gauge latent talents and skills. In the early 1990s, in order to learn more about career testing, I spent two days taking tests administered by Johnson O'Connor Research (www.jocrf.org), a nonprofit research group with offices in ten large metropolitan areas nationwide. Far from revealing some exotic and hidden traits, the tests simply confirmed that I should stick with writing and discard any idea of being a late-blooming lawyer or artist. The cost for ten hours of testing and a results assessment is nearly $500.

Vocational or career tests need to be administered, analyzed, and reported to the test-taker by a career counselor. College or university career services often administer these tests for a fee, or they can recommend an appropriate independent organization.

Try It On for Size

Paid or volunteer workplace experience can provide insights into new career possibilities and will help prove to prospective professional schools that you're not merely an older student who lacks a realistic notion of the profession you hope to enter. Some employers find "job hoppers" suspect. Admissions officers also are wary of people who collect degrees or whimsically decide at age 38 to be a lawyer.

In medicine, premed programs weed out romantics. Nearly all career-changing students spend one or two years taking chemistry, physics, and biology courses and labs just to qualify to apply to med school. Columbia University's postbaccalaureate premed program required Michael Stern (profiled in Chapter 8) to work or volunteer in a health care–related facility before entering medical school. Stern did both; he was paid to coordinate several clinical drug trials and he volunteered in a hospital emergency room.

Dub Gulley (profiled in chapter 3) took a different route. Gulley, a retail novice before opening an outdoors-clothing store, designed his own on-the-job training program by picking up practical know-how in visits to similar stores in Virginia and North Carolina.

Temporary work is one option for career changers to consider. Temp workers are no longer the Kelly Girls of yore, primarily women doing secretarial and lower-level administrative work. Temporary work, though still heavily skewed toward administrative jobs, has broadened into nursing, engineering, and law. Temp work can give career changers a way to make money during the transition period and provide a peek into a different career. It's like tryout practice: a way to play ball without signing up for the team.

Back to School?

Late bloomers continue to return and flower in the classroom. According to the U.S. Department of Education's National Center for Education Statistics (www.nces.ed.gov), 20% of all undergraduate students are between the ages of 30 and 50. In that age group, 45% of the enrolled graduate students are studying for master's and doctorate degrees, and another 20% are seeking professional degrees, such as law and medicine.

Many of these students are undoubtedly career changers, and others need an undergraduate, graduate, or professional degree to qualify for promotions or different jobs within the same career track. In addition, an unknown number of students are taking noncredit or nondegree technical or how-to courses at community colleges and vocational schools to change careers. Greg Vimont (profiled in chapter 5) switched careers from commercial photographer to computer systems analyst. Vimont was not interested in another college degree but rather a certificate to qualify for an entry-level computer job. He took two courses each semester at Columbia University; after eight courses he was ready for the job market.

Online programs provide an attractive option to potential career changers who don't have the time to attend class, or don't want to let employers know about their future plans.

Anyone considering returning to school will have to decide between a daytime and an evening program. Evening programs take longer to complete but they permit students to work at daytime jobs, which is a good way to avoid or at least lower tuition loans. To attract students, graduate business schools offer degree candidates day, evening, weekend, and online schedules.

Online programs, which are being integrated into a growing number of higher-education curriculums, provide an attractive option to potential career changers who don't have the time to attend class, or don't want to let employers know about their future plans. Courses cover a broad range of topics. UCLA (www.ucla.edu), true to its location in the center of the entertainment industry, offers a series of online entertainment courses, including writing publicity for radio and television and writing a business plan for an entertainment or new-media venture. New York University (www.scps.nyu.edu) has created a virtual college with courses as diverse as the elements of fiction writing and legal issues in electronic commerce.

The MBA program at Duke University's Fuqua School of Business (www.duke.edu), which combines classroom attendance with interactive education, typifies what's happening in graduate business and management education.

Long-distance education via online computer conferencing and e-mail has become popular at the University of Maryland (www.umuc.edu/online), which offers bachelor's degree programs in accounting, English, psychology, and several computer specialties, and graduate degrees in business, computers, and international management. According to the university, students can get their degrees "without setting foot in a classroom."

Career changers who downshift from the lifestyle of a big-city lawyer or corporate executive to practice in a small community should expect to earn less money.

And, of course, there are still programs designed to teach vocational skills and get you back into the workforce as quickly as possible. The French Culinary Institute in New York City (www.frenchculinary.com) appeals to career changers with an advertisement in the *New York Times* telling readers about its six-month "total immersion" program: "It's how, in just six months, you could cook up a whole new career."

Financial Planning

Money facilitates changing careers. As ministers, teachers and craft workers will attest, there's a good chance that the pay in some careers will not match the pay of one's previous work. Career changers who downshift from the lifestyle of a big-city lawyer or corporate executive to practice in a small community should expect to earn less money. Bob Calhoun (profiled in chapter 12) experienced a shortfall in his take-home pay when he closed his profitable home-building company to join the Habitat for Humanity staff.

Financial planning means putting money aside before changing careers. Sally Bates (profiled in chapter 6), brown-bagged lunch to cut her expenses before entering divinity school, and for the next three years she lived off savings, proceeds from stock that she sold, and the cash value of her life insurance—and enjoyed a free room in a friend's home.

How the Military Helps Career Changers

Since the early 1990s, the armed forces have been steadily downsizing in an orderly procedure that gives personnel ample time to prepare for civilian careers.

Unlike most corporate employees, 20-year military veterans can retire as early as their late 30s. Others leave the military in their 30s with five to ten years of service.

The transition to the civilian workplace is a particular challenge to people who have never had a full-time civilian job. They need to learn how the job market functions. Those who have portable skills have a decided edge. An Air Force computer technician or systems analyst can move with ease from the military to civilian workforce. The same can't be said for a tank commander, although he or she may have significant leadership skills. As an artillery officer in Vietnam (who was also a West Point graduate) once told me, there are no comparable jobs in corporate America for former artillery officers.

John Shemwell (profiled in chapter 9) is more fortunate than most former members of the armed forces. When he left the Navy, he had a master's degree in nuclear engineering and related naval experience—a body of knowledge that would be valuable in the civilian job market. His engineering degrees from the Naval Academy and Johns Hopkins University were ideal credentials for a job with General Electric. Eighteen months later, however, Shemwell left GE to teach high school physics.

Ramona Ramirez (also profiled in chapter 9) became a teacher, too, although by a different route, after retiring from 20 years' service in the Army. The Defense Department's Troops to Teachers Program enabled her to earn a college degree that took her from administrative work in the Judge Advocate General's office to a public-school classroom.

Career-service offices are located on most military bases to help personnel plan the next step months, if not years, before the date of separation. Contrary to its name, the Army Career & Alumni Program (www.acap.army.mil) provides career services, primarily job-hunting assistance workshops, counseling, and job leads to active personnel before they leave the armed services. Career-placement services are also available through the Non-Commissioned Officers Association (www.ncoausa.org), the Retired Officers Association (www.troa.org), and the U.S. Department of Veterans Affairs (www.va.gov).

A key academic incentive available to former military personnel is the G.I. Bill of Rights, which furnishes up to 36 months of paid education for a degree, certificate, apprenticeship program or correspondence course.

A Handy Planning Checklist

- **Look at the "10 best career lists"** but don't be put off by the rankings. There's always room for one more good person.
- **Take an aptitude test** to confirm that your passion for a new field is validated by the facts.
- **Moonlight in the same field or a similar one** to acquire new skills and experience and to sample what the work will be like before you burn any bridges.
- **Start saving money.**
- **Cut expenses.**
- **If relocation is part of the plan,** spend time in the area in advance to see what life there is really like. For example, from a brief business trip, Phoenix or Denver might seem like pleasant places to live, but what do you really know about either community? You might have a son who requires a school with special-education facilities. If your spouse is professionally employed, what are the job opportunities for him or her? If you like to fish, how many miles will you have to drive to find a decent stream or lake? In short, do your homework. Pick up and visit Phoenix or Denver for a few days. Go beyond the chamber of commerce and real estate company literature. Visit residential areas. How costly are homes? Visit the special-education school. Read the classified section of the daily newspaper for a few weeks to learn more about the job market. In short, do your homework. Even then, relocating is a gamble. But at least find out all you can about a new area before asking a moving company for an estimate on relocation costs.
- **Use the Internet and how-to books** to gather basic facts about

the field you would like to enter, but supplement these facts through one-on-one talks with earlier career changers in the same field.

- **Don't change careers unless your mate supports the idea.** A new career often means less income, different and perhaps longer working hours, and in some instances a different lifestyle that will affect everyone in your family.
- **Let teenage children know and appreciate what's taking place.** They should understand how career changing differs from getting a job. Explain to them how career changing may mean less money for what they consider to be "necessities."
- **Be prepared to increase your level of personal debt** to offset the cost of buying or starting a business or attending graduate school.
- **Don't expect a strong return on investment.** A lawyer turned minister, or a corporate manager turned schoolteacher has little chance to duplicate previous earnings. Both accept the trade-off in order to do something that they really wish to do.
- **If the career change involves self-employment,** be prepared to say goodbye to corporate health and benefit programs.
- **Expect your leisure hours to decrease** during the transition.

POINTS TO REMEMBER

- **Good planning** starts long before a career change is executed.
- **Begin with** a personal mission statement.
- **Discuss the career switch** in advance with family members, including teenagers.
- **Personality tests** are a good way to take a look into the mirror.
- **Paid or volunteer work** provides opportunities for insight into a new career.
- **A large proportion of** people over age 30 go to college to pick up new skills.
- **The armed forces** have programs for people who leave or retire from the military in their 30s and 40s.
- **It is important** to start cutting costs and increasing savings if you contemplate a career change.

Some People Who Made the Change

Some workers have little time to prepare a career change. On Friday, they lose their job; over the weekend, they launch a new career. Most others take a bit more time to change careers. Good planning is mandatory for anyone other than young people in their early 20s who have few obligations. People who are 30 to 40 years old need a plan that foresees family needs and likely problems during the switch. Why invest time and money to switch careers without a written plan? The people described in this chapter, as well as most of the others in this book, didn't shoot from the hip; they prepared and used a roadmap to guide them throughout their transitions.

PREACHES WHAT SHE PRACTICED

Fay Krapf
CAREER COUNSELOR WAS ONCE A POTTER

Fay Krapf, now in her early 50s, is a career coach who practices what she preaches. She spent 15 years making and selling pottery before taking the plunge into a new career.

Krapf attended Texas Woman's University to become an occupational therapist, and while in school, took a pottery course and loved it. Two years later she left school without completing her degree in order to marry. She moved to Maine to join her husband and got a job as an occupational therapy aide. After a year, she and her husband moved to Iowa so she could finish school, getting a degree in home economics, a good skill when you know that the next year would be spent raising children. Then back to Maine and three children later—a daughter and two sons—"I started doing pottery again while the children took naps."

Krapf bought her own kiln and joined the local Potters Guild. She outgrew her small in-house workroom and built a standalone studio on the family's property. She called her business Friedendorf Pottery Studio, incorporating the German phrase for Peaceful Village.

As her pottery business grew, she moved again; this time she opened her studio a few miles from home, in Bryant Pond, which Krapf describes as a busy summer tourist destination

about 90 miles northwest of Portland. She started an apprenticeship program, employing about three apprentices at a time. Her apprentices worked nine months to one year learning how to be potters. In return for their work, they received free room and board plus a small stipend.

> After 15 years as a potter, Krapf had begun to ask herself, Is this what I'm going to do the rest of my life?

When Krapf developed tendonitis, she was forced to find another career. The transition actually had started before the onset of the condition, but tendonitis accelerated the process. After 15 years as a potter, Krapf had begun to ask herself, Is this what I'm going to do the rest of my life? To answer the question for herself, she used a form of career development that she had previously used in her studio with her apprentices—one that she has applied ever since in her teaching, consulting and coaching work.

Krapf wanted to learn more about communication to handle the challenge of dealing with the apprentices. Looking for some practical solutions, she took courses at the National Training Institute in Bethel, ten miles from her home, where she learned about human inter-action, team building, conflict manage-ment, and diversity. Little did she realize in dealing with her apprentices that she had arrived at the threshold of another career.

Relocating to California while her husband did graduate work, Krapf earned a master's degree in organizational behavior from the California School of Professional Psychology in Berkeley. Getting this degree was an important step if she intended to find a job in this field. After returning to Maine, she opened her pottery studio only during the summer tourist season. Two years later, in 1989, she closed it permanently.

For the next two years, she worked as director of organizational develop-ment for a utility company, where she initiated a succession planning and career development program, coached executives and managers, and provided employee-development and organizational-development services. Corning, in upstate New York, hired her to consult with its various plants and divisions as it redesigned its organization to be more efficient and team-oriented.

After living most of her life in Maine and the Northeast, Krapf wanted to relocate to a warmer climate. Selecting Chapel Hill, N.C., she spent five years at the University of North Carolina's Kenan-Flagler Business School teaching an undergraduate business communi-cations course and a peer-counseling course in the MBA program. Her UNC schedule enabled her to serve as a consultant and career-transitions coach, helping people who had been laid off from their jobs.

Krapf then left UNC to work full-time as a career coach, leading individual and group sessions on ways to conduct a job search, improve interviewing techniques, and negotiate successfully with current and prospective employers.

"I continue to apply to career coaching and counseling many of the lessons that I learned 15 years ago."

To Krapf, nothing she has learned is ever discarded. "I continue to apply to career coaching and counseling many of the lessons that I learned 15 years ago, when I was supervising my pottery apprentices."

Once or twice a year, Krapf teams up with Lou Raye Nichol, another organizational-development consultant, to run a one-day continuing-education seminar on leadership for women at Duke University. "Using my experiences in two distinctively different careers, I show younger women managers how to develop an action plan to help them achieve their goals."

LIVING—AND LEARNING—ON THE ROAD

Louis Reyes
NAME THE CAREER AND HE'S DONE IT

Luis Reyes, in his early 50s, has been changing careers all his life.

"I've worked as a school handyman, waiter, restaurant manager, fireman, bank teller, security driver, welder, and bread-truck driver, and I spent four years on active duty in the Coast Guard." Reyes is from Puerto Rico and has two children in their 20s from a previous marriage. He graduated from high school and has about 28 college credits.

An important change in Reyes' life occurred in 1989, when he met Joyce, a recent college graduate from South Carolina, at a Coast Guard Reserve training session at the Great Lakes Naval Station in Illinois. Unlike Reyes, Joyce had two college degrees, one in philosophy and the other in biology. If they were to get married, Reyes needed a more stable job.

What they did sounds somewhat bizarre: They became truck drivers because they saw the opportunity for good wages that would provide them with the savings they needed for a sound financial start to their marriage. Luis already had a commercial license, and Joyce got her license so that she could share driving. They bought a large rig on a lease-back arrangement with a Charlotte-based trucking company and crisscrossed the country for ten months a year. Working at least ten hours a day,

they drove an average of 20,000 miles a month and paid the lessor $2,000 a month. They often spent as much as seven months on the road before returning to their home base in South Carolina. The truck was home, office, and just about everything else. Their personal expenses, which were minimal,

"We set practical goals, and we created a plan so we would be independent."

included food, insurance, gasoline and maintenance and some other operating expenses. They considered their truck to be a small business, in which they were partners and co-workers.

This was hardly the lifestyle one might expect of a 25-year-old woman who had planned for a science career. "We knew there was going to be a change of lifestyle for both of us from the moment we decided to get married," Reyes says. "We set practical goals, and we created a plan so we would be independent." Trucking made the dream possible. The bottom line: profits of $900 to $1,200 a week.

Neither of the pair felt that truck driving would be a social or professional obstacle because they did not expect to be driving for more than a handful of years. Even so, it took them about nine years of driving to tire of it. When the couple was on the road, they were basically on call 24 hours a day, since the truck had a small compartment behind the driver where the co-driver could sleep. "You need a break to rest, shower, exercise, to sleep in a real bed and to relax. When we were in Chicago, we visited visit the museums, and in San Diego we went to the zoo. It was all part of our learning experience."

Long trips gave Luis ample time to think of the kinds of work he'd like to do when he was no longer a trucker. He read and listened to tapes on subjects as diverse as philosophy, psychology, and religion, getting ready for the day when he hoped to get a college degree.

About two years before they sold their truck, they started to put down local roots. They rented an apartment in Durham, N.C., and bought their first furniture. "We picked Durham," Luis said, "because it has a hospital (Duke Medical Center) where Joyce could work, and a growing Spanish population where I knew I could work as a translator and attend college."

After nine years, as truckers Joyce got a job at Duke as a technician doing behavioral research, while Luis became a part-time certified court translator in Durham County working for the judge and prosecutor. "I like this work since it is exacting. It requires me to be precise in English and Spanish." While waiting for approval for a full-time translation job with the state, he sells sporting goods at Wal-Mart. He has not yet pursued his dream of a college degree.

Since the couple left trucking, their

"Nothing happens by accident—driving, the move to Durham, and my career. It's all part of a plan," declares Reyes.

marriage has broken down and divorce is imminent. But even with this turn of events, Reyes doesn't miss the life of a trucker. "Nothing happens by accident—driving, the move to Durham, and my career. It's all part of a plan. And I know I can find a job anywhere due to my diverse background."

BETTER THAN GOING TO COURT

Peter Travis

TRIAL LAWYER BECOMES AN EXECUTIVE-SEARCH CONSULTANT

Growing up in Topeka, Kan., Peter Travis, now in his early 40s, once thought he would be a physician like his father. But as a Vanderbilt University undergraduate, Travis was a premed student who had trouble with organic chemistry. He transferred to the University of Kansas, switched to business and English, and ended up at law school there.

"I clerked for a Topeka estate- and tax-planning firm following my second year in law school. I found that the work was the most boring aspect of law possible. When I graduated, I took a job with a new firm in Kansas City (Missouri), where I had clerked the previous summer." It was a relatively small firm consisting of a handful of former big-firm partners with a specialty in trial practice and litigation law.

A few years later Travis realized that although he and some of the other younger lawyers were the lifeblood of the firm, they were not being fairly compensated for their work. "We were working 70 or more hours a week. None of us were even close to a six-figure income while the senior partners were making several hundred thousand a year. They were hesitant to bring any of the associates into the partnership. It was a fight every time they did. When a new partner was named, the equity buy-in was oppressive."

In his eighth year at the firm, Travis became a junior partner. He had already decided that he wouldn't leave the firm until he was made a senior partner. "It's not a good idea to leave before then. Otherwise, people say that he or she left because they were not partnership quality. I considered other job

> **"I wanted to know if my parents thought I was crazy for leaving a profession that I had spent so much time and energy pursuing."**

opportunities but I had no desire to relocate."

Meanwhile, a variety of problems hit the firm. "It was hard enough doing battle in multi-million-dollar cases against highly skilled opponents, let alone to protect yourself against internal attacks." Travis left the firm in February 1995. His only regret now is that he didn't do it sooner.

Besides his wife, Terrie, Travis shared his thoughts with only a few others. "I sought my parents' counsel. I wanted to know if they thought I was crazy for leaving a profession that I had spent so much time and energy pursuing. Not only did they encourage me, but they offered to act as a financial backstop if necessary."

Travis fortunately had an ace in the hole. Several years earlier he had been asked to fire a younger associate with whom he was friendly in the law firm. "It was one of the hardest things I ever had to do, but I must have done it right because we remained friends. He went into recruiting, and he offered me a job."

Travis now works for the Howard Group, an executive-recruitment franchise of Management Recruitment International, where he specializes in recruiting sales, marketing, and operational workers for jobs in group-insurance benefits and managed care. The firm has only eight employees and is located in Overland Park, less than 15 minutes' drive from Travis's home.

Whereas he spent three years training to be a lawyer, his executive-search education was acquired on the job. "Being a lawyer has been helpful. Law taught me how to be disciplined, and it showed me how to be organized."

The skills that Travis used in trial preparation—anticipating questions and issues, figuring out what could possibly go wrong and preparing for it—have proved useful. "Our firm just landed the exclusive recruiting contract for a national organization. The flat-out paranoia ingrained in me and my training as a lawyer to filter out the junk and focus on what really matters to the client are transferable in how I prepare

for a recruitment assignment."

In contrast to his more than nine years in a law firm where his goal was to become a partner, Travis enjoys his work in the Howard Group without any partnership or managerial responsibilities. He was able to leave his job in law, where he made $76,000 a year, because he and his wife were saving money long before he left the law firm, living in a small house and keeping a lid on their expenses. This frugality was critical, because Terrie, a social worker

"Being frugal, I had the luxury of making the change from a steady paycheck to a 100% commission job."

and teacher by profession, was staying home with their two daughters.

Although Travis was at times indecisive about quitting the law firm, Terrie supported the career switch from the outset. "Terrie and I discussed whether she should return to work. We felt that we had already given up many of the material goods our peers possessed, so that she could stay home with our daughters when they were young. To change that philosophy would have invalidated the sacrifices we had already made.

"Being frugal, I had the luxury of making the change from a steady paycheck to a 100% commission job. This was a big part of planning my transition. We budgeted and 'guesstimated' my income as a head-hunter for the first 12 to 18 months. I wasn't even sure I'd like or be any good in this work.

"The first year, however, was frankly worse than even my most conservative estimate. As it turned out, my income was cut in half. To be truthful, I cannot say with certainty that we would have made the same decision had we been equipped with 20/20 foresight, because there was more financial stress than I had anticipated. Had it not been for my resolve to distance myself from the legal profession and Terrie's support, it would have been a dismal time."

By 2000, Travis's five-year gamble was beginning to make financial sense. "The first year I made $31,000, the next year $68,000, and the following year $89,000. I now make over three times what I made as junior partner." And the family has a bigger house.

DENVER TO RURAL NORTH CAROLINA

Jennie Lorette Keatts
FORMER CORPORATE MARKETER HANDCRAFTS JEWELRY

"Do you have a fax?" I asked Jennie Lorette Keatts? "Of course, I do," she said. "Remember, I used to be in sales and marketing." That was a surprising reply from a jewelry designer in Seagrove, a rural town tucked away in the rolling hills 40 miles south of Greensboro, N.C. But Keatts, in her mid 40s, has only recently been making gemstone jewelry for a living. "I'm now doing what so many people living in the fast lane would like to do," said Keatts.

Born in Mont Vernon in southern N.H., Keatts attended the University of Colorado in Boulder, where skiing was one of the attractions of student life. "At the time, I thought I'd be a veterinarian, but my science grades weren't good enough to get accepted into vet school. I realized this early on, so I switched to environmental biology. My professor said this was a good thing to study since there were good job opportunities."

After graduating from Colorado, she put her college education aside and started a catering business with a friend. "Cooking was and still is a passion. I like to cook Northern Italian and Asian food. It comes naturally to me without any formal training. It was a good thing I had a job as a cocktail waitress, since I needed the tips to survive as a caterer. After one year, I called it quits. Our

biggest mistake was that we didn't have a business plan."

Moving to Denver, Keatts became a bartender in the state's largest Sheraton hotel, and over the next six years she had a series of jobs in the hotel. By the time she left, she was Sheraton's beverage manager, supervising three

She left corporate stress in Denver but brought along 15 years of marketing know-how.

bars, and wine and liquors for several dining rooms and the banquet department at a salary of $35,000.

When her boss, the Sheraton general manager, took a similar job at the Warwick International Hotels, also in Denver, Keatts followed. Six years later, she was the hotel's senior sales and marketing executive with responsibilities for supervising these functions at some of the other Warwick hotels in the U.S. and Europe.

By now, Keatts had a reputation in the international hotel and tourism field, and she was hired as manger of tourism-industry sales for the Denver Metro Convention and Visitors Bureau. The job required her to travel to Europe and Asia about 30% of the time.

Keatts married in 1989, and at about the same time, she became interested in jewelry design as a hobby and a way to relax. "I had a studio in our house. When I was divorced a few years later, I moved into a one-bedroom apartment and a closet became a studio."

By the late 1990s, job pressures had mounted. Passed over for the Visitors Bureau top job, she considered a similar job in North Carolina, but quickly dropped the idea because the salary was considerably less than the $55,000 she was then making in Denver.

Fate stepped in. Keatts's younger sister, Pam, is a potter who had moved to North Carolina in the early 1980s to study and work. She married Vernon Owens, another potter and a member of a family that has produced a number of notable potters in Seagrove over the past 80 years.

Up to this point, jewelry design had been a hobby for Keatts, but Pam helped her make it a new career. Pam began sending miniature pots and figurines to Denver, which Keatts combined with beads and silver to make necklaces, the forerunner of her current jewelry pieces. In 1998, this "extracurricular" work netted her about $2,000. In 1999, she took Pam's advice, quit her job, and, on July 4, arrived at Jugtown, the name of the Owens family's operation. "I didn't make the same mistakes I did with my catering business," Keatts says. "I had a business plan. I had my own tools."

Jennie Keatts describes her work as "turning mud into gems." She fashions hand-rolled and -cut pieces of pottery or natural stones and semiprecious gemstones, and fashions them into necklaces, pins and earrings. She uses glazes made at Jugtown, a feature of the Owens' pottery. The pieces cost from $40 to $170.

Keatts was fortunate in many ways. Jugtown provided all the facilities she needed: a guest house adjacent to her sister's home, a studio, a drying room and kiln, and a showroom and museum. As a result, she was able to break even

"I didn't make the same mistakes I did with my catering business. I had a business plan. I had my own tools."

in less than six months; after one year she was ready to start paying herself a salary. Single, with no children and an ability to live modestly, she lived on savings during this period. However, she did not become a jewelry designer as a way to recapture her former income, but to gain independence and to run her own business.

Keatts left corporate stress in Denver but brought along 15 years of marketing know-how, including skills for preparing a brochure and sales kits, and for doing market research on the Internet. "My intention is to build the business my way. My business is primarily wholesale. I started off by marketing to a few museum shops, which I visit. I also use e-mail to contact other suitable retail outlets. My Web site (www.jlkjewelry.com) is used primarily for stores whose owners or buyers are unable to see the jewelry themselves." After one year in business, her jewelry is being sold in some 15 museum shops, from North Carolina to Massachusetts.

In late 2000, Keatts signed a contract with an online specialist, Wholesalecrafts.com, to bring her jewelry to the attention of several thousand prequalified potential customers. "The cost for this service is less than attending one wholesale show, and although meeting in person and being able to handle the jewelry is important, I know from past marketing jobs that this service will save me lots of time. To me, time is money and more time to spend in design and production. Even so, I still do two North Carolina retail shows."

Everything Keatts does, from buying equipment or supplies to billing and payment, is supported by her computer. She researches design and fashion trends on the Internet, a carryover from her previous jobs. After a year in business, she took a month's "vacation" and built two Web sites—one for Jugtown and the other for her business. And when it came time to illustrate the Web sites, she used her digital camera to photograph her jewelry and the Owens' pottery.

RETURNED FROM THE FAR EAST

Jerome Watson-Peters

FORMER MARYKNOLL PRIEST FINDS A NEW IDENTITY AS A CARPENTER

For many career changers, the transition merely involves moving from one occupation to another, but not so for Jerome Watson-Peters, now in his early 60s. Switching careers meant breaking ties with an institution that he had embraced emotionally and vocationally for nearly 40 years. Watson-Peters' experience is akin to that of career military officers and enlisted personnel who go from a disciplined workforce and lifestyle to civilian jobs with different traditions and expectations.

At the age of 10, when many boys of his generation wanted to be firefighters, pilots, or baseball players, Watson-Peters, reared in Mishicot, Wis., a small town 80 miles north of Milwaukee, had already decided to become a priest. In high school, he shifted his goal from parish to missionary priest, and started training for the career of a Maryknoll overseas missionary.

Ordained at age 26 from the Maryknoll Seminary in Ossining, N.Y., he was assigned to Mindanao, the second-largest island in the Philippine Archipelago (slightly smaller than Tennessee). To communicate with the local population, Watson-Peters learned Cebuano Visyan, a dialect spoken on Mindanao.

After 13 years, Watson-Peters returned to the U.S. for seven years to serve as a Maryknoll recruiter, educator, and fund-raiser in Cleveland, Los Angeles, and San Francisco. Denied a visa to work as a priest in Indonesia, he journeyed to Nepal and began the opening round of a career shift. Nepal was a totally different challenge for a missionary priest. In contrast to the

After a retreat and 16 weeks of counseling, he knew it was time to step out of the priesthood and into his own identity.

Philippines, where more than 80% of the people are Roman Catholics, Hinduism is the national religion in Nepal. This meant that Watson-Peters and other Maryknoll missionaries had to avoid proselytizing and many other of their priestly duties.

The break in his focus on missionary work began in his mid 50s, when he attended a retreat for Maryknoll priests in Southeast Asia at which he discovered that he was no longer comfortable working as a missionary. He returned to the U.S. for 16 weeks of counseling, after which he concluded he no longer wanted to return to Nepal. "It was time to step out of the priesthood and into my own identity."

Waiting for the Vatican hierarchy to release him from his priestly vows, Watson-Peters returned to Mishicot, and for the next nine months worked as a laborer in a foundry. Physical work was nothing new to him. "I always liked staying in shape. In the Philippines, I rode a motorcycle on jungle paths, and often walked 30 to 40 miles visiting parishioners."

In addition, he had learned carpentry as a youngster, and enjoyed working with his hands. At one point as a priest, he had taken a course in small-motor repair, a skill he had thought would be invaluable if he was going to be assigned to Indonesia, where priests visit parishioners by motorboats that are often in disrepair.

During this transition period he considered what to do as a "civilian." He had to have a paying job. Other than anticipation of small social security payments and other government benefit programs, based solely on his token Maryknoll salary, Watson-Peters had no financial resources to support him in his retirement years.

Unlike some priests who are trained health care specialists or educators, Watson-Peters was a generalist. "While I felt that I was good at the work of mission education, fund-raising, and recruitment, I am more of a hands-on guy and I love hard physical labor. As a priest, I was convinced of Maryknoll's mission. I felt that I could 'sell' the product effectively. If I had had another

such 'product' to sell, I might have considered sales or administrative work."

By the time he was discharged from his vows, in October 1997, he had left Mishicot and was working as the assistant director of a large program for the homeless in Middletown, N.Y. He had also married Carolyn Watson, a clinical social worker whom he had met years earlier while living in Mindanao. As part of their marriage vows, they combined names.

Watson-Peters left Middletown for

During this transition period he considered what to do as a "civilian."

Framingham, Mass., and a job as a full-time maintenance worker at the Learning Center for the Deaf where Carolyn was already a staff social worker. A year later, he changed from full- to part-time status, and set himself up as an independent carpenter.

Then Watson-Peters took another important step, this time purchasing a house in Framingham. This was the first time that he had ever owned or co-owned a home, or had lived so long in one place. "Since childhood, I'd been taken care of, first by my parents, then at seminaries, and as a priest. It's exciting doing things for myself after so many years of living a sheltered life. It's as simple as when I went back to Mishicot, and I was living by myself, I had to learn how to cook."

John Brown Jr.

CLASSICAL AND JAZZ BASS PLAYER LIKES LITIGATION

Ask John Brown Jr., age 30, for a résumé, and he sends you Brown, the classical and jazz musician, and Brown, the May 2000 graduate of law school. Variation is a key to his two careers, law and music.

Brown grew up in Fayetteville, N.C. "I've been playing the bass since I was nine, and at 14, I played with the Fayetteville Community Symphony Orchestra, and got paid $10 a performance."

Music plays no small part in his family's life. His sister Tammy, now a dentist, also plays the cello, and his mother plays the piano. Brown likes jazz and classical music, or just about any music without words.

A passion for music and an equal passion to be a lawyer made it difficult for him to select a college. "I went to the University of North Carolina's Greensboro campus because jazz musician Jack Burdow was teaching bass there. I would have gone just about anyplace to study with him." Brown originally declared a double major of music and prelaw, but music ultimately won out, and he graduated with a bachelor's degree in music performance. "I didn't take college seriously. I was more interested in music than my studies, but I did well enough to qualify later on for law school."

When Brown graduated from UNCG in 1994, the challenge he faced was akin to that faced by college athletes who want to play professionally yet also want to go to graduate school. Should they turn professional, deferring graduate school for several years, and face the risk of never continuing their education? Becoming a lawyer had not

Musicians, like athletes, must decide: Should they turn professional and face the risk of never continuing their education?

lost its luster, but at the time, Brown wanted to take advantage of his opportunities as both a jazz and a classical musician.

For the next three years, he played with the likes of Wynton and Ellis Marsalis, Rosemary Clooney, and Nnenna Freelon at the Kennedy Center and Carnegie Hall and on tours to Japan, Brazil, Mexico, and France. During the same period, he started, and managed, "In the Black," a regional jazz quartet. He also taught bass at Guilford College and was a member of the North Carolina Symphony Orchestra.

After ten years devoted to playing

and teaching music, he decided it was time to apply to law school. "If I hadn't gone then (in 1997), I might never have gone. I didn't want to have future regrets about not being a lawyer. I went to UNC because North Carolina is where I want to live. When I told friends my plans, they couldn't believe me. They asked how could I give up the good life and the overseas trips for law school. It's hard to tell them that the trips were work, and I was doing too much traveling. Law school is where I wanted to be, and being a lawyer is where I can help people."

Entering law school did not mean an end to Brown's musical career, but just a redirection of some priorities. He reduced his musical schedule but continued as a substitute with the North Carolina Symphony, performing in one concert a month and attending several days of weekday rehearsals prior to the weekend performances.

In Brown's first two years of law school, he was an adjunct professor of music at the North Carolina Central University in Durham, and in his third year, he had a similar position at UNC. "It required about eight hours of teaching and lessons a week. I had to practice about five hours a week myself. How could I ask students to practice if I didn't do the same?" Teaching also helped to pay some college expenses and to maintain his musical skills.

"My original goal was to be an entertainment lawyer. Sounded like a perfect way to mix my two main interests. But I discovered that entertainment law is actually paper driven—contracts and transactions, and that's not where I want to be. In the first year, we all took the same courses, but in my second and third years I took courses in trial advocacy, criminal procedures and medical malpractice." Brown enjoys the mental contrast between law and music, law being literal and music abstract.

For law students, the summer break is the time for internships. Summer

"If I hadn't gone to law school then, I might never have gone. I didn't want to have future regrets about not being a lawyer."

internships often produce permanent jobs. Brown worked his first summer for the North Carolina Attorney General's office and the following summer in a Greensboro law firm. In the last term at law school, he worked in the Orange/Chatham County District Attorney's Office. By then, he had decided he wanted to do advocacy and litigation.

In the spring of 2001, a year after graduating from law school, Brown opened a law office in Chapel Hill. He expects to build his client base by serving as a trial attorney and by handling wills and contracts. Music, however, won't take a back seat. He'll continue to teach bass students at UNC, Duke, and NCCU, and to perform with the North Carolina Symphony.

"I've never had a desire to work for a large and structured law firm or any organization," said Brown. "I want my freedom to practice law and play the bass. Music is what I am, and I have a need to preserve my own identity. Working for a law firm, and being required to bill 2,100 hours a year, is not who I am. My place is in court. I like litigation, the diversity of clients, and the drama of the courtroom. Remember, I am a performer, so I feel at ease in front of an audience."

Recycling Existing Skills

N THE OLD DAYS FOOTBALL BACKS COULD RUN, KICK, AND pass. No wonder they were called "triple threats." Although such versatility has long been forgotten, a similar spirit still exists in the workplace, especially among people, like Shawna Lemon, in her early 30s, who fuse different skills into a single career. For Lemon, obtaining multiple skills is consistent with a long-term career plan. For others the path is more haphazard but the end result is the same: One career piggybacked onto another, resulting in a hybrid.

"While I was in college, I really wanted to be a lawyer," Lemon says, "but my parents thought that law was no career for an African American woman. They felt it was a 'good old boys' network, and no place for me." As a premed major at Wofford College, in Spartanburg, S.C., Lemon had enjoyed science, but she had no passion for medicine.

By the time Lemon was in her mid 20s, she had earned a doctorate in biomedical sciences and pharmacology from the University of South Carolina and had gotten married. She lived in New York City and worked for Merck, marketing an osteoporosis product, while her husband, Brian, earned a law degree from New York University.

Even with a doctorate, Lemon never intended to do research. She wanted to use it in conjunction with training in another field, like law, in which her interest had never really flagged. "In my job, I found that there was only so much information that I could tell doctors. Merck's lawyers called the shots. I realized that law affects everything we do. I now had an incentive to go to law school."

Career changers are packaging experts, capable of blending two or more related or even unrelated skills into single career.

Lemon returned to the South in 1997 and entered the University of North Carolina Law School in 1998. She had a child in 1999. Her professional interest is intellectual-property law, a specialty that blends her training in bio-medical sciences and law. A summer 2000 internship with the patent-law firm of Myers Bigel Sibley & Sajovec in Cary, N.C., resulted in a job that started in September 2001, just a few months after her graduation. Described as North Carolina's largest independent intellectual-property firm, with nearly 25 intellectual-property specialists, Myers Bigel has a client base that includes a large number of pharmaceutical and health care companies.

Career Changers Are Packaging Experts

Career changers have a common bond; like Shawna Lemon, they rarely abandon their former careers even after they've completed their transition. For example, whatever field an accountant enters, he or she remains a numbers person. Past careers are an indelible part of everyone's signature; they show who you are and where you've been.

Career changers are packaging experts, capable of blending two or more related or even unrelated skills into single career. For example, Tom French, profiled later in this chapter, is a librarian who took a law degree as an entrée to his present career as a law-school librarian. David Hutchins (profiled in chapter 6) is a one-time commercial banker turned minister who has the skills to discusses business and personal finances with parishioners at his church.

Michael Reid, a Roman Catholic parish priest, (also profiled in chapter 6) is a former naval officer and attorney. In recognition of his legal training, there's a good chance that his church might send Reid to study canonical law.

It's not only virtually impossible to dump past work experiences, but it's short-sighted. Why totally disregard former skills when they provide a niche expertise and an invaluable gateway into many specialty careers? That's one reason why so many graduate and pro-fessional students are candidates for degrees that mix some combination of law, medicine, environmental sciences and business admini-stration into a hybrid career. Nearly a third of the class of 2001 at Duke University's Fuqua School of Business, for example, were under-graduate engineering or natural-science majors. After five to six years in the workplace as engineers or researchers, these MBA candidates have found a way to join two skills together.

> **It's not only virtually impossible to dump past work experiences, but it's short-sighted.**

Perhaps surprisingly, the current age of specialization puts a premium on workers with varied experience, a lesson that David Blomquist (profiled later in this chapter) learned. A former political reporter, Blomquist saw the opportunities available in online delivery of news, and, with news-gathering and editing skills in hand, became a new type of news editor: online reporter and editor.

While I was in the Air Force's Air Rescue Service, I had a roommate who was both a physician and a parachutist, trained to jump into remote spots to furnish medical treatment to downed airmen. In recent years, technology has been responsible for a spurt in hybrid careers. Consider the array of skills that astronauts need to perform multiple in-flight assignments.

An Opportunity to Be Creative

The generalist is dead; long live the specialist. In many ways, this is the motto in today's workplace. Chapter 7, on careers in the law, provides insight into the amazing number of hybrid careers open to people with a law degree. Contrary to some opinion, hybrid specialists are hardly dilettantes; those profiled in this book are skilled in two or more fields.

Mystery writers are a special breed. They instinctively understand the value of their past careers and, as writers, know how to harness that experience. Take a look at the books by Dick Francis, a jockey; Andrew Greeley, a Roman Catholic priest; and Margaret Truman, a Washington, D.C., insider—not to mention Arthur Conan Doyle, a physician. Fans know that Francis's mysteries feature either horses or race tracks, Greeley draws on his clerical training, Truman employs her knowledge of the Washington scene, and Sherlock Holmes and his sidekick, Dr. Watson, represent an extension of Conan Doyle's medical training.

Similar logic can be applied in any career. It can be as simple as taking a current job and adding a new dimension, the step taken by Richard Schneyer (profiled in chapter 12) who left commercial banking after 15 years to become a fund-raiser. Schneyer finds that his understanding of finance and his ability to deal with lawyers and accountants help in his negotiations with potential donors.

> ### POINTS TO REMEMBER
>
> - **Nearly all career changers** blend two or more careers into a single career.
> - **Career "A"** usually has job skills that are applicable in career "B."
> - **To some extent,** all career changers recycle past skills in their new work.
> - **Whatever the work,** it's impossible to dump past work experience.
> - **Some people are "simultalented,"** working in two different careers at the same time.
> - **Law and graduate business schools** are filled with students building hybrid careers.

Are You Simultalented?

In her doctoral dissertation, Susan Lawley, a career changer who left her job as human-resources manager at Goldman Sachs, in New York City, to form her own outplacement firm in New Jersey, identifies the "simultalented" as career blenders who use overlapping sets of talents to achieve peak performance in concurrent work activities. John Brown, the concert bass player (profiled in chapter 2), who taught the instrument to college students and played in a symphony orchestra while attending law school, is a self-employed trial lawyer. Brown is intent on pursuing two separate careers simultaneously. For 'simultalented' workers like Brown the "other" career is not a hobby, an avocation, or a moonlighting job, but a career they pursue with equal vigor and talent.

Lawley describes the seven characteristics of simultalented people she studied:

- **They approach work with passion,** in contrast to their sense of duty with which their parents approached work.
- **They are high achievers in multiple areas.**
- **They are not motivated by money;** two-thirds of the people in Lawley's survey said that they would relinquish the career that provides the higher income for the one that satisfies them the most.
- **They feel enormous time pressure** and face constant scheduling conflicts, which they resolve imaginatively.
- **They find little need to belong to groups,** and tend to be nonconformists.
- **They make particularly difficult career choices** and dramatic career changes.
- **They experience both the rewards and regrets** of a career-blending work style. It is challenging enough for most people to have one full-time job, but two jobs surely strain one's lifestyle and personal relationships.

Some People Who Made the Change

To a large extent, career changing amounts to blending one or more past skills into a new career. Whether they realize it or not, the teachers, ministers, artists, writers, physicians, Web managers, and craftspeople described in this book are drawing on past job experiences. Specifically, this chapter discusses career packagers who already have at least one workplace skill, learned new skills on the job or at school, and reentered the job market with a new persona. If the process could be expressed mathematically, it would be $1+1=3$.

NO LONGER WALKS A BEAT

Phillip Berran
FROM COP TO LAWYER TO DOCTOR

The only other person in Philip Berran's family to become a policeman was his grandfather. Unlike his grandfather, Berran has added a career-switching twist: He's also a lawyer and a physician. At present, he uses his varied professional skills as an Army doctor.

After Berran, now in his mid 30s, graduated from high school on Staten Island, he went to New York University for two years until he was eligible at age 20 to be a policeman. He spent the next six years, including six months' training, as a cop with the New York City Housing Authority, which was subsequently integrated into the New York Police Department. During this period, he graduated from NYU and started the four-year evening program at the New York Law School.

"While I was going to law school, I was reassigned to the police department's Office of Legal Matters. I also got the idea of becoming a physician from one of my instructors, who taught a course in medical law. I became interested in being a medical examiner, better known as a coroner." For the next few years, as Berran was preparing to be a physician, he was managing attorney in both the NYPD's Office of Legal Matters and in its Special Prosecutor's Department.

Qualifying for medical school required taking premed courses and preparing for the Medical College Admission Test at NYU for two and a half years. "When I was a student at NYU and New York Law, the police department was very supportive," Berran says. "They like the idea that cops go to college. It helps them recruit young people. I knew one cop

> "When I became a cop, I never thought anything would get me out of police work but I found something more interesting that combines all my skills."

who received a Ph.D., and another who went to medical school while continuing to work as a cop, and a third one who worked for the Emergency Medical Service throughout his four years in medical school." As a rule, however, most medical schools discourage their students from holding full-time or even part-time jobs.

After resigning from the NYPD as a sergeant in 1996, Berran began medical school. Divorced, with a daughter (now a teenager) who lived on Staten Island, he went to the State University of New York at Stony Brook so that he could see his daughter on weekends. About ten of the 110 students in Berran's class were over age 30, a high proportion for medical school.

No longer working as a cop and a lawyer to pay the bills, Berran attended Stony Brook as a participant in the U.S. Army's Health Professional Scholarship Program. The Army paid his medical school and lab expenses, along with $1,000 a month in living expenses. In return for an all-expenses-paid medical-school education, Berran was commissioned a second lieutenant and owed the Army four years' total service after graduation—and additional years for any specialty training and fellowships.

"I found medical school no more difficult than law school," said Berran. "The difference is that, in medicine, there's a need to memorize tons of information. In some ways, I was ahead of the younger students. Most of the them had never held a job other than a summer job or an after-school job at a fast-food restaurant. They had never filed an income-tax return, or made enough to have paid social security. Nor did they know about being married, divorced, or being a father.

"As a cop, I learned to ask questions and write it up in a report. A doctor does the same thing in writing up a patient's history. And in medical examining, a doctor doesn't have to be a lawyer, but it is helpful to know about the legal rights of individuals, and something about the ways people can be killed. Forensics combines medicine and law. Add to this

my training and practical experiences as a cop."

Legal knowledge is useful in dealing with traditions and religious rituals associated with death. To illustrate, Orthodox Jews are reluctant to permit autopsies and want the body buried within 24 hours of death. While Berran hasn't yet encountered this situation, he's confident that being a lawyer can be a useful skill for a medical examiner.

"My interest in pathology began with my admiration for the work of New York

"As a cop, I learned to ask questions and write it up in a report. A doctor does the same thing in writing up a patient's history."

City's medical examiner. By the time I had finished my first year in pathology and organ systems, I was sure that I had made the right choice of medical specialty. My desire is to practice pathology in a military or academic setting."

Like other medical-school students, Berran worked during the summer in hospitals. After his first year in medical school, he spent his summer vacation rotations at Walter Reed Army Medical Center, in Washington, D.C.; at Tripler Army Medical Center in Honolulu; and at Officers Basic School in Houston.

After graduating from Stony Brook in May 2000, Berran was promoted to captain and went on active duty with pay that exceeds most civilian medical residencies. After a one-year internship at Tripler, Berran started a multiyear pathology residency as part of the National Capital Consortium, which includes training at Walter Reed, the Bethesda Naval Hospital, and the Armed Forces Institute of Pathology. The additional training means that Berran's military obligation will end in nine years, when Berran will be in his late 40s.

"When I became a cop, I never thought anything would get me out of police work. Then I found something more interesting that combines all my skills—policing, law, and medicine. But in many ways being a cop will be with me forever."

HISTORY, TECH, AND THE LAW STACK UP

Thomas French
LIBRARIAN GOES TO LAW SCHOOL

Tom French, in his early 50s, represents the new breed of law-school librarians, a librarian with a law degree. Born and reared in upstate New York, Tom graduated from the State University of New York in Oswego just before the end of the Vietnam War. He joined the Navy and served three years on a destroyer as an operations specialist third class. The highlight of his naval career came when the Navy selected his destroyer to make a nine-month worldwide goodwill tour. "It gave me the chance to visit about 30 to 40 countries. My commander kidded me that I was the only sailor on the ship who acted like a tourist."

After finishing his stint with the Navy, French resumed his academic career. Following in his older brother Mike's footsteps, he got a master's degree in library science from Geneseo, a branch of the New York State University system. His next stop, the doctoral program in history at Xavier University, in Cincinnati, turned out to be a detour. "I only went as far as a master's degree," said French. "I realized that there were quicker payoffs and more opportunities as a librarian. Anyway, being a college librarian is where I wanted to be. A history Ph.D. would have been more for my personal satisfaction; I decided it was not worth it."

French was named associate professor of library services and head of technical services at Northern Kentucky University's law-school library in Highland Heights, across the Ohio River from Cincinnati. Modern librarians, unlike those coming out of school two decades ago, are trained as information specialists, for which computers are the tools of the trade. French was no stranger to

"When I was in law school, my class was filled with people trying to enhance their skills or change careers."

the technical side of librarianship.

Mike, now a librarian in Toledo and in many ways his brother's mentor, suggested that French get a law degree if he wanted to work in a law school. "At the time, the American Bar Association was recommending that law librarians of law schools accredited by the ABA should also be lawyers. Going to law school as an evening student was my way to qualify for future jobs. I had little intention of ever practicing law. The ABA feels that being a lawyer provides greater insight into the field. Interestingly, medical schools do not require their librarians to be doctors." While attending Northern Kentucky as an evening student, French switched jobs, working at the Cincinnati Law Library Association, where he did both law-library and administrative work.

"When I was in law school, my class was filled with people trying to enhance their skills or change careers. Our class had cops, teachers, physicians, and college administrators. None of them were planning to practice law, but, like me, they were interested in furthering their current careers." To make it official, French passed the bar exam and was admitted to practice law in Kentucky.

With his law degree in hand, French became assistant law librarian at the University of Maine School of Law in Portland. Then an even higher-level job with more pay beckoned. In 1993, French left Maine to become associate director of the University of North Carolina law-school library.

"I like Maine. When I left to go to North Carolina, I wasn't able to sell my house near Portland at the price I wanted, so I rented it for seven years until I got the money I wanted. If I hadn't sold the house, I might have considered retiring there."

In addition to his UNC library duties, French taught "Introduction to American Law," a course on the American legal system that was designed for foreign exchange students, primarily those from England, Holland, France, and Scotland. Twenty years earlier, during his brief stint as a doctoral student, his history minor related to the British Empire and Commonwealth, a topic that came in handy in teaching this course.

French's job at UNC lasted seven years. He moved back north in July 2000 to become director of the library at Syracuse University's School of Law. "I heard about the Syracuse job from the scuttlebutt among law librarians, advertisements and friends. They sent me e-mails of the job notice, knowing that I was from upstate New York and not afraid of wintry weather.

"I had always thought that if I was to leave UNC, I wanted a job north of Washington and east of Lake Erie. I had come to dislike the hot North Carolina summers. The money was not the reason I left, since I'm making about the same pay as I did at UNC, but it was a chance to be director of a law library. And the move didn't affect my retirement, since I've contributed to the same retirement program in my different jobs." (French's retirement is in TIAA-CREF, the Teacher's Insurance & Annuity College Retirement Equities Fund.)

At UNC, French had a five-year contract, whereas Syracuse gave him tenure as head librarian. In several years, he expects to also qualify as a tenured member of the law-school faculty.

"Sure, some people might not want to live and work in upstate New York, but I see a number of benefits: Besides the job itself, I'm familiar with and even like upstate winters. I still have family in the area, and buying a house was no problem since prices are much lower than those in Chapel Hill."

EARLY INTO ONLINE

David Blomquist
BLENDS NEWS AND WEB SITE SKILLS INTO A SINGLE CAREER

While attending the University of Michigan as a political science major during the mid 1970s, David Blomquist, now in his mid 40s, little realized that working with computers while doing quantitative research would help to set the stage for a career change 20 years later. Blomquist was also a movie critic and the entertainment editor on the university's daily campus newspaper. The experience gave him sufficient editorial know-how to launch his journalism career as a news intern with the *Detroit News*.

Blomquist ultimately left Detroit for Harvard and graduate study in political science. "My parents were disturbed that I was not going to law school, so Harvard was actually a compromise." Blomquist departed Harvard with a master's degree in 1982.

For the next two years, Blomquist received his first real taste of the relationship between news and computers. He worked for CBS on a very early Internet venture. For the pilot project, designed to test consumer buying habits on an early version of a Web site, AT&T built 100 desktop computers for CBS to install with 100 families in Ridgewood, N.J. Blomquist was the features editor for the forerunner of what would someday become Prodigy.

When the experimental project ended, Blomquist looked for a job as a newspaper reporter, which was consistent with his career goal. "I was preparing to take a job as a reporter for the *Rochester Democrat* in New York when a CBS associate recommended me to her next-door neighbor, who was an editor on *The Record*." Located

Blomquist's work with computers in college would set the stage for a a career change 20 years later.

in Hackensack, N.J,. *The Record* is the state's third-largest daily newspaper. After a tryout, he joined the paper; at 24 he was the youngest reporter on the news staff.

For the next three years, Blomquist's beat was local government news in Bergen County, in northern New Jersey; then he spent seven years in the newspaper's Trenton bureau, as the chief political writer, covering state government and political news and managing the bureau. He was reassigned to *The Record*'s main office in Hackensack, but the new editorial job proved to be a dead-end position.

"I was politely told that *The Record*

was overstaffed: I should find something else to do on the paper if I wanted to stay as a manager. Otherwise, I would be back working as a reporter. By then, I did not want to do daily news reporting."

Blomquist heard that *The Record* was preparing a series of cable TV programs to promote its operation and that it needed someone to head the project. "I put my hand up, and for the next two years I was a cable TV manager." The work ended when *The Record* sold the cable operation to Cablevision.

At this point, *The Record* had been running an Internet system for a year. A small venture with only a few employees, it lacked a manager. Blomquist, a computer enthusiast, saw the opportunity, volunteered, and was named to head this group.

"Up to then, I had never built a Web site. I knew what Web sites did, and I used them, but that's about it. Over the weekend before starting my new job, I read books about the Internet. I became the manager on a Friday and on Monday I was at work." For the next six months, like any good reporter, he asked lots of questions, and he learned about Internet technology on the job.

In 1999, the *Detroit Free Press* recruited Blomquist as its new-media director. He returned to his hometown to work more than 20 years after leaving Detroit for Harvard. "What I had to offer was the creditability and experience of 15 years as a reporter and an editor. I realized that one part of my life was over and a new one was about to start."

Blomquist is responsible for the content and development of the newspaper's four Web sites: www .freep.com features daily news; www .auto.com covers auto-industry news; www.alldetroit.com provides a sort of online Yellow Pages; and www.yakscorner .com (yak as in yakking, or talking), a Web site for youngsters.

Blomquist manages a staff of eight computer and Web-site professionals. His staff is in a constant state of flux, as other employers recruit his experienced

"What I had to offer was the creditability and experience of 15 years as a reporter and an editor."

Web site professionals. As a result, Blomquist often works 70 to 80 hours a week to cover a staff shortfall.

As the newspaper's Web manager and Internet expert, he is expected to take the news and prepare it for Internet presentation. Reporting to the executive editor, he participates in the paper's daily editorial meeting, when the editors decide what news will appear on page one; to be invited to that meeting represents a step up from his status at *The Record,* where he reported to the marketing director. Blomquist's work with the paper's Web site enables him to contribute a unique perspective to the meeting. He knows which parts of the paper have had the biggest number of "hits," and whether more or fewer readers have accessed the paper online. He can provide a quick "read" of readership.

But it also places a burden on him. "Unlike my days as a reporter, now I'm judged differently," said Blomquist. "The Internet has the ability to rapidly show absolute numerical measurement. I can tell the editors how many hits I had yesterday. I'm held accountable for these numbers. Compare this with being a reporter, when the most I ever heard was 'that was a nice lead on your story.'

"My readers are really in charge. If they don't like my Web site offerings, they can easily click it off and might never return. Web-site users have little loyalty. In many ways, they're the ones who decide what we will provide for them to read."

In sum, Blomquist enjoys the best of two newspaper environments, old and new: taking the daily news and presenting it in online.

FROM COMMUNITY ACTIVIST TO BUSINESS ADVOCATE

Dub Gulley

RETAILER USES HIS KNOW-HOW TO COUNSEL ENTREPRENEURS

As a teenager, Dub Gulley, now in his early 50s, wanted to get away from Little Rock. He and his twin brother, Wib, went to Duke University and graduated in 1970 at the height of the Vietnam War.

A student activist at Duke, Gulley, like many people his age, ducked the draft and went to the West Coast, doing odd jobs. His first job was working for Arby's. His father, a banker in Arkansas, wondered if this was the way his son was going to use his Duke education.

"I wanted to change the world," said Gulley. The answer for him was to take a series of grassroots, nonprofit jobs. "At the time, I was interested in community-sponsored housing groups. I worked in Massachusetts for the Cambridge Tenants Organizing Committee, and I then returned home for a job with ACORN (Arkansas Community Organization Reform Now)." Fortunately, Gulley was single at the time and could live on pay of $200 to $300 a month—not much even then. Gulley later went back to Durham to work for several more community action groups.

In 1978, Gulley and his brother took a year off to go around the world. "It was an important year in our lives. Afterwards, Wib went to law school. By now, I considered myself a builder of community organizations."

Gulley married Libby Patterson in 1984. "Libby and I discussed what would be next for me. I decided to go into business. We both liked the outdoors, camping and hiking, and I saw a hole in the local market. There was a need in Durham for an outdoor store."

Gulley had little retail or business experience other than a brief period in

Gulley picked up some business savvy, spending 18 months visiting outdoor stores and speaking with the owners.

the late 1970s, when he worked as the general manager of a cooperative auto-repair shop. What's more, his knowledge of outdoor equipment was limited to his own personal likes and dislikes. "Few people were interested in my first business proposal. I circulated 12 business plans, but only two bankers would speak to me, because my business history was nil. They said, 'Why should I take a risk?'"

As a result, Gulley picked up some business savvy, spending 18 months visiting outdoor stores in Virginia and the Carolinas, and speaking with the owners. What he observed there formed the basis of his new marketing plan.

Despite his inexperience, in late 1985 he opened Eno Traders, named for a local river, with a personal investment of $25,000 in savings and an equal amount in collateral loans. The store operated in the black for three years, with Libby working there until she got pregnant. Gulley put in 50 to 60 hours a week, and like many retailers, he had trouble hiring good people. After the first three years, sales and profits sagged. "I had several bad seasons. We had too much inventory as a result of some bad buying decisions. Banks were reluctant to lend us money, yet we survived and paid our debts. I thought about opening a second and perhaps even a third store, but then I asked myself, How many headaches did I really want?

"About a year before I closed Eno Traders, after 12 years in business, I started to think of career options— go to work in corporate sales or marketing, do fund-raising work, or get involved in Durham downtown-property development." By then, the Gulleys had two sons, and Libby, who had completed her master's degree in public health, was working as a Duke health-care administrator.

Rather than sell the store—which is the advice he now gives to others— Gulley decided to sell all the merchandise in three days. Then he networked with people he had known from his days as a community activist and retailer. One of these was the president of Durham Technical Community College, who was looking for someone to direct the nearly moribund Small Business Center sponsored by the college. Gulley's combination of retail and community activist credentials was considered ideal for the position.

Besides sponsoring an ongoing series of workshops on business-management topics, Gulley now counsels about 100 wannabe entrepreneurs or recent start-ups a year. "While I might not be an expert in their field, I play the role of the devil's advocate. I rain on their parade. I ask the hard questions that they often don't want to face. From my own experience, I tell them the last thing they want is to be prisoners in their own businesses by being in debt."

HOME AND PRINT-SHOP UNDER ONE ROOF

David Deiss
SMALL—PRESS PUBLISHER IS SMALL—TOWN LAWYER

When David Deiss, who is now in his mid 40s, was growing up in Galveston, Tex., his family thought that he would become a lawyer. At Duke University, Deiss studied political science, a first step toward a law degree. At the same time, he also became interested in a number of excellent, though overlooked, French and British pre- and post-World War II authors. His literary interests would spark a future career.

After graduation, Deiss put off law school for two years to help run a low-income cooperative housing project in Orland, Maine. Then, at the Vermont Law School, he was managing editor of the law review, had a six-month clerkship with Vermont's secretary of state, followed after graduation by an appointment as counsel to the state senate's judiciary committee. Even though he had done well academically in law school and recognized the opportunities open to him, Deiss had doubts about a full-time legal career.

He built a house in North Pomfret, Vt., a village with a population of 500 about 20 minutes from Dartmouth College. He felt it was an ideal place to live and run a small-town legal practice. An avid book collector— he had learned book collecting from his father, a physician—Deiss also needed space for a growing library.

Meanwhile, he began retreating from a more active law practice to concentrate on collecting and publishing books. He learned how to do letter-press printing a pre-electronic form of printing, from a printer who worked for Dartmouth. A local typesetter creates "hot," or metal, type for Deiss, which he

Deiss's early interest in overlooked French and British pre- and post–World War II authors would spark a future career.

places in a page form and uses to press ink directly to paper. For purists like Deiss, letterpress provides a direct relationship with the printed page that computer-set pages can't duplicate.

In 1989, Deiss started Elysium Press in his home, which serves as a combination office for Elysium Press, letterpress and other printing equipment, and a law practice. "The name Elysium is derived from the Greek concept of Valhalla, where the mortals live forever. My goal, then and now, was to print and publish letterpress books by authors whose works are either out of print or out of fashion, with a focus on gay authors."

A one-person operation, Deiss runs Elysium Press to satisfy his personal literary interests and the purchasing habits of his niche customer base.

In contrast to other publishers, who usually have much larger press runs, Deiss produces either 30 copies of a book, priced to sell for $1,000 each, or 200 copies, to sell at $75 to $100 each. "To produce a steady flow of books, I usually have three to four books in the works. To do this, I visit England once a year in search of manuscripts. For one of my first books, Jean Cocteau's *Les Enfants Terrible,* I lived in France for six months. Being a lawyer has its advantages. I'm able to write my own publishing contracts."

Deiss's press produces spring and fall catalogs, which he mails to a list of 600 names. He also promotes his books via his Web site (www.elysiumpress.com) as well as on several Web sites that sell his type of books. Many of his customers are private collectors and libraries. "Interestingly, Amazon sells my books. It has been a good source of sales, but I'm reluctant to sell my books in bookstores, because the books are too specialized and too costly, and they might get damaged in stores."

Publishing is Deiss's prime venture. Even so, he spends about 10% of his time doing family law, title law, and some general legal assignments, and, of course, representing Elysium Press. To maintain a Vermont license to practice, he takes continuing-education law courses.

Other than a few legal clients, Deiss derives most of his income from distribution of his twice-yearly, 40-page catalogs that list books produced by other publishers on topics that appeal to him; sales of books that Elysium Press has published; and from fees generated by purchasing books for others. The general catalog also lists Deiss's Asphodel Editions, a name derived from the place where the Greeks believed more common folk lived.

As Elysium Press's only employee, Deiss has diverse duties: letterpress operator, editor, proofreader, marketer, promoter, company lawyer, and manager. "When I started out, I didn't know in what direction Elysium Press was going, even though I knew it would become a bigger part of my life. I did know that my legal practice was in conflict with an even greater interest in publishing."

Improving the Quality of Your Life

MARCIA BROOKS, IN HER EARLY **40**S, IS WHAT CAN BE called a "lifestyle worker." Like millions of other Americans, Brooks makes her career choices revolve around her choice of a desirable lifestyle— in her case, working from home so that she can care for her two young children herself. Brooks scrapped a career as an art-edu- cation teacher to become a furniture designer. "Initially I though that teaching was great. I like art. I like kids. And I like to teach. When I became pregnant with Zeke, I realized that teaching was not the best career for raising children. You go to work at 7 in the morning, work all day, and, in the evening, you prepare for the next day."

Brooks's career goal, which has been delayed temporarily by the birth of a daughter in January 2001, is to complete the master's program at North Carolina State University's School of Design by 2002. Her field of specialty is furniture design, a craft that she's already pursuing from an at-home office. "I design custom furniture pieces and have them built to my specifications. I like the flexibility of this type of work, which lets me use my drawing skills and spend time at home with my children."

There's no single formula for achieving a desired lifestyle through one's career choices. Some of the factors that affect lifestyle are fundamental to specific jobs, while others are incidental or as superficial as corporate dress codes. Lifestyle goals may influence whether we want to leave one job or profession to try a new one. Some people's goals are satisfied only with a high-paying job that provides the income necessary for them to enjoy the "good life," regardless of whether they like the work. In the name of lifestyle, some people are content working for a small rural bank, while others are satisfied only with the pressure-cooker lifestyle of big city investment banking. In short, our lifestyles—and our career choices—are specific to our interests and needs.

The first part of this chapter considers five common lifestyle considerations in today's work world: Working from home, simplifying one's life, dressing down at work, working full- or part-time schedules or on temporary assignments, and converting a hobby into a full-time career.

Working at Home or Anywhere

The statistics vary on the number of people who work at home, and they are, at best, estimates. The U.S. Department of Labor's Bureau of Labor Statistics (www.bls.gov), which usually issues more conservative workplace tallies, reported that over 21 million people work full- or part-time at home. According to the BLS, that number includes everyone from teachers catching up on lesson plans, to wage-and-salary telecommuters on the company time clock, and people who are self-employed and operate home businesses.

A report in *American Demographics* finds that "Telecommuting is finally taking hold and people are starting businesses at a rate of 2 million a year, with technology turning households into telecommunications centers and flexibility becoming the war cry among workers not only coast to coast but worldwide; home business is big business. And it's expected to get even bigger in the millennium."

The makers of computer, networking, and software products and systems are elated with the growth in home-office usage. It's no longer a matter of owning just one computer. Computer-industry researcher International Data Corp. predicts that the number of home-office households with multiple PCs will soar from 7.8 million homes in 1998 to 12.1 million by 2002.

In a work-and-family study, the Conference Board (www.conference-board.org) found that only 6% of employees telecommute, and they are almost three times as likely to be women. The Conference Board also noted that nearly two-thirds of telecommuters work outside the office two or more days a week. As a result, telecommuting gives workers an increased sense of control and independence. What's more, morale seems to improve because employees can balance priorities in their personal lives with work.

Nearly two-thirds of telecommuters work outside the office two or more days a week.

It makes sense for corporate telecommuters to work two days at home and the rest of the week in a more traditional office setting, especially if their career goal is management. This way telecommuters can enjoy the convenience of working at home while directly participating on the corporate team.

Working at home is also a logical place for writers, artists and craftspeople who normally work by themselves, for shut-ins and handicapped people, and for people like Marcia Brooks, who want to combine home, family, and job into a single package. At-home offices can be the ideal incubator for start-up businesses, which can operate rent-free.

Cost is hardly a factor. The price tag to outfit an office declines each year. Ten years ago, a computer, printer, fax, and copier would easily have cost $5,000 or more for a modest configuration. Today, better equipment, along with Internet communications gear, costs between $2,000 and $2,500. Some enlightened employers will either subsidize or pay this cost in full, and some even allow their employees to take their equipment home.

But all is not paradise in at-home offices, and I have some reservations about their long-term viability. Working at home can be a lonely experience, a view shared by Marc Wallace, a partner in Workplace Effectiveness, Inc. Wallace sees certain other disadvantages, including a loss of creativity. "The inventiveness and energy that drive innovation can get lost when people are not interacting with one another on a regular basis, and there's an assumption in telecommuting that, somehow, the home is going to be a friendlier, easier, quieter place to work than the office. That's not always the case."

AT&T received contradictory results on the question of productivity when it interviewed its telecommuters: 71% of the workers said they concentrated better from at-home offices, yet one-half of them also indicated that frequent interruptions impeded productivity. One necessary solution for parents of young children is to hire caregivers. A productive work environment requires a business day with a minimum of intrusion, and that goes not only for corporate telecommuters but for entrepreneurs and artisans, too.

> **It is highly convenient to walk a handful of steps to my office, but, still, something is missing that cannot be replaced with the telephone, e-mail, and chat rooms.**

I've been working from my home office for ten years now. I admit that it is highly convenient to walk a handful of steps to my office, but, still, something is missing that cannot be replaced with the telephone, e-mail, and chat rooms. As a writer, I recognize that telephone interviews are only a matter of convenience, and that, no matter how good my technique, I receive, at best, a black-and-white picture. I miss out on the opportunity to observe that my interviewee collects paperweights or grows African violets. In some instances, the observation has no bearing on the story, but many times it does.

Brian Gillooly, an *Information Week* editor said, "It's no longer a case of balancing work and home life where the implied result is that one must make sacrifices on either side to achieve some measure of security. Instead, we've got to learn to merge work and home life. To integrate some aspects of each into the other. And the very technologies that are often blamed—justly or not—for having created this complexity in our lives are precisely what can be leveraged to help create a workplace that engenders happier, more productive employees.... Mobile computing, telecommuting distance learning, flex time, the Internet: They've all been cited for having changed the way people work—and play. They've created a new style of worker where boundaries between work and home are dissolving."

Seeking Simplification

When T. J. Johnson, a former corporate manager (profiled later in this chapter), tired of traveling on business trips 60% of his time, he quit his job, relocated with his family, and changed careers. Johnson's decision is consistent with a Hilton Hotels Corp. survey that found that more than half of the Americans in its study wanted to simplify their lives. The problem is that they want to make more money at the same time they want more leisure time. In this equation, something has to give. Some of the other Hilton findings are worth noting:

- **Our focus** seems to be on cramming more things into a day, rather than concentrating on what is important to us.
- **We say we don't have much time** for plain old fun, even on weekends.
- **We seem to be more interested** in keeping up with life's rapid pace than in taking steps to slow it down.
- **About one-half of those surveyed** said they wish they could slow down and enjoy life.
- **We spend about twice as much time** each day doing things we have to do rather than things we want to do.
- **What we actually need** is a 28-hour day to accomplish every thing we need to do.
- **Part of the reason we're always so busy** may be that we're trying to live up to the expectations of others.

Americans reportedly put in the longest workweek in the industrial world, surpassing even the time the Japanese spend on the job. *American Demographics* reported that "the average married couple labors a staggering 717 hours more each year than a working duo in 1969. The tools that were supposed to free us from the shackles of our desks have bound us to our jobs in ways unimaginable just a decade ago. They are electronic umbilical cords to the workplace."

Moreover, unlike their European counterparts, Americans rarely receive six weeks of vacation.

Some alternatives for simplification are emerging:

Like a number of American cities, Durham, N.C., my home, is rebuilding its downtown area. The development plan calls for a combination of apartments, stores, offices, and entertainment facilities. The Durham plan will help residents achieve what their grandparents might have experienced as part of everyday life, namely, working, living, and playing in a centralized community. It eliminates the need to commute and be as dependent on a car to attend to errands. Some "lifestyle" workers seek such communities or neighborhoods and relocate to them.

Although sabbaticals are a rarity outside academia, some workers are finding ways to create them.

Career downshifting is the goal of many career changers, according to the message in *Downshifting* by Amy Saltzman (HarperCollins, 1991). Saltzman suggests a number of different ways to achieve a lifestyle with greater "inner karma," such as voluntarily choosing a demotion in order to gain more personal time, moving to a smaller community, or transferring skills to a job with less pressure.

British consultant and author Charles Handy has posed some refreshing ways to look at workplace and lifestyle issues in *The Age of Unreason* (Business Books Ltd., 1989). Handy created the concept of a "portfolio career" as a work and lifestyle formula. The portfolio combines wage-and-fee work, work around the home, volunteering, and study, in proportions to be set by the individual.

Although sabbaticals are a rarity outside academia, some workers are finding ways to create them. Jonathan Beard (profiled later in this chapter), a mental health specialist, and Greg Vimont (profiled in chapter 5), a photographer turned software specialist, structured their own sabbaticals. Each took time off in his career to take care of newborn children while their wives worked. Besides the parental bonding, Beard and Vimont got the "space" away from their jobs to assess the direction of their careers.

Do Clothes Really Make the Man?

It was big news when a New York law firm, Cadwalader, Wickersham & Taft, retained *Esquire* magazine and fashion designer Ralph Lauren to conduct a seminar on the acceptable clothes that its lawyers and paraprofessional staffers could wear to work. Of concern, would the male three-piece suit and wingtip shoes, and the female fashion equivalents, be replaced by chinos, Docksiders, and sport shirts?

What started out as dress-down Fridays has spread to a Monday-through-Friday fashion statement. In high-tech companies, informality is the only dress code. In the 1980s, when Bill Gates was a rising young software developer trying to get IBM to buy Microsoft's DOS software operating system, he would arrive at IBM's offices wearing a sweater, shirt, no tie, of course, and slacks. To IBM, Gates's informality was a 1980s version of "in your face," even though his attire was already accepted in the software industry.

In the name of lifestyle, corporate as well as at-home workers seek informality. Who needs to don a shirt and tie when you won't see anyone except the FedEx delivery person all day? John Mingis (profiled in chapter 5) is an exception. A year after starting a consulting firm for nonprofit agencies, Mingis still wears a suit and tie to an office down the hall from his bedroom.

An informal dress policy helps to attract or, better yet, does not discourage future employees. New York investment banker D. E. Shaw headlines a recruitment advertisement for software personnel this way: "Suits don't run this business. Code does."

Perhaps Scott Omelianuk, a fashion expert and *Esquire's* executive editor, said it best. "Relax, it's only clothes. If you are something of a traditionalist and you are comfortable in your suit, keep wearing it." And "remember that the workday isn't the weekend. What's appropriate for washing the car ain't the togs for closing a deal."

Full-Time, Part-Time, or Temporary

A flexible work schedule is another of today's lifestyle options. About eight million professionals, double the rate in 1989, now work part-time.

It is expensive to recruit employees, especially in fields with a shortage of trained managers and professionals. Flexible work options, such as job sharing or telecommuting, or the choice of working full- or part-time, are ways to recruit and retain employees.

Workplace flexibility in many ways is a reaction to the "Silicon Valley syndrome." Aon Consulting (www.aon.com) describes that pattern as "working all hours and all-nighters in anticipation of a big, future payoff. More commonly, though, people are working longer hours just to keep up. Whatever the reason, the increase in the number of hours on the job means that people need help managing the demands of work and life. The present generation wants to know what an employer is going to do to enhance their work experience and help balance their work and personal life."

> **The increase in the number of hours on the job means that people need help managing the demands of work and life.**

Until recently, temporary jobs consisted of blue-collar or lower-level corporate administrative workers. It was rare to find a "temp" engineer, lawyer, or accountant. Then in the early '90s, along came massive downsizing, in tandem with a generally soft employment market. Downsized managers and professionals turned to interim jobs as a way to tide them over until they found permanent employment. Some liked the flexibility or so mistrusted corporate management that they took the next step and became independent contractors. In some instances they were retained by a former employer.

Surveys by the American Staffing Association (www.natss .org) show that 64% of assigned temporary workers indicated that a flexible workplace environment is important to them. Nearly three out of ten temps noted that a temp job provided the flexibility needed to pursue nonwork interests.

Don't, however, count on being a long-term temp. The average tenure for temp employees ranges from three to five months. The Bureau of Labor Statistics reported that temporary employees with more than 24 months of tenure constitute only about 0.1% of the American workforce.

Summarizing a study of part-time work arrangements, the Conference Board noted that part-time jobs are a popular workplace option among mothers. They are also a good option for career changers who need the additional income while they attend college, upgrade their skills, or work in a field with a lower pay scale. Chris Schafale (profiled in chapter 11), a psychologist with a doctorate, supplements her income as a self-employed potter by working full-time for a social services agency.

Where Should I Live?

It's fun to read recruitment ads. They often focus on lifestyle issues, especially when the company is located in an area with a reputation for casual living. Cymer, a San Diego–based technology company, caught the spirit with a headline "Cymer— where sun and science go... hand in hand." (The illustration shows a man and woman emerging from the ocean hand in hand, with a palm tree in the background.) Nice idea, but for most of us, what are the odds of getting a well-paying job in such vacation spots as Vail, Key West, or Myrtle Beach, or even in smaller communities not abutting metro centers?

Admittedly, in the Internet Age and with overnight delivery systems, small-town America is no longer so isolated as it once was, but such places still have their limitations. Husband and wife George Radwan and Stephanie Green (profiled in chapter 11) moved twice, from New York City and Chapel Hill to rural Vermont and New Hampshire, in search of a better lifestyle. They found that the scenery was great, but acceptable jobs were limited.

The more general your skills, the more easily you can relocate. For example, a legal generalist is not restricted to specific communities, but an admiralty lawyer will most likely find the best jobs in large coastal cities. Geography rarely affects internists or pediatricians, but that's not so with medical specialists who require larger medical facilities. That's why, when planning a career change, it's smart to think in terms of portable skills that won't confine you to a particular location.

If you're thinking of relocation, there are some side issues to consider. What about your spouse? Will he or she find comparable work in a new community? My alma mater, Colgate University, in rural upstate New York, often loses out in faculty recruitment when a prospective professor's spouse can't find a corporate or professional job at an appropriate skill or pay

POINTS TO REMEMBER

- **Working part- or full-time** at home continues to grow as an alternative lifestyle.
- **Temporary work** is increasing in popularity.
- **Would-be at-home workers** need to consider whether a home office is the best work environment for them.
- **Managers and professionals** want to simplify their lives.
- **Clothes** make a fashion statement. The question: three-piece suit or chinos?

- **Relocation** is not always the way to improve one's lifestyle.
- **Workers need to consider** whether cell phones, pagers and laptops enhance or hinder one's lifestyle.
- **Converting a hobby** to a full-time career is a tempting career alternative, but one that's often unrealistic.
- **Outside academia,** sabbaticals are a rarity for most workers. When available, sabbaticals offer time to think and to retool.

level. And how will your children, particularly teenagers, adapt to a different community?

Relocation often means costly housing. Corporate relocation specialist Runzheimer International (www.runzheimer .com) offers this sobering comparison: The annual cost (including mortgage payments, homeowners' insurance, realty taxes, utilities, and maintenance) for a 2,200-square foot, eight-room home in San Jose, Cal., the unofficial capital of Silicon Valley, is nearly $64,000. The annual cost for a similar home in Boston is $32,000, and $14,000 in New Orleans. State income taxes are similarly diverse. Texas, California, and five other states are still tax-free.

So if relocation is your "lifestyle" goal, it's best to do your homework. Start with a visit to the area. For a broad overview, lots of comparative data can be found in David Savageau's *Places Rated Almanac* (IDG Books Worldwide, 1999), which highlights the cost of living, jobs, education, health care, recreation, transportation, climate, crime, and the arts in 345 metro areas.

Converting a Hobby Into a Full-Time Job

When an injury forced Lydia Gabor (profiled in chapter 11) to leave behind her career as signer for the deaf , she had little trouble picking a substitute career. Ever since childhood, Gabor had enjoyed baking, a skill she learned from her grandmother. With a year or so of training, Gabor turned her teenage hobby into her new career. And Bob Page (profiled in chapter 10) left a secure job as an auditor to start Replacements Ltd. when his hobby, collecting dishes and glassware, became his prime focus.

Hobbies provide a special advantage. They are often a passion, sometimes more so than one's paid work. As most dedicated hobbyists realize, a hobby can provide escape from workplace pressures. It is a way to relax, to be creative and to express feelings.

It's natural for a wannabe career changer to turn to a hobby, but before taking the next step, look realistically at your hobby. How skilled are you? Discard compliments from friends and family, and start with a cost analysis. How long do you take to make a chair, what do the lumber and the other supplies cost, and what is the selling price for the chair? If you make two chairs a week and each one nets $100, can you afford to live on $200 a week?

Hobbies can be the source of a sideline business or the basis of a small cottage-industry company, but even skilled hobbyists will probably have difficulty justifying the cost of exchanging one's well-paid vocation for a financially iffy avocation.

Some People Who Made the Change

The people profiled on the following pages have based their careers on lifestyle choices, whether becoming a stay-at-home mother, downshifting to a job where more time can be spent with the family, taking a paternity leave, or tailoring a work schedule to meet personal needs and family responsibilities. In each case, the career changer is recycling his or her skills.

PUBLISHES ALTERNATIVE NEWSPAPER

Sioux Watson

SHIFTED HER SOCIAL–WORK SKILLS INTO ADVERTISING SALES

Sioux Watson, now in her late 40s, is from Mississippi. Her first name dates back to the fifth grade, when the four other Susans in her class decided to make things easier for themselves and their teacher by using different first names. "I hit upon Sioux, which I've used ever since."

After graduating from the University of Mississippi in 1974, with majors in sociology and social work, Watson moved to Chapel Hill where her father, a General Electric employee, had been transferred. Like many recent college graduates, she did a number of nondescript things before she settled into a full-time job with the Durham Exchange Club, a social-service agency where she supervised mentally retarded adults who assembled materials for IBM. Over the next three years, Watson's other tasks ranged from testing people to coaching the club's basketball team.

Working at the Durham Exchange Club, however, was not Watson's first experience working with a social-services agency. As a teenager, Watson had been a camp counselor for youngsters with developmental problems.

"I left to take a job with the Durham County Mental Home, where I supervised the renovation of group homes for patients," says Watson. About this time,

I started to get disillusioned with the way social-service agencies operated."

Still single at the time she quit the job, Watson took the small amount of money in her county retirement account and bought a sailboat, learned how to make baskets, and sold them at street fairs. She also thought about future jobs

> **"It was a perfect job without any executive responsibilities. I was only rated for selling ads, nothing else. I just did my job."**

and careers. During this period, Watson married Paul Savery, a Durham County mental-health worker whom she had met at her former job. When she became pregnant she began to think about increasing her income to meet the family's growing needs.

"What I really wanted was a nine-to-five job. The best way to get it, I thought, was in sales. Without any experience, I got a sales job with an import record company. But my timing was bad. Along came compact discs, and the record company was out of business."

In 1983, she answered an ad for a job selling advertising space in The Inde-

pendent, a local alternative newspaper that had just published its first issue. "I liked what *The Independent* stood for, with a mission that I could support: 'to publish the nation's best alternative journalism, to help build a just community, to create a good workplace for every employee, and to make a profit doing it.'"

The pay was only $13,000 a year, but it was a straight salary, not a commission. Watson's first child was born the next year and the job was compatible with the way Watson wanted to balance motherhood with a job. "I made calls on advertisers Monday through Friday during the business day. It was a perfect job without any executive responsibilities. I was only rated for selling ads, nothing else. Nothing to do with management. I just did my job."

Four years later, a second daughter was born. Watson continued in the same job because it was convenient to her home and children. In 1996, Watson's career took a different direction when she was promoted to advertising director. "As advertising director, my assignment changed. I was responsible for budgets and administration. I knew something about budgets from my days as a social worker." By this time, her daughters were 11 and 7. Her promotion also came at a time when *The Independent*'s founder, publisher, and principal stockholder started to step back from day-to-day operation.

In June 1999, the founder resigned as publisher, naming Watson as his successor. *The Independent* was no longer a small weekly published by a small staff; it employed 28 full-time editorial, advertising, and management workers, plus many freelancers and part-timers. Once again, Watson reached for her skills from years back, when, as editor of her high school yearbook, she came to know and appreciate the editorial process.

With Watson, little from the past has ever been discarded. "I began to realize that mental-health workers often make good business managers. They are good listeners, good at solving problems and good at dealing with people with difficulties. I also realized that parenting skills have carryover into the workplace. To raise children, you have to have a consistent message, learn to stick to your guns, and have an ability to stay focused."

RECORDING IN A ONE–TIME CHURCH

Will Russell
ANALOG AND DIGITAL MUSICAL RECORDINGS ARE HIS GIG

Music has been a passion of Will Russell's, now in his early 40s, ever since he heard his first Beatles' recording in the 1960s. Not that you'd ever call him a virtuoso. "I was in the high school band, but my trumpet playing was such that, if there were five seats in the band, they'd ask for a sixth one for me."

Russell, originally from Westfield, N.J., graduated from Ithaca College in upstate New York. "I studied psychology, but I was more interested in staging concerts, and doing things in live sound. I'm a lifelong audiophile. I made recordings in my room when I was 15. I was the technical person with the college's concert bureau. This was a volunteer job, but to make some money, I rented out sound systems to bands in bars and clubs."

Unlike many college students who can't wait to go somewhere else after graduation, Russell remained in Ithaca. With a degree in psychology, he was recommended by a college professor for a job as a counselor in a high-security school for troubled girls. The job lasted six months. "I got married, and my wife bugged me to get a real job that paid more. I went to the local community college for an associate's degree in electric technology." That was Russell's formal introduction to computer systems.

Wang, then a leading computer manufacturer, recruited Russell as a customer engineer. "I believe I was hired because I was one of the few people they talked to who had the slightest clue what a customer engineer does." Given a territory of several upstate New York counties, Russell drove about 1,000 miles

"I have no aspirations for the business to grow any larger than it is; I do what I love with people I enjoy."

a week to provide technical support and service for Wang's computers. "I liked the work, the pay was good, and I got all the benefits that a large company can offer. In many ways, I was my own boss, since I was reporting to a boss who was in Syracuse about 60 miles away."

With popular acceptance of PCs in business, Wang's business began to slip and the company started to lay off employees. Good at his work, Russell schemed with his boss to allow him to retain company benefits during the transition to another job. "My job at Wang was not in jeopardy. Customers liked me. I was more than a service rep who told them that their computer was broken. I helped them solve many of their technical problems."

Russell had been doing some freelance recordings, using his 16-track system and charging $25 an hour for studio time. He reasoned that if he was no longer with Wang, he could do this work full-time. When he left Wang in 1990, Russell received severance pay. He also received one-half the net profits from the sale of his house in Ithaca. After 10 years of marriage, he was getting divorced.

No longer a Wang employee, he switched his part-time recording business into full gear. "My relationship with a customer is more than being a techie. People look to me to help them understand what's taking place technically in their recordings." In many ways this was what he had been doing during the 1980s for Wang—blending technology with customer relations.

Russell also discovered that he had a different perspective on working in the music field at age 30 than he did at 21. "Back then, I pictured myself in New York City, sweeping floors in a recording studio so I could pay my dues and work my way up. Now I was a lot less interested in that idea."

Russell's company, Electronic Wilburland, started out in a 400-square-foot studio with carpets on the wall to enhance acoustics and a $500-a-month rent. In 1998, Wilburland moved, with the help of a guaranteed loan from the Small Business Administration, to a renovated church with a nearly acoustically perfect 1,400-square-foot soundroom, or as Russell puts it, "the best sound within

100 miles." Russell describes the setting as ideal. "It has a comfortable lounge, a kitchen overlooking a lovely backyard, a creek, a wooden covered bridge and a two-bedroom apartment available for overnight accommodations."

The new recording studio, the purchase of an array of more sophisticated recording equipment, and the addition of one full-time and another part-time employee have increased overhead sixfold.

By standards for success in some

Russell may not be "making it big," but he is making it, doing what he likes to do in the area where he wants to live.

urban areas, Russell may not be "making it big," but he is making it, doing what he likes to do in the area where he wants to live—and the cost of living in Ithaca is comparatively low.

Ithaca continues to be a good recording market for Wilburland (www.wilburland.com). Ithaca College and Cornell University, along with the bars and clubs in the area, attract considerably more musicians, bands, and musical groups than many towns of 30,000 do. Many of these performers, with colorful names like the Horseflies, Madder Rose, Sunny Weather and the Burns Sisters, record at Wilburland. The studio does everything from carrying out one-day projects to producing full CDs, which can take several months.

Russell is considered a "townie," enjoying the informal lifestyle in rural upstate New York. "I have no aspirations for the business to grow any larger than it is; I do what I love with people I enjoy."

Russell's second wife, Susan, who he married in 1995, has supported his music-related career. Content with his occupation and lifestyle, don't expect him to open a Wilburland recording studio or a franchise operation near you.

PUTTING DOWN ROOTS

J. T. Johnson
TRADES IN COMMUTING FOR A LOCAL JOB

By the mid 1990s, J. T. Johnson, now in his early 40s, had tired of corporate traveling. His drive to work took more than one hour each way, and he spent nearly 60% of his time on U.S. and overseas business trips.

Exhausted with this routine, he left his job in 1996 and moved with his wife and two children (a third child was born in 1998) from New Jersey to Raleigh, N.C., without a job or even a hint of one.

Relocation was in Johnson's blood. Growing up with a peripatetic Air Force father, Johnson had gone to high school in Germany. After graduating from Lafayette College, in Easton, Pa., as a chemical engineer in 1981, he had taken a job as a researcher with Exxon Research & Engineering. Within a year, Exxon downsized its Florham Park, N.J., research center, and Johnson found himself unemployed at age 23.

Engineering was the last type of job that Johnson wanted. Instead, he went to work in 1982 as a production manager for a $30-million company, then called Cascdam. Through mergers and acquisitions, Cascdam became Cambrex Corp., a life sciences company, and over the next 13 years of Johnson's employment with the company, it grew into a $750 million operation.

In 1984, single, and living and working in Bayonne, N.J., Johnson began commuting after work to New York University's Graduate School of Business, one hour each way from Bayonne. Three years later, he received an MBA degree, which enabled him to make the break from production and join the company's corporate staff.

"The company had completed five

> ## "I had no clue of how I would earn a living in Raleigh. My goals were to enjoy life with my family, and no longer travel on business or commute to work."

acquisitions, each with a different accounting system, and I was responsible for centralizing accounting and installing a companywide computer system." Johnson's management responsibilities broadened. Over the next several years he was director of management information systems, director of materials management, and business manager of a division that sold chemicals to the fiber-optics and electronic-component markets.

After 13 years, Johnson felt it was time to do something different. The company was no longer a small organization. Its growth meant that there were too many levels of management and administration for him. "I was also traveling much too much for my liking. I looked for something different, a chance to manage a smaller operation. I found a *Wall Street Journal* ad that looked promising. Gibson Guitar was looking for an engineer, with an MBA, who had plant engineering, marketing, and sales experience to become general manager of its $2 million startup Slingerland Drum Division. "It seemed liked a perfect fit. It looked like a good way to return to a smaller-company environment."

There was only one hitch. Gibson was located in Nashville, Tenn. By that time, Johnson, his wife, Kristine, whom he had married in 1987, and their two young children were living in Clinton, N.J. The couple chose to defer moving their family until after he was settled in his new job. Johnson ended up working in Nashville, renting an apartment, and commuting home to New Jersey on weekends. The pressure of living in two places caused him to leave Gibson Guitar nine months later.

Kristine, knowing how miserable he was in this job, encouraged him to change jobs, his career, or both. The fact that his family had not relocated to Tennessee made the choice easier. With no employment ties to bind them, the Johnsons moved to Raleigh to be nearer to Kristine's mother who had been diagnosed with terminal cancer. "I had no clue of how I would earn a living in Raleigh. My goals were to enjoy

life with my family, and no longer travel on business or commute to work. I knew I wanted a job where I had greater control over my life."

It took him six months to find that job, during which time the Johnsons lived off savings. Prudential Securities presented a job possibility. Prudential employed many career changers, and the average age of its new brokers was 40. The company liked Johnson's manage-ment experience, and it wanted to train him in its New York offices to

"I knew I wanted a job where I had greater control over my life."

be a branch manager.

Taking such a job would mean further relocation for his family because he might well be assigned back to the New York area or, conceivably, to any Prudential branch office in the U.S., and that was exactly what he had been trying to avoid. "I didn't wanted to be a supervisor or return to corporate management, so I became a Prudential stockbroker." Johnson knew a little about the stock market, because he had handled his own investments and had set up a corporate 401(k) program in one of his former jobs.

As usual with all new brokers, Prudential hired Johnson on a provisional basis. He spent the first five months learning the business in Raleigh, and then spent a month in New York for more training before taking the required broker tests. "After returning to Raleigh, I looked at the computer screen in my office: no telephone calls and no business. It was all uphill from there."

Prudential gave him an advance on his salary for the first two years. In the third year, Johnson was on his own. During this transitional period, he used additional savings to supplement his income. Next, he developed a business plan. From his previous jobs, he was familiar with the factors that motivate the management of smaller companies. Johnson put that background to work by developing a plan to sell individual and 401(k) retirement plans to smaller companies, those with 20 to 100 employees, in central and eastern North Carolina. He selected these areas because there were fewer brokerage firms competing for business.

When Johnson left Gibson, his Nashville job, he was making $130,000 a year. He hopes to regain that salary level by 2002, five years after becoming a broker, a goal Johnson still considers feasible even with a declining stock market. Even more important, his lifestyle has changed. He works six miles from home. On the day I interviewed him, his son's Little League team at the last minute needed a substitute coach. Johnson left his office to coach, something he would have found impossible to do in past jobs.

ENJOYS SPLIT WORKWEEK

Lucia Greene
MAGAZINE WRITER TAKES A BREAK AND RETURNS TO WORK

Lucia Greene, in her mid 40s, comes from a family of writers. Chapter 11 describes her sister, Stephanie Greene, and mentions her mother, Constance Greene, both of whom write books for children. Lucia Greene's career as a writer has a different twist.

Upon graduation from Colgate University in 1976, Greene, a French and English major, wanted to get into publishing. Her goal at the time was to write children's books.

Twenty-five years ago, it was common for women to start a publishing career as a secretary. Lucia Greene became secretary to two senior editors at E. P Dutton, a job that elicited some advice from her father, "Never become too good a secretary."

Two years later, taking her father's advice to heart and having been promoted to assistant editor in Dutton's children's book group, Greene left Dutton. "I was paid about $7,000 a year. Harper & Row then wanted to hire me at $8,500 a year. Before I took this job, my father suggested that I try to get a job at Time, Inc."

Greene was hired by *People* magazine as a photo researcher. Her relevant experience was restricted to a few photo projects at Dutton. Greene's first assignment on the magazine's unusual editorial ladder was to tie photos and text together to support a *People* article. The next rung was text researcher and the first real step to becoming a staff writer. Then came another trial, editing copy into the magazine's own vernacular and style, commonly called "Peoplese," and some rewriting. Finally, Greene became a full-fledged writer and an assistant editor,

When the youngest child was 11, Greene was ready to go back to work.

primarily rewriting features prepared by the magazine's reporters.

In 1980 Greene got married. In two years she had the first of three children and left *People* to stay at home with her kids. She freelanced from her home in Connecticut for *People* and *Family Weekly*. IBM even hired her to write a brochure to launch an employee program called "Just Say Yes."

"With three children under four, I gave up writing in favor of diapers. When the youngest child was 11, Greene was ready to go back to work. She was hired as a part-timer with a local advertising agency, Mason & Madison, to edit and revise client promotional copy for Konica, Scandinavian Airlines, and Delphi Automotive Systems. Hired as a contingency worker, she was on call five days a week, but there were periods when she had no assignments.

"When I was home with the kids, I wrote a few children's books. I peddled them and almost had one accepted, but it was rejected at the last moment. I felt like a failed writer; I never thought I'd be one again."

Greene's husband, Tom Connolly, a marketing executive, got a new job that was closer to home and required less travel. "With Tom more available as back-up, I was now free to look for work outside the local area. Tom encouraged me to go back to *People*." By that time, Greene knew very few people at the magazine; nearly all the writers and editors of her day were gone. "Luck was on my side. I wrote the managing editor, Carol Wallace, one of the few people remaining on the staff from the old days. She had had the office next to mine. I was back with *People* 16 years to the day that I had left. They weren't even interested in seeing my résumé."

Greene had interviews with several editors before she was assigned to the New York bureau, which covers New York, New Jersey, Pennsylvania and New England. She believes she is the oldest of the 14 staffers in the bureau. Greene requested a job with flexible hours. She commutes on Thursdays and Fridays from Connecticut to New York, a two-hour, door-to-door trip each way. On Mondays and Tuesdays she works from home, researching articles or doing what *People* likes to call "phoners," or telephone interviews.

When she first worked for *People*, Greene was a writer, mostly taking files of information sent by reporters and writing them into the editorial style popularized by the magazine. Now roles have been reversed. As a reporter, she typically prepares a 20-page file that becomes the basis of a two-page piece written by other staff members.

Greene's schedule at *People* fits her personal and family needs. She works but she can still be a "soccer mom" for three teenage children. "What's even more important is that a few years ago I thought my career was over. It was the end of my creativity. I discovered that I could go back to a paid job after an absence of 16 years."

TOOK A PATERNITY LEAVE

Jonathan Beard
LIFESTYLE CRITICAL AS A CLINICAL SOCIAL WORKER

Jonathan Beard, now in his mid 40s, has been a social worker since 1977, but his career in social work actually started earlier. Beard's father was a mental-health practitioner who was one of the founders of the "clubhouse," a rehabilitation method to help adults with severe mental-health problems. As youngsters, Beard and his sister, Margaret, also a social worker, helped out at Fountain House, in New York City, where their father was the director. "I feel I literally grew up at Fountain House, working in the kitchen or doing odd jobs around the place."

After graduating from Florida Southern College in 1977, Beard worked for the next 12 years as a social and mental-health case worker and supervisor, first in New Jersey and then in Texas. Working at Independent House in Dallas set the stage for a master's degree in social work from the University of Texas and the next stop in Beard's career. In 1990, he was hired as executive director of Threshold, a clubhouse rehabilitation center based in Durham, N.C., and modeled after Fountain House.

Six years later, the birth of a daughter stimulated a switch in his career. Beard took vacation time to help out at home, followed by a paternity leave of approximately three months. He was taking advantage of a policy he had proposed several years earlier. "No sooner had the Family Leave Act gone into effect than we implemented the policy at Threshold. I had just gotten married, and Grace and I had not yet decided whether we wanted children. But I thought it would be a good idea to offer paternity

His sabbatical was preceded by family discussions about home finances, and professional ones about how the leave might affect Beard's career.

leave to attract and retain employees."

Beard returned to work in early 1997 as did his wife, who was part-owner of the Mad Hatter, a bakery and coffee shop in Durham. Mad Hatter was only two years old, and Grace was needed in the business. "At first, we had a full-time caretaker for Josephine. Then I resigned from Threshold, looking at the time away from the workplace as a detour in my career." After 20 years in the mental-health field, Beard felt ready for a break. After that, the couple shared the child's care.

His sabbatical was preceded by family

discussions about home finances, and professional ones about how the leave might affect Beard's career. The loss of Beard's income was balanced by Grace's salary at the Mad Hatter. He had some income from work he did as a mental-health consultant in his spare time. Grace's schedule allowed her to cover the home scene if an assignment required him to visit a client for an hour or so. In some fields, "time off" might be harmful to future employment, but Beard reasoned that most mental-health employers would understand and approve of his actions.

Beard's consulting practice began to grow, and he was hired as a part-time clinical social worker at Duke University Medical Center. Five months later, the University of North Carolina's School of Social Work offered him a job too good to refuse: a half-time position directing the continuing-education program, and a chance to teach a nonprofit and public manage-ment course.

Still, Beard had some reservations about the job. As a newcomer to college administration, he asked his sister, who had also switched careers, whether the move was sound. "Margaret told me that this job would permit me to reinvent myself. The skills used in my past jobs could be applied in a different setting." While Beard liked the idea of being part of the UNC scene, his first love was working directly in the mental-health field, so after becoming a UNC part-timer, he spent his Fridays continuing to do mental-health consulting.

Nearly a year later, Beard left UNC when he learned that the part-time job in which he was expanding the continuing-education program at UNC would not become a full-time assignment.

He had mixed emotions about making yet another career move, but he missed clinical work. In September 2000, he joined the staff at Dorothea Dix Hospital in Raleigh, one of the four psychiatric hospitals in North Carolina, as an advocate for patients. Beard investigates the abuse and the neglect or exploitation of patients to ensure that their rights are not violated. The assignment is consistent with his long-time concern for patients' rights, drawing on more than 20 years of professional training and previous mental-health jobs.

SHE LEAVES THE URBAN FAST TRACK

Lauri and Kirk Michel

BUYING A COUNTRY INN IS AN ANTIDOTE TO A NEW YORK CITY LIFESTYLE

Lauri Michel, in her mid 40s, estimates that she has changed careers at least ten times, although all have been based on her architectural education and experience. Lauri and her husband, Kirk, are co-owners of the Hillsborough House Inn, in a small city of the same name about ten miles from Chapel Hill, N.C. Guided by a game plan, the Michels relocated from New York City with their 13-year-old twins; Kirk, who has an MBA from Columbia University, continues to commute three days a week to his midtown New York financial advisory firm, the Bahia Group.

Lauri Michel graduated from the University of Pennsylvania and the University of California in Los Angeles with bachelor's and master's degrees in architecture. "I worked for about five years as an architect, but I discovered that studying architecture differs from its practice. It was time to change careers."

Lauri's entrée into business followed a path different from Kirk's She was recruited by Chemical Bank when it was hiring people with industry or professional expertise as commercial loan officers.

After a year's training she spent the next seven years with Chemical's real estate group doing commercial loans in the construction field. During this period she took a year's maternity leave.

Other bank jobs followed, all of which fused her knowledge of architecture, building and now banking. As a Canadian Imperial Bank loan officer, she took a two-year leave of absence when Mayor Rudolph Giuliani appointed her as deputy commissioner in charge of affordable housing with the New York City Housing

> "In 1998, I made a New Year's resolution that 'This is the year I'm going to figure it out.'"

Department. Then back to the bank and the start of her break with the New York City business and social lifestyle.

"For several years, I wanted to leave banking, which I had been doing for 14 years, and do something else. What I really like to do is somewhat artsy-craftsy. Money is actually not high on my agenda. So why stay in banking other than to make a good living? In 1998, I made a New Year's resolution that 'This is the year I'm going to figure it out.'"

"A career coach asked me to prepare a personal mission statement, starting with five major goals. My list included lifestyle, family and friends, but never making more money. I took the Myers-Briggs test, which indicated that I was a people person and an extrovert. Thinking about it, what I liked about banking was meeting with customers, but not returning to the office and crunching numbers. Based on these tests, I was definitely in the wrong place."

When Lauri and Kirk got married, they discussed their dreams and their retirement fantasies, one of which was to own a bed-and-breakfast inn. "A few years ago, Kirk said that we should do it now, not wait until our retirement. At my Canadian Imperial Bank exit interview, I told them that it was important at this time in my life to run my own business."

Other than being regular B&B guests, they knew little about their operations. "I took a weekend seminar on buying and operating a B&B. Even with my banking experience in evaluating houses and property, I knew nothing about financing a B&B. I learned this at the workshop. In meeting with other B&B people at the seminar, I realized that they were people like me who had diverse interests."

The couple decided to select an existing inn, not build their own. They already were somewhat familiar with central North Carolina because some members of their family lived there. When they could not find a suitable inn for sale in either Raleigh or Durham, they purchased the six-bedroom Hillsborough House Inn, a historic home in a historic community. Built in 1790, it remained family-owned until its conversion to a B&B in 1991.

Unlike many B&Bs where the owners often live in cramped quarters in the inn,

Hillsborough House, located on seven acres a few blocks from Hillsborough's center, has separate residential quarters—important for two teenage children—and sufficient space for Lauri's art and sculpture collection.

Purchasing an Inn was not a real estate investment, but rather a way to achieve a different lifestyle for Lauri and the children, while Kirk continues to commute to New York three days a week. "Lindsey and Matt no longer need a housekeeper to walk them to school,"

"We faced some unplanned problems… but through it all, I can safely say that this is the best decision I ever made in my life."

said Lauri. "They have a sense of freedom they rarely enjoyed in New York, and it takes me a minute or two to get to work. For lack of a better term, we own a home-based business."

B&Bs are rarely big money makers. In 1999, their first year as innkeepers, the Michels grossed over $90,000, a figure consistent with their business plan, and they expected to break even or make a small profit in 2000, slightly ahead of their projection "But we faced some unplanned problems, just about every challenge a small business can have, including staff turnover, unexpected capital expenditures due to a tornado and the January 2000 blizzard (24 inches), exorbitant natural gas prices, and a cash crunch. But through it all, I can safely say that this is the best decision I ever made in my life.

"I continue to become more involved in the community, a luxury I did not have in my previous life. But my involvement also allows me to give something back to the town while at the same time promoting the Inn."

Unlike many B&Bs that primarily serve tourists and vacationers, the Inn is adding to its revenue base as a daytime and overnight retreat. It draws upon Duke and the University of North Carolina and the area's large number of corporate offices. "What guests like about a B&B is that they can disconnect, with no TVs or telephones in the bedrooms. When we have retreats, talks continue in the evening on the porch or sitting room instead of everyone going to their rooms to watch TV," says Lauri. As an incentive to attract retreat customers, the current 600-square-foot meeting room is being modernized with data-communications lines. The computer age has affected the inn in other ways. Although telephone and B&B directories and referrals are the main sources of guests, about 20% of the guests make reservations via the Internet (www.hillsborough-inn.com).

The biggest challenge is finding reliable workers. Lauri prepares breakfast and on weekends Kirk pitches in on different inn chores and keeps the books. When the housekeeping is short-staffed, Lauri also does hands-on work.

It's been more than two years since

"I have a closet filled with suits and pumps that I never wear."

the Michels sold their house in the Fieldston section of the Bronx, withdrew the twins from private school, and relocated as novice innkeepers to North Carolina. "I don't miss New York City one bit. When we visit, we play tourists. I enjoy my new freedom. In Hillsborough, I have a closet filled with suits and pumps that I never wear."

Meeting the Future Now: Information Technology

CAREER OPPORTUNITIES CONTINUE TO BE STRONG IN the information technology field. Despite recent set-backs in the Internet world, the Web and e-commerce are not disappearing. The Internet field will continue to be the place to be when your goal is an exciting and still somewhat unstructured career.

For the rest of this decade, computer-related jobs, according to the Bureau of Labor Statistics (www.bls.gov), should expand faster than any other job category. Employment in the four fastest-growing occupations in the economy—computer engineers, computer support specialists, computer systems analysts, and database administrators—are expected to grow at rates of 108%, 102%, 84%, and 77%, respectively. In short, opportunities in these occupations will double, or nearly double, by 2010. Nearly 13% of all information technology jobs require workers with Internet talents, according to the Information Technology Association of America (www.itaa.org), a business group that represents software, computer and communications companies with roughly $2 trillion in worldwide sales.

On the basis of hiring projections at more than 1,900 companies who employ 447,000 computer professionals, Computerworld reported in early 2001 that information technology (IT) staffs would grow nationwide about 4% for the first quarter and 23% for the year. Although the overall size of IT staff won't be increasing dramatically in these companies, hiring should remain brisk as managers try to cope with staff attrition. If nothing more, it's a case of hiring just to stay even.

At the same time, about 35,000 Internet workers were discharged in a three-month period ending in late February 2001, 12% more than in the preceding year combined, according to Challenger, Gray & Christmas (www.challengergray.com). However, the outplacement firm speculated that programmers and network managers should have little difficulty finding new jobs in other technology sectors.

> **Who can forecast what will happen technologically in the next ten years to create computer-related jobs that are unknown today?**

The information-age career track is like a mass of gelatin—difficult to grab and to hold. Job descriptions, salary scales, and entry-level requirements exist, but the field is in continual flux as new equipment, systems and software are introduced. Who other than a few futurists and technical gurus could have forecast with any precision in the mid 1980s how widespread the use of the Internet only a decade later, and how it would affect the way we live, work, buy, and play? The Internet has created the kind of career excitement that woos traditional computer systems and software analysts, as well as nontechnical workers who want to be part of the action. And, just as interesting, who can forecast what will happen technologically in the next 10 years to create computer-related jobs that are unknown today?

More on the Job Market

The Bureau of Labor Statistics appears to have trouble tracking the number of Internet professionals. Rather than breaking them out as a separate category, it includes them among the 2.2 million systems analysts, programmers, computer engineers, and scientists that it does categorize. Within that group, the BLS does break out approximately 150,000 independent consultants or contract workers with skills in new programming languages or specific software applications. Many of these independents work through temporary agencies and, after completing the assignment, they move on to the next job. John Clendinen (profiled later in this chapter) is a freelance Web site consultant with an informal approach to the workplace. He designs and maintains Web sites for clients either from his at-home office or from local coffee shops, where he sets up shop.

Looking for a job is no problem. Sources of leads include Internet job banks, classified newspaper and business magazine ads, trade shows, and career fairs. The starting salary is $45,000 plus. The choice of employer is up to you—say, the private sector, a nonprofit or government agency, an advertising agency, a graphics firm, or, like John Clendinen, yourself as a freelance consultant. And that's probably not the half of it.

David Blomquist (profiled in Chapter 3) traded in 12 years as a political reporter, columnist, and editor of the *Bergen Record* and his knowledge of computers as a long-time user, to become Webmaster at the same newspaper. A year later, he was recruited by the *Detroit Free Press* as its new-media director, heading an eight-person Web operation. Blomquist credits his newsroom savvy and acquired computer skills in getting him the job.

The Web Workplace

Web work has its ups and downs, says Ken B., a Washington, D.C., Webmaster who prefers not to be named. He runs a one-person department for a trade association where he is, by necessity, a jack of all trades. A college math and philosophy major, Ken learned about computers and communications on previous jobs. Ken is responsible for the daily updating and maintenance of more than 1,000 Web pages.

"In my job, I'm creating a product that has daily visibility, which is great, but there are times when I think I'm working in a vacuum. Few people in my organization have any idea of what I'm doing or can be helpful to me in my work."

A Web manager needs to be more than a "computer nerd

in a basement," which is the way Ian Worthington, public information technology coordinator for Durham County, N.C., describes Web work. Worthington is not a career changer, but he has some interesting observations to share about the work. He got into computers in the mid 1990s with a master's degree in information systems and operations management. Worthington finds that software, hardware, and communications skills are not enough. Webmasters must understand their organization's work and culture just as a lawyer or an accountant must do.

Webmasters must understand their organization's work and culture just as a lawyer or an accountant must do.

"There's never a dull day in my work. It's an ever-changing job; I never know enough about my work. There's no end of things to do, which is both good and bad." His most frustrating moments occur when something goes wrong with the county's Web site. Just as people have little patience with a power or telephone failure, people want the computer system updated and fixed immediately.

Web-related careers still have many of the informal characteristics of the software industry of the early 1980s, when an unknowing public often spelled the word *softwear.* People used software but couldn't describe what it was. As is true of any occupation in its formative stage, the job characteristics change with the introduction of new technology and new protocols. A year before the debacle that faced all too many dot-com companies, Boston University's Corporate Education Center described Internet trends this way: "Everywhere you look, dot-com companies are springing up like mushrooms after a rainstorm. Industry gurus compare the Internet to such society-altering inventions as the electric light and the telephone because its impact is just being felt and its potential seems limitless." The report went on to say that the fields of e-commerce and e-business are so new there "hasn't been enough time for information-technology professionals to gain much experience in these exploding areas. That means there is no existing talent pool, which spells opportunity for anyone who wants to jump in."

Who Does What and How Do You Obtain the Necessary Skills?

There are several different Web jobs: a Web developer is a computer programmer who creates interactive Web sites; a Web designer blends technical skills with graphic or commercial art skills; and a Webmaster combines the work of the programmer and the designer while also maintaining and sometimes creating the content of a Web site.

Art Langer, who heads the department of computer technology and applications at Columbia University's School of General Studies, said that the school's classrooms are filled with people who want to switch from law, teaching, and even ballet dancing into something they believe is more exciting, but to get a good entry-level job what they need is a certificate. He describes his mission as training people for leading-edge technical jobs, not what Langer describes as "bleeding edge" or way-out jobs.

The best bet for the career-changer is a daytime or evening certificate program at a community college or university.

The first Web professionals were self-taught; they learned on the job. As a field matures, classroom education replaces on-the-job training. Even though there are few "official" work requirements, Web professionals need to know how to work in a variety of programming languages, such as HTML, Perl, and Java.

Unless another degree is the career changer's goal, there is little need to enroll in a four-year college program. The best bet is a daytime or evening certificate program at a community college or university, which will take from 12 to 24 months to complete. Brita Sofra (profiled later in this chapter), who heads a community college's information-technology department, has among her students a biologist, a former police officer, and a technical writer, all of whom intend to use their IT training to switch careers.

A few years ago, college computer curriculums consisted of courses in systems development, systems analysis, software applications, and data communications. In response to student and marketplace demands, many of these schools have retooled, and are teaching courses relating specifically to the Internet and e-commerce.

Mercer County Community College (www.mccc.edu) in Trenton, N.J., developed its curriculum to train students in Web site design and e-marketing; it also offers basic and advanced courses in building e-commerce Web sites. The courses reflect Mercer's aim to help students become owners of an e-business, get a job designing and maintaining Web pages, or work as a Web developer or Web editor.

Although classroom education provides a number of the tools needed by career changers, there are other ways to approach the job market. Remember that Bill Gates, who started out as a software designer, did pretty well for a college dropout. Career changers can learn a lesson along the way. Gates took an idea, and created a software product. This same spirit still exists throughout the information technology field. Take a look at Web development work executed by teenagers and college undergraduates. In their way, they are similar to basketball players who quit college to play as professionals because the money is "too good." These younger technologists

POINTS TO REMEMBER

- **Web design** and development are the stages for today's glamour jobs.
- **Two- and four-year colleges** offer degree and certificate courses in Web design and management.
- **Some career changers** learn their Web or information systems skills on the job.
- **Previous workplace skills** complement computer skills and help people over age 30 get good jobs.
- **There's more to Web management** than just computer skills.
- **New technologies** are continually emerging.
- **Web-related jobs** are ideal for workers who prefer to be self-employed.
- **Even with the downturn** in the number of dot-com enterprises, other career opportunities open up each day.

see greater opportunities in doing it rather than studying it. What about you?

Some People Who Made the Change

The best crystal-ball gazers have trouble talking with any degree of accuracy about what's going to take place in the computer software and data communications field. What seemed like an accurate forecast as recently as 1996 seems outdated a few years later. The bottom line is that good jobs abound for skilled professionals. Some of the people described in this chapter learned about computers in their 30s; others have been computer users since college or even high school. Career changers in this field have one thing in common: They're using past skills in furniture design, photography, law, or journalism in their current computer jobs.

SHOWBIZ MEETS DOT-COM

Tony Dunne and Rosemary Breslin
NONTECHIES IN A TECHIE WORLD

Tony Dunne and his wife, Rosemary Breslin, are low-tech workers engaged in e-commerce. They aim to apply Web technology to the sale of medium- to high-priced furniture. Techies would hardly be impressed with Dunne or Breslin's credentials prior to their starting HauteDecor.com in 1999. Dunne, now in his mid 40s, spent nearly 20 years as a film and television set builder, and Breslin, now in her early 40s, worked for nearly as long as a newspaper reporter and television scriptwriter.

Dunne attended both Williams College and the University of Indiana but did not graduate from either institution. When he left college in the mid 1970s, Dunne lived briefly in California with his uncle, writer John Dunne, and his wife, Joan Didion. "I grew up with good furniture; I understood its place in the home. I was impressed with their carpenter, Harrison Ford (on the verge of becoming a Hollywood star), who was doing work at their house. What impressed me was Ford's pride in his craft. He made raw space beautiful, and that's what I wanted to do."

Returning east, Dunne became a woodworker. "I owned a small home that doubled in price in two years, so I sold it. Once I had some money, I could do what I wanted to. I moved from Connecticut to New York City." Dunne went to work for Don Russo, then one of the city's premier furniture designers.

"Russo gave me a job. Everyone else in his shop was in his 60s, and Russo needed some fresh blood. Over the next four years, he taught me how to work hard, to be more disciplined, and to take new approaches to solve what

> **"I never planned to do movie sets all my life, and I started to think seriously of other things I might like to do."**

seemed like unsolvable problems."

While working for Russo, Dunne also taught furniture making at the Woodsmith Studio, a New York City specialty school for furniture design. One of his students was a film producer, for whose home Dunne started to make furniture. "We discovered that each of us was doing what the other wanted to do. He gave me an opportunity to build film sets. I left Russo, went on my own, and started Dunne & Company."

To Dunne, the logistics of building movie sets was as important as the creativity it required. He found that an ability to transport materials, along with an ability to accurately project costs, was key to running a successful set-design and building business. This insight served as a precursor to the eventual startup of HauteDecor. Dunne also found that many of the techniques used in designing film sets could be applied in the design of home interiors and decor.

Unlike other film-set designers, Dunne worked only on one assignment at a time. He found the assignments too complex to simultaneously build sets for such movies as *Addicted to Love, Ransom, The Out of Towners,* and *Die Hard: With a Vengeance.*

Dunne's business philosophy emphasized the use of sound business systems throughout his operation:

"We started to use computers to visualize different sets, and to schedule the building and delivery of completed sets. We found it was less expensive to design sets on a computer. The visualization via computers helps them avoid problems that with paper design that they otherwise wouldn't have found until they started building. Unlike some of the older set builders, I was young enough to understand the benefit of computers."

Then a personal tragedy struck. "My brother, four years older than I, was killed in a plane crash. We had been talking about our futures. He was a successful lawyer and a partner in a law firm, but he was also looking for more personal fulfillment. I never planned to do movie sets all my life, and I started to think seriously of other things I might like to do."

Dunne had never totally abandoned his interest in interior design, but he had limited his work to family members and a few close friends. The death of his brother, however, marked Dunne's transition. He and Breslin discussed the next step, and in early 1999, Dunne left the movie-set business and returned to full-time work as an interior designer. The couple was prepared to take some financial risks, including a drop in income for about a year and the accumulation of personal debt during the transition.

Having seen the virtue of computer technology in designing movie sets, Breslin wondered, Why not apply similar systems to interior design?

Having seen the virtue of computer technology in designing movie sets, Breslin wondered, Why not apply similar systems to interior design, a field that in many ways operated at a very low-tech level? An idea perked. Dunne created the concept which would soon evolve into HauteDecor.com (also its Web address). It would initially bring together 15 to 20 leading interior designers, each creating a room where individual pieces or all of the furniture could be purchased online. Unlike static print or TV ads or a sales brochure, HauteDecor's Web site shows online customers a chair or table from different angles. Six months after creating the concept behind HauteDecor, Dunne received the first round of venture-capital financing, sufficient to hire a staff of software experts and marketers and to develop software and a Web site. And in June 2000, HauteDecor raised an additional $14 million in venture financing needed to launch its online interior design marketing concept.

Until they formed HauteDecor, Dunne had used computers solely as a design and production aid; Breslin's usage had been restricted to word processing and Internet research. After graduating from Hamilton College in Clinton, N.Y., Breslin had worked as a reporter for *Newsday,* the *New York Times,* and *Rolling Stone;* she had written a number of television episodes for *NYPD Blue;* and she was the author of *Not Exactly What I Had in Mind,* a book that recounts some of her own health problems.

"When we started HauteDecor, I had little intention of joining the company," said Breslin. "Up to then, my income was only supplemental to Tony's. I wanted to continue as a freelance writer. It became apparent that scenario writing was critical to a virtual interior design center." Breslin signed up as the second employee in the company and became its editorial director.

A HauteDecor script, which accompanies the visual materials online, differs from the text written for the movies or TV. It needs to be continually tweaked to meet changing market and customer needs That's where Breslin's skills come in handy—namely, the ability to meet daily deadlines, rapidly revise a script, and make it work in an Internet environment.

SELF–TAUGHT COMPUTER SKILLS

Roylee Duvall

A SERIES OF CAREERS LEAD TO THE COMPUTER CLASSROOM

Roylee Duvall, now in his late 40s, grew up in Kannapolis, N.C., a cotton-mill town and the home of Cannon Mills. He worked on the company's looms during his high school summers. Duvall married right out of high school and was divorced before moving to Chapel Hill in 1972, minus a job or a career.

His first job, building prefabricated homes, lasted six months; then Duvall turned to photography, a long-time hobby. "I was offered two different jobs in photo studios. One was in Raleigh, an hour's drive from Chapel Hill, and a local one with the University of North Carolina."

Duvall took the latter. He didn't actually work as a UNC photographer but operated a small printing press in the School of Continuing Education. When the job was abolished a few years later in a cost-cutting and consolidation move, it was time for another youthful career change.

"I liked cameras, so I went to work in the camera department at J. C. Penney in Durham. I enjoyed selling and working with people, but the department was run as a 'loss leader,' and it soon became apparent that there was no real career or future in selling cameras for Penney."

Duvall's career alternative was to open a 600-square-foot camera store in a Chapel Hill shopping center, with the backing of a Small Business Administration loan. "Called Photosynthesis, like the photosynthesis process, we took light and made it into green, which for us was the color of money. We did rather well until the early 1980s, when a bad economy and catalog sales of cameras did us in."

"I'm a gadget person, no matter whether it is a camera or a computer."

Duvall was not despondent. The store had received good ratings from customers and photo suppliers. His immediate goal was to remain in the photography field as a freelance photographer doing weddings, parties, and portraits. "The trouble is, I didn't really want to do weddings, so I was a freelancer for less than two years, but photography still fascinated me. The technical side was more interesting than taking pictures."

His interest in photography led Duvall to a job as a sales representative for a photo-supply manufacturer. This provided a chance to do some traveling.

"I went to a photo-supply trade show in Atlanta, passed out some résumés, and got several favorable responses. On my first job, I was assigned to sell photo supplies in a territory that included all of Kentucky, Mississippi, western Alabama, Tennessee, western North Carolina, and parts of Virginia. I stayed only four months. I would leave Durham and be gone for 30 days. Even for someone who wanted to travel, it was too much for me."

Duvall got another photo-supply sales job, this time with a smaller territory, North and South Carolina. He quit several years later when his second wife, Barbara, a high school Latin teacher, asked him to work closer to home.

By then, Duvall had become interested in computers. As a sales rep, he used a computer to record and maintain photo-supply sales and marketing data. Without any formal computer training, Duvall created his own database systems. The next career step combined his interest in computers with his sales skills.

Carolina Computer Stores, a small local chain, seemed like a good place to work. "The owner believed in training, and employees spent a few hours each week at workshops. But as much as I liked my job, I was ready to move on after three years."

Duvall was hired to market a digital printer to advertising agencies. To further his professional skills, he took community-college courses in advertising and graphic design.

Then he took a job as a contract worker with a local trucking company that was ahead of its time in computerizing its tracking of shipping information. The job expanded and he was hired as

the trucker's network administrator.

Duvall's computer career soon took a different direction. A friend he had known at Carolina Computer Stores suggested that he teach a computer course at Durham Technical Community College.

"'That's not for me' was my immediate reaction. But my friend persisted. She even called Durham Tech and suggested that they hire me as an instructor. They liked my diverse computer background, and the fact that

To keep current in the fast-moving computer field means an ambitious personal continuing-education program.

I knew both Apple and IBM desktop systems.

"The school called at 10 A.M. and told me that I could start teaching later that day. I had only a few hours to prepare for my first class. I walked into class at 6 P.M., scared to death, but in less than 15 minutes I felt comfortable in front of my students. It was like the retail photo business when I was scared at first, and then found I could work with customers. The same personal approach applied in the classroom."

To keep current in the fast-moving computer field means an ambitious personal continuing-education program. Duvall keeps up by spending about

$1,500 a year on publications and books relating to computers. For a person who has been a retailer, waiter, photographer, and a photo-supply and computer salesperson, Duvall now concentrates on his teaching and work as an independent Web designer. "I never had difficulty making the transition from one job or career to another. I'm a gadget person, no matter whether it is a camera or a computer. Sometimes I wish that I were in a field like wood-working, where the technology changes at a much slower pace."

COLLEGE OPENED HIS EYES

Robert Cress
A TRUCKING ACCIDENT LEADS TO A CAREER AS A COMPUTER ANALYST

Robert Cress, in his late 30s, describes his career as "being late into the tunnel." Hardly a pun for a one-time truck driver, Cress refers to the nearly 20-year route he took from trucker to his new career as a computer analyst.

After graduating from high school in Buena, in the southern part of New Jersey, in the late 1970s, he learned how to drive a truck from an uncle who then hired him to drive one of his trucks. "I finished high school, but that was about it. I saw a chance to make some money, and I looked at things very short range. I didn't understand at the time that while I was driving a truck, people who went to college weren't making any money, but they would surpass me once they went to work."

The next 18 years were similar. Cress was a trucker for several companies, driving either local or regional routes in New Jersey and New England states. A member of the Teamsters union, he earned about $40,000 a year. Cress was single and his earnings provided a fairly good livelihood until the mid 1990s, when severe disc problems limited him to light physical work and ended his career as a truck driver. "I never thought of college while I was driving. I was comfortable doing the work. I got used to getting up at 2 or 3 in the morning, and working 12- to

14-hour days. I took six months off after leaving trucking and went to Gloucester Community College to get an associate degree. Up to then, I had never used, or been interested in, computers."

After completing the two-year program, Cress decided to finish his undergraduate education at Drexel University,

Job opportunities, new technology, good pay, and nonphysical work beckoned.

in Philadelphia. Job oppor-tunities, new technology, good pay, and nonphysical work beckoned.

Drexel's curriculum stresses cooperative-education programs that enable students to mix classwork and jobs. There are two, ten-week terms followed by a six-month placement in a job relating to the student's field of specialty. To offset $16,000 in annual tuition and personal expenses, Cress relied on a $6,000-a-year Drexel scholarship, savings, and co-op education jobs like one he had in Cigna Corp.'s computer operation.

The next challenge after graduation was to get a full-time job in information systems.

"Until Drexel, I had never had a

corporate job interview. My previous jobs came from reading want ads in the newspaper or from the Teamsters. Now I had some other things going for me. I'm from the old school. I show up for work on time, and work the full day. When I worked for Cigna, some of the younger Drexel students came to work late. Trucking taught me how to work hard."

Now that he has left trucking, he says, he has lost touch with most of his former truck-driver buddies. "I no longer party like they do, and we no longer speak the same language."

WORKS FROM HOME OFFICE

John Clendinen
TOOK THE LEAP TO FREELANCE WEB-SITE DESIGNER

John Clendinen, in his early 30s, is a young career changer. Unlike so many people who spend years in careers they no longer enjoy before making a break, Clendinen decided when he was 27 that he didn't like the corporate life at Blue Cross or, in fact, in most companies. His solution was to become an independent computer consultant.

As a freshman engineering student at Duke University, Clendinen switched to liberal arts, studying public policy. Returning home to Florida after graduation, he held a few brief jobs with several management consulting firms, which were not to his liking. With his wife, Heather, a speech pathologist, Clendinen left Florida, returned to Durham, and took a new job with Blue Cross. It, too, was short-lived; as Clendinen put it, "It was numbers-crunching and data-management work, and not very exciting."

His career options were to get another job or do something on his own. "Heather encouraged me to go into business. My parents felt the same way, but Heather's folks are more conservative and felt that I should have a 'real' job."

Clendinen had become fascinated with computers in the fourth grade, when he received a computer as a present from his parents. "In every job,

I became 'the computer guy,' even though I had no formal training other than a Fortran class in a freshman engineering course." So, in his late 20s, Clendinen decided to become an independent computer consultant. Clendinen doesn't consider himself to be much of a risk taker. He just feels more comfortable

"In every job, I became 'the computer guy,' even though I had no formal training."

being self-employed and not being a permanent part of an organizational team. Paramount among his goals is the maintenance of the personal freedom he has found in self-employment that he never found as an employee. His start-up, which he initially called Clandestine Productions, was renamed Qblue (www.qblue.com), in the hope that the name inspires curiosity.

Clendinen, an Internet-development specialist, concentrates on purchasing Web space in bulk, subdividing it according to each client's need, and then building Web sites. Part of his job is to help clients make the transition from the "real" world to the virtual world. Clendinen's clients are mostly smaller companies and entrepreneurs who want to develop a Web site but do not have the know-how or staff expertise to do the work themselves. "In the case of a local church, I started as a volunteer, and then worked my way into doing fee work. I can personally handle about 20 different projects at once, but above that number, things get confusing." He derives his income from different sources: He is a host and reseller for Internet operator Mindspring, he has a consulting agreement with a company for half his time to develop and maintain its various Web sites, and he has a series of Web development assignments. "I find it more exciting to create a site than to update and maintain it. My work already pays me a living, and, best of all, I'm self-employed."

Relatively young, with an informal work attitude, Clendinen works in an office behind his home in a 240 square-foot former shed that he remodeled and equipped with the gadgets necessary for Web development. Before his daughter was born in early 2000, he worked in his home. "I like working at home and not being an absentee father, but I also need some privacy in my work. That's why I have a place of my own behind the house."

I met Clendinen at Foster's, a local restaurant and coffee shop, where he was transmitting data to a client on his laptop via a cell telephone. I stopped at his table to chat and to watch his online technique. His mobile office serves as a billboard for Clendinen and Qblue in action. "I work from home, Foster's, and Barnes & Noble, and just about anyplace where I can use a laptop, work, and drink coffee."

Clendinen meets people his age who seem dissatisfied with their corporate jobs and expects to find more and more

"I work from home and just about anyplace where I can use a laptop, work, and drink coffee."

of his college classmates switching careers as they find that corporate life is no longer fulfilling. "Along these lines, our generation is redefining jobs and careers. In fact, who knows where this work will take Heather, Anna, and me? In five years, we might want to live in France. I'm free to work anyplace. "What problems I have are related mostly to figuring out how to keep growing without eliminating my favorite part of the job—that is, freedom."

SURVIVING IN A TOUGH JOB MARKET

Greg Vimont

A PROFESSIONAL PHOTOGRAPHER BECOMES AN E–COMMERCE WEB PROGRAMMER

Little did Greg Vimont, now in his early 40s, realize in the early 1980s that his childhood passion to take things apart and see how they worked would take him from photography to computers. Vimont satisfied his first interest as a photojournalism major at the University of Texas. It led to a job as a staff photographer for Texas Governor Mark White. From there, Vimont moved to New York, apprenticing for three years with Bernard Vidal, a commercial photographer with studios in Paris and New York.

"I then went out on my own as a photographer. What I enjoyed the most about photography was solving problems." Those included getting a photo crew from point A to point B, arranging the lighting, working with props and especially communicating effectively, which he feels is the essence of photography. To achieve these objectives, he began to use PCs and Macs in his work.

In the mid 1990s, Vimont became a photographer and production manager at Rockefeller University in New York, where he did digital imaging for the university's research faculty and doctoral candidates. Vimont was responsible for training a staff of six in the use of a number of different digital systems. His job required the use of such software applications as PhotoShop,

Quark, PageMaker, Illustrator, Freehand, and Canvas. Computers and software, rather than photography, became his prime focus. The longer he worked with Rockefeller's information systems people, the more Vimont knew that's what he wanted to do.

In 1996, Vimont's son, Ben, was born

"From my past jobs, I had acquired skills that are applicable in most business settings."

with some health problems. Vimont's wife, Celia Slom, took a three-month maternity leave and, when it ended, Vimont took a similar leave. "One of us wanted to be home with Ben. So I left Rockefeller. Why go back? I was in a dead-end job with little opportunity for growth. Anyway, Celia had a better job and better hours with the American Lung Association."

Although he was no longer in the workforce, Vimont thought perhaps he'd take a few computer courses. Instead of taking random courses, he opted for a Columbia University certificate program in analysis and design of information systems. He reasoned that Columbia's demanding certificate program would position him for a better job. The family's low overhead enabled them to survive on one salary. They don't own a car, and the monthly rent on their two-bedroom apartment is modest by New York standards. If they had both worked and hired a nanny, it would have been a financial wash. Savings paid Columbia's $11,000 tuition.

In September 1997, after nearly a year as a stay-at-home dad, Vimont started classes. His wife got home about 5 P.M., giving him one hour to get to Columbia in time for class. For the next 18 months, he concentrated on his studies, declining any freelance photo assignments.

Certificate in hand, along with a 3.9 grade-point average, Vimont posted his résumé on several Internet job banks and heard from several search firms. "At the time, I was interested in discovering what jobs were available and for what jobs I was most qualified as a former photographer."

Vimont found that his background in photography, design, and journalism impressed job interviewers. "From my past jobs, I had acquired skills that are applicable in most business settings. I could have gone with some large companies, but as a former entrepreneur, I like the flexibility of smaller companies."

Within a few months he was hired by an e-commerce firm that did Web programming, and he doubled his former Rockefeller salary. But the job ended eight months later when the company closed as a result of the dot-com shakeout.

While he looked for a full-time job, Vimont worked as an independent consultant with WNET, the public broadcasting station serving New York City, and as a computer workshop instructor at Columbia.

Six weeks after the demise of the dot-com firm, Vimont's WNET relationship paid off. Through an associate at the TV station, he found a job at retailer J. Crew's corporate offices in New York, where he works on data-warehouse applications in the company's data-management group.

His wife, Celia, a freelance health care writer, works several hours a day at home while Ben attends school.

ART AND WEB–SITE DESIGN BLEND

Brita "Bree" Sofra
FROM SPEECH PATHOLOGIST TO COMPUTER EDUCATOR

Brita "Bree" Sofra's career provides testimony to the Internet opportunities open to career changers. As a high school graduate in northeastern Ohio, she put aside her intention to study art in college and instead got an under-graduate degree at Kent State University and a master's degree from the University of Akron in speech pathology. After 12 years' experience as a school and nursing-home speech pathologist, Sofra, who is now in her early 40s, changed directions for a new career as an Internet professional.

Sofra got hooked on the Web in the early 1990s, when Internet technology was comparatively crude by today's standards. With little self-help informa-tion available, Sofra taught herself how to use the Internet and began designing Web pages. "And being an artist at heart, I was able to indulge my desire to create, draw, and paint. There is no limit to what you can do artistically on the Web."

Several years after moving to Cary, N.C., for a job in speech rehabilitation at a nursing home, Sofra lost the job when Medicare changed its formula for reimbursing speech pathologists. By then, however, she was already designing Web pages on a freelance basis. "After I was laid off, I did Web-site maintenance for just about anyone who would employ

me. I wanted to build a portfolio to show new clients." Her business, Webbildr (www.webbildr.com), grew with free-lance assignments from another speech pathologist, a greeting-card designer, and two local universities.

Her introduction to computer instruction had actually come years

> ## "I did Web site maintenance for just about anyone who would employ me. I wanted to build a portfolio to show new clients."

earlier when the principal of the Hattiesburg, Ms., school, where she was working as a speech pathologist, discovered that she was computer liter-ate and asked her to teach the other teachers how to use computers.

Then she started to take computer-graphics courses at Wake Technical Community College. Wake Tech was beefing up its computer-related curriculum by adding courses in data communications that reflected industry trends. When Sofra's instructor learned about her classroom experience in Mississippi and her knowledge of how to start and operate a Web site, he asked her to teach class as a full-time temp and to serve as acting chairwoman of Wake Tech's new Internet Technology department. She accepted the offer and progressed to become a permanent faculty member; in August 2000 the school dropped "acting" from her title.

Sofra is responsible for developing a series of courses in Web graphics, Web development, and Web management. In one of her classes, the career changers include a biologist, a police officer, and a technical writer.

"Even with my new Wake Tech job, I'm still an artist at heart. What I do in my own Web-design work and in the classroom bring together my interests and training in speech pathology, communications, and art. And one thing I'm sure of is that there are no experts in the Web field because it's evolving so rapidly."

SEGUEING FROM THE FAMILY BUSINESS

John Mingis
NONPROFIT CONSULTANT GOES ONLINE

John Mingis, now in his mid 30s, walked away from a secure management job with a family-owned business for a new career as a nonprofit consultant—with an online twist.

Mingis was a third-generation member of his family to work for Pepsi Cola Bottling of Greenville, N.C., a franchised company started by his grandfather in the early 1930s, which bottled and sold Pepsi products in 13 counties in the eastern part of the state.

As Mingis was growing up, Pepsi Cola was a large part of his early life. "I worked at Pepsi every summer in junior high school and high school, and all through college. I was involved in every aspect of the business." Mingis attended East Carolina University, also located in Greenville, where he majored in criminal justice and sociology. He considered getting into law enforcement, but he gravitated toward the family business.

After working at Pepsi for a number of years, Mingis started to think about other things that he might want to do. At Pepsi, he had worked in human resources and community relations, and was the company's community representative. He was appointed to the Governor's Crime Commission, a natural volunteer assignment, considering his college major, and he served as a director of the Greenville Boys and Girls Club.

Eventually, Mingis became less satisfied with being a company employee during the day and a volunteer at night and on weekends. "I approached my family. At the time, my father was alive, and I proposed to him that I leave the

> **Eventually, Mingis became less satisfied with being a company employee during the day and a volunteer at night and on weekends.**

company and get a full-time job in the nonprofit field. He was against it. He said that if I tried to do something different, I could never return to the company, because I'd never be respected by the other employees."

While remaining at Pepsi, Mingis was responsible for processing requests from nonprofits looking for money. Mingis realized that the nonprofits needed management assistance, as well as funding. As a consultant, he began developing business and marketing plans for smaller nonprofits that lacked management expertise and staff.

The transition from paid executive

with Pepsi Cola Bottling to owner of Mingis & Associates was less difficult than Mingis had anticipated. As a director of the bottling company, he continued to serve on its board and collected a director's fee. "Fortunately, Sarah and I are low-maintenance folks, and we could manage on less income."

Like many entrepreneurs, Mingis looked at office space outside the home when he left Pepsi. "But I couldn't justify the cost. I decided to try working at home for year, and if it didn't work out, I could always rent an office. We had a number of telephone lines installed at home—a basic line, a rollover line, and two computer lines."

Mingis also installed a dedicated telephone line for the Greenville Foundation, for which he has served as part-time director, for an annual fee, since the late 1990s.

Mingis finds that working from home has certain disadvantages. "I have a hard time getting away from my work, until Sarah says it's time to have dinner. I also miss the day-to-day contacts of an office job. I still put on a suit in the morning and walk down the hall to my office."

Fortunately, Mingis knows the key nonprofit players in the Greenville area, for whom he writes brochures and solicitation letters, and whom he counsels on ways to operate more efficiently.

A small consulting firm like Mingis & Associates has limited local or regional growth potential because it can serve only a few clients from its home base in Greenville. To expand his business, Mingis created a Web-based consulting service (www.fundraisingexpert.com) with various sections on fund-raising, general management, and networking techniques for nonprofits. Mingis fulfills requested services and bills online customers at an hourly rate. From his own and some linked sites, he averages several thousand "hits" a month. Naturally, most hits are from curiosity

From his own and some linked sites, he averages several thousand "hits" a month, which are producing online consulting assignments.

seekers, but the traffic has reached the point at which it is producing online consulting assignments.

In early 2001 Mingis took another step to further his dot-com marketing concept by rolling out a database of more than one million nonprofit names and addresses, including about 400,000 nonprofits that are located outside the U.S. but are registered to do business in this country. He's able to sell customized databases and names for less money than similar online services, and turn a profit on these transactions.

Blending Many Skills in the Clergy

THE RELIGIOUS LIFE IS A FIELD WHERE YOU CAN "MAKE a difference," and some career changers find the call to become a minister, priest, or rabbi appealing. The ministry requires diverse job skills: the ability to participate in a congregation's series of events from birth to death, to conduct the weekly or more frequent worship services, to write and present sermons, and to champion one's faith. If that's not enough of an incentive, add to the mix the need to be a politician, diplomat, public speaker, community activist, counselor, teacher, fund-raiser and business manager.

Msgr. Francis Kelly, president and rector of Pope John XXIII National Seminary (www.geocities.com/bjxxiii), in suburban Boston, knows first-hand about career changers. For the past 40 years, this seminary has been dedicated exclusively to training career changers who are 30 to 60 years old. Monseignor Kelly's message on second-career priests applies equally well to older divinity-school students of other faiths:

"The priest's empathy rings true as that of someone who has lived many of the challenges and decisions—some about pleasant conditions, others not so pleasant—that face people throughout life. People relate well to advice and counsel from a priest who they believe understands them.

"The older priest has a wealth of experience to relate when

he delivers homilies at Mass. The homilies often are memorable when they include an anecdote about a personal experience, and they relate to real life as lived today."

The Job Market

There's no shortage of career changers at 237 Protestant and Roman Catholic divinity schools, according to Association of Theology Schools (www.ats.edu). In 1998–1999, of the 28,283 students working toward a master of divinity degree, which is the entry-level degree for ministers and priests and the degree needed for ordination, nearly one-half were between the ages of 30 and 49.

At present, approximately 400,000 Protestant ministers, 47,000 Roman Catholic priests, and 5,000 rabbis serve an estimated, nominal 91 million Protestants, 61 million Roman Catholics, and 3.5 million Jews in the U.S. population.

The job market depends on the denomination. A number of the more traditional Protestant denominations have either declining or static church-going memberships. The evangelical churches, however, are growing, acquiring more churches and more members. Does this mean that those churches are a natural job market for divinity-school graduates? Not necessarily. Some have ministers who followed a different academic route into the ministry, or simply responded to a "call to the ministry," with little formal theological education.

The Jewish Theology Seminary, which trains conservative rabbis, and the Hebrew Union College/Jewish Institute of America, where reform Jews receive rabbinical training, have an increasing number of career changers, but their rate remains below the rate at many Protestant seminaries.

The number of Roman Catholic Church worshipers in the U.S. is expanding largely because of the immigration of Roman Catholics. The church's 47 seminaries are unable to educate enough priests to serve 61 million parishioners or to replace priests who retire, die, or leave the priesthood. To keep pace, the use of ordained deacons has grown fivefold in the past 20 years. Deacons participate in baptism, weddings, and funerals but are not permitted to celebrate Mass or administer the sacraments.

Members of the clergy seldom take early retirement, perhaps because they can't afford to retire. Nonetheless, 12% of the working clergy are more than 65 years old—a rate that is four times the rate for people in other professions. Like professionals in other fields, members of the clergy enjoy their work and have a strong relationship with their congregations and communities; in some cases, they have been given lifetime tenure.

The ordained clergy have other outlets for their religious and pastoral training, as chaplains in hospitals, universities and the armed forces, or in social-service and community assignments. Of the 94 graduates from Princeton Theological Seminary in 1998, 11 went to work as chaplains or in other specialized ministerial jobs. In Judaism, there is a separate though closely related career track for cantors who sing or chant liturgical music and train at the same seminaries as rabbis.

In some religions and denominations, women have made significant inroads into this job market. One-third of the 13,500 divinity-school students who are 30 to 49 years old are women.

In some religions and denominations, women have made significant inroads into this job market. One-third of the 13,500 divinity school students who are 30 to 49 years old are women. At the Hebrew Union College, over half the rabbis ordained in 2000 were women—a remarkable change considering that the first woman rabbi was ordained only 28 years earlier. Of the 405 master of divinity students at the Garrett-Evangelical Theological Seminary, in Evanston, Ill., 246 are women.

It is quite a change from a generation ago, when most Protestant and Jewish denominations refused to ordain women. Nonetheless, women are excluded from ordination as Orthodox rabbis, as Southern Baptist ministers, and as priests in the Roman Catholic Church. But unlike other professions, the clergy to date is guided by ordination rules rather than equal opportunity employment guidelines.

The Calling

The epiphany, as priests and ministers put it, is the mystical perception of a divine being. It is the key reason that motivates lawyers, accountants, and executives among others to switch careers. While Jews do not have a "calling," Ellen Lippmann (profiled later in this chapter), a reform rabbi in Brooklyn, said that the sense of mission that moved her to go to rabbinical school was the nearest thing to a calling.

Don't be concerned if, as a potential minister, your past includes personal indifference to religion or church or synagogue attendance that was limited to Christmas and Easter, or the Jewish High Holidays. Divinity schools are more interested in your changing religious attitude that stimulated a "calling."

Even so, a sudden act or perception of faith is not enough to qualify for divinity school and a new career as a minister. It needs to be balanced with practical acts of faith—such as working at a food bank, counseling the poor, or teaching Sunday school classes—that goes beyond a two-month commitment simply to meet a divinity's school's entrance requirements.

Preparing for Divinity School

Students should be realistic when they prepare to enter a field where the future financial prospects are not very good. It differs, said Gregory Duncan, director of admissions and student life at Duke University's Divinity School, from the experience of career changers who enter other professions where the financial return is better.

The candidate's spouse and any older children who are still at home will have to buy into the pastoral life of a minister. At times, says Duncan, who is also an ordained Methodist minister, "I have urged some career changers to delay applying to divinity school for a year or more so they can get their life and finances in order." Many need to learn about the minister's daily life. Being a church volunteer is one way to see that there's more to a minister's life than preaching Sunday sermons.

A peripatetic lifestyle, though less severe than in past generations, continues to exist to some degree in some denominations. Until recently, Methodist ministers were assigned to a different church every four to five years. This policy is softening because families are no longer so mobile. A minister's spouse is not always able to find an equally good job in another community, or children cannot be easily yanked out of school. This means that reassignments are made to accommodate a family's personal, not just the church's personnel, needs.

It's never too early to start preparing for divinity school. It is important to speak to your minister (or priest or rabbi), and to ask the hard questions about career changers in the ministry and divinity school. It's also wise to make the minister an ally, because the minister is a necessary, if not mandatory, divinity school reference.

Divinity schools are interested in your changing religious attitude that stimulated a "calling."

Some divinity schools include psychological testing and screening interviews with faculty members and other clergy members to determine the applicant's sincerity and to discourage romantics who lack the personal and people skills needed in the ministry. To determine whether her decision to leave the theater for divinity school was sound, Sally Bates (profiled later in this chapter) spent nine months in pastoral counseling with a psychologist who also was an ordained minister.

Divinity School

The Master of Divinity degree qualifies Protestants and Roman Catholics for ordination. Reform and Conservative Jews receive a similar degree, a Master of Arts in Hebrew Letters, to qualify to be ordained rabbis.

The choice of a divinity school is similar to selecting any graduate school; one must consider the school's course of study, locality, tuition, cost of living, size of classes, and reputation. There are approximately 200 Protestant, 47 Roman Catholic, and 40 Jewish seminaries in the U.S. Some divinity schools require applicants to take the Graduate Record Examination, while the majority rely on a combination of college, and, if applicable, professional- or graduate-school grades, workplace and related life experiences, and personal interviews, in which school officials explore the applicant's "calling."

The course of study is three years; in addition, many churches require students to spend a year as a student pastor. Some fundamental Protestant denominations employ less structured academic guidelines to prepare people for ordination.

This career change requires a willingness and an ability to replace a corporate or professional lifestyle with that of a job with low pay that most likely will not rise significantly in the years ahead.

Even traditional Protestant denominations have alternative routes into the ministry. Since 1994, the United Methodist Church has offered the "Course of Study," an abbreviated part-time academic program that is used primarily to recruit pastors to work in rural areas. The assignment combines the duties of a pastor with a requirement to complete 32 hours of graduate theological education within five years. Over 2,000 pastors are being trained with the Course of Study, compared with 3,000 full-time divinity school students.

A liberal arts education is considered the best training for divinity school. As part of the training at the Hebrew Union College/Jewish Institute of Religion (www.huc.edu) and the Jewish Theological Seminary of America (www.jtsa.edu), students learn Hebrew during an academic year in Israel. It's common for Roman Catholic students to learn Spanish if they intend to take church assignments in Spanish-speaking communities.

Costs vary. Of course, the states don't sponsor low-cost state university divinity schools, because such sponsorship would violate of the Constitution's principle of separation of church and state. Some divinity schools have tuitions and expenses that match those at law and medical schools, while others are subsidized by their denomination. Protestant, Roman Catholic, and Jewish divinity schools structure programs to permit students to do paid part-time church and community work during the school year and vacations.

Getting a job after graduation differs within each denomination. Newly ordained Roman Catholic priests return to their home dioceses for parish assignment. A similar approach exists for the Episcopal Church, with its structured hierarchy and to a lesser extent among other Protestant denominations. For most Protestant and Jewish denominations, a recent graduate is a free agent who gets a job via seminary career-services offices or denomination-sponsored placement offices. An alternative path resembles the route taken by law-school and graduate business-school interns, who make job connections during their summer work.

An equally important question concerns where to work: a smaller church, where one can immediately become the pastor in charge, or a larger church, where as an associate minister, one can have the opportunity to be supervised by an experienced minister?

The Pay

More than faith is needed to become a second-career minister. It requires a willingness and an ability to replace a corporate or professional lifestyle with that of a job with low pay that most likely will not rise significantly in the years ahead. Spiritual satisfaction notwithstanding, the financial transition for people in their 30s and 40s is not easy. Churches in rural areas and inner cities pay less than those in more affluent suburban markets.

Ministers, priests, and rabbis are usually permitted to keep part, if not all, of their in-kind cash or gift payments given for officiating at weddings, christenings, funerals, and the like.

PROTESTANT MINISTERS. Most churches pay new ministers from the low $20s to low $30s. Paid or contributory retirement and health care benefit plans are provided by the church, or through a national or regional church office. Part of the package includes either a house or a housing allowance, and sometimes a car. On paper a "free" house sounds like a good benefit. In practice, however, many of these homes are in disrepair or do not meet the minister's family or personal needs. The more satisfactory arrangement is often a housing allowance that gives the clergyperson flexibility in selecting a home. Some churches peg the salary to the average pay earned by members of the congregation. An employed spouse is usually necessary to enable a family to balance its books. Gone is the day when the minister's wife served as the unpaid assistant to her husband.

ROMAN CATHOLIC PRIESTS. Each diocese sets the salaries for its priests. Cash salaries range from $13,000 to $15,500 along with room and board in the parish rectory, health insurance and retirement plan, and a possible car allowance, reports the National Federation of Priests' Councils (www.nfpc.org). The council reports that annual salaries for parish priests, including in-kind income—namely, room and board—brought the gross to nearly $31,000. Religious priests such as Jesuits and Dominicans take a vow of poverty, and are supported financially by their orders.

RABBIS. Each synagogue sets its own salary. As is true of Protestant denominations, the financial package includes a home or housing allowance along with a fringe-benefit package that also factors in in-kind income. The package for entry-level rabbis is typically valued at $40,000 to $50,000.

POINTS TO REMEMBER

- **A minister, priest, or rabbi** has a job that defies a simple description.
- **Divinity schools** are wary of career-changing romantics.
- **Seminaries** welcome older students.
- **A number of churches** and denominations still exclude women from ordination.
- **Some denominations** ordain ministers with little or no formal academic training.
- **A "calling"** is critical to becoming a minister.
- **The course of study** at most theology schools is three to four years.
- **A minister** needs to believe that there's more to life than a high salary.
- **Previous workplace experience** is invaluable in the ministry.

Some People Who Made the Change

C areer changers who decide to become ministers go through a decision-making process that differs from that in other professions. Besides responding to a "calling," candidates are putting aside one kind of life and entering a new one that is demanding in terms of time, energy, and commitment. The process goes from divinity school to ordination and, often, assignment to a small inner-city or rural church. Many career changers in this field have saved money from their past careers, or have spouses or other family members who can make an all-important financial contribution to help balance the family's books. In short, the ministry is not an easy career, but it offers other rewards. The men and women described in this chapter wanted a different workplace experience, and were interested in using their religious faith and nonreligious skills to help others.

FULFILLING A LIFELONG DREAM

Michael Reid

FROM NAVAL OFFICER TO LAWYER TO ORDAINED PRIEST

Early on in his naval career, Michael Reid, now in his mid 40s, made a pledge to God that someday he would become a priest. "Over time, I forgot about this deal. In my last four years in the Navy, I thought about it again, but I was still not ready to say yes."

Reid's father had set the example for a military career. In 1968, Reid was 14 when his father resigned from the Air Force and the family settled in Harrisburg, Pa.

"I received an Naval ROTC scholarship to Notre Dame. I majored in sociology and I took some criminal-justice courses. When I graduated from Notre Dame, I expected to make the Navy my career." For the next ten years, Reid was a line officer, serving on a carrier, a destroyer, and a destroyer tender. When he was not promoted to lieutenant commander, his naval career was cut short earlier than he expected. "Now what do I do?" Reid asked himself?

"Ever since college, the idea of being a priest had always been in my mind, and I continually asked myself whether I should go to a seminary. First came my naval obligation, and then I decided to go to law school, which was my way of procrastinating once again."

Widener University had just opened a law school at its Harrisburg campus, and Reid, who was unmarried, had saved enough money in the Navy to put himself through law school. After graduating from Widener, Reid became a solo practitioner, handling general law and criminal cases. To make additional money, he was a part-time student recruiter for the another new law school, the Roger Williams School of Law in Providence,

> On a number of occasions, his parish priest, with whom he shared his reflections, asked him if he wanted to become a priest. Finally, Reid said yes.

R.I. After nine months as a solo practitioner, Reid took a one-year clerkship with a Pennsylvania superior court judge. After returning to his own practice, he continued to reflect on his life. "As a lawyer, I liked working with people, but something was still missing in my life. I remembered an ordination ceremony that I had attended years ago as a Notre Dame student. From it I felt inner joy; the feeling stayed with me as I reflected on becoming a priest." On a number of occasions, his parish priest, with whom he shared his reflections, asked him if he wanted to become a priest. Finally, Reid said yes.

In 1995, Reid entered Pope John XXIII National Seminary in Weston, Mass., the first seminary in North America to educate career changers between ages 30 and 60 to become priests. Reid's Harrisburg diocese paid the $13,500 tuition for each of the four academic years at the seminary. St. Cecilia Parish in Lebanon, Pa., paid a stipend for the year that Reid spent at the church between his second and third years at the seminary. He received another stipend from Saint Paul, a church near the seminary where Reid served during the academic year.

Many of the skills that Reid used as a naval officer and as a lawyer came into play at the seminary. "The Navy taught me how to speak with different types of people, distill what they had to say, and to help them understand what they need. While I was a law student and then as a lawyer, I learned to question and to reason." But, he added, "As a seminarian I had to learn that I was not in charge."

Reid admits that classroom discussions were rarely dull, considering the makeup of the student body, which included people who worked as physicians, teachers, corporate managers, and social workers. "Adult students bring different life perspectives into the classroom. They also represent many different academic, theological, and practical experiences, which would be less true in a classroom of younger students."

Seminary life moves with the times. "We used both desktop and laptop computers to prepare reports, papers, presentations, and homilies. Some seminarians, though not me, brought laptops to class to take notes. We did our research on the Internet, and we all have personal e-mail addresses."

Ordained a priest in June 2000, Reid was assigned as the parochial vicar to St.

Seminary discussions were rarely dull; the student body included physicians, teachers, corporate managers, and social workers.

John the Baptist in New Freedom, Pa., a parish serving an expanding population—1,700 families, up from only 400 in the mid 1960s. Even with his current responsibilities, Reid doesn't think his legal career has come to an end. The church, which draws upon priests with applicable skills, could at some future date send him to Catholic University in Washington, D.C., to study canon law, which is the body of law of the Catholic Church.

IT'S ALL ABOUT COMMUNICATION

Sally Bates

"THERE'S NO BUSINESS LIKE SHOW BUSINESS"

The religious upbringing of Sally Bates in Brielle, N.J., was nothing exceptional. "I had a modest church upbringing; I went to church on Sundays."

In 1972, Bates, now in her early 50s, graduated from Mary Washington College, in Fredericksburg, Va., having majored in theater arts, a skill that provided the backdrop for many of her future decisions. "I worked for two years at the Children's Theater in Wilson, N.C., got a master's degree in theater arts from the University of North Carolina in Chapel Hill, and returned to Wilson as executive director of the Wilson Arts Council." Eight years later, she became executive director of Artspace, in Raleigh, and from there moved to Charlotte to become director of its community theater.

"For the first ten or so years after college I was rebellious, and uninterested in religion. Then I began to see the part God played in my life and my life in God's life. This was the beginning of a calling."

While living in Charlotte, Bates became involved in various church activities, from singing in the choir to being a volunteer. "It got to the point that it seemed to me I was more involved at church than in my paying job. I didn't aspire to more power, more money or another job. I basically liked my job and I felt I was well paid, making

$44,000 a year. But I needed something more in life to motivate me."

The watershed event took place when Bates was directing a theatrical production of *Annie*. "Imagine 12 little girls, a dog on stage, and 12 sets of different costumes. Everything that could go wrong went wrong in rehearsals.

> # "I began to see the part God played in my life and my life in God's life. This was the beginning of a calling."

Then on opening night, the caterers blew some fuses in the theater. Everyone in the audience saw what they thought was a perfect performance, but I thought it was chaotic. At that moment, I said if I ever was to work this hard again, I wanted to do it for something more important and on a higher level."

Deciding to become a minister, she discovered, is not a simple task. "I was then about 40, and I went into pastoral counseling with a person who was both an ordained Methodist minister and a psychologist. It took me about nine months to come to any decision, even though the counselor recognized in about six to eight sessions what my decision would be." Two years later, Bates enrolled at Duke Divinity School, 14 years after receiving her master's degree from UNC. She felt that a Duke education and her work experience in North Carolina would make it easier to remain in the state once she was ordained.

Bates, who was unmarried, had no family pressures in planning a career change. Her father died when she was 29 and her mother died six years later. But she wanted to share her decision with someone who had known her mother. "I called my mother's closest friend in New Jersey. Her reaction when I told her was, 'Your mother would have been thrilled.' What made it most interesting is that my mother's friend was Jewish." Bates continues to call this woman whenever she wants to talk over some important event.

When Bates told her friends and theater associates of her plans, their jaws dropped, but seconds later, nearly all affirmed her choice.

"Some suggested that I was tired, and just needed a vacation. Little did they know that during the period before I made my final decision to go to Duke, I was haunted by an advertisement that I had clipped from *Christian Century* magazine, which said, 'Is God keeping you awake at night?' It was attached to my refrigerator door, and the question was with me day and night until I made my decision."

After leaving her Charlotte job, Bates took her final paycheck to the bank. "I

said to myself that this would be my last paycheck for three years. I partially paid for Duke with savings, cashing in my life insurance, and selling some inherited stock. Fortunately a friend in Raleigh let me have a free room in her house while I was a Duke student."

Bates was at first a hesitant divinity student.

"I wasn't sure that I could hack it, be able to tax my memory, or even carry 30 pounds of books. This concern lasted 48 hours. I soon discovered that most of

"I am considered a lively teacher, since I bring subject matter at Sunday school or adult classes to life."

my fellow students faced the same fear, regardless of their age. I had some advantages. I was a bit more mellow than the younger students, who were fresh from college with lots of exuberance and some cynicism."

Ordained as a Methodist minister in 1995, Bates spent the next year as the pastor of three very small churches about one hour northeast of London, England. Returning home, she was assigned by the bishop as the associate pastor of Hayes Barton United Methodist Church in Raleigh, a church with 2,100 members, a $1.2 million budget, and a paid staff of 15. The congregation paid her a starting salary of $26,500 a year, along with a housing allowance.

Many of Bates's church responsibilities fuse her theatrical experience and religious training. She directs the Sunday school, preaches one sermon a month, conducts Bible classes, and does pastoral counseling.

"Much of my current work is about communication, and I've been a communicator most of my working life," says Bates. "This is most evident in my dramatic affinity for gestures and theatrics. I am considered a lively teacher, since I bring subject matter at Sunday school or adult classes to life."

Unlike many other ministers, Bates came into the profession as a seasoned business manager with many applicable carryover skills. "I already knew about marketing, bookkeeping, and financial budgeting, and writing grant proposals."

At age 50, Bates realized that she had about 15 years to work as a minister, because 65 is the age at which Methodist ministers typically retire. "This does not bother me. I am not interested in becoming a bishop or in climbing the ladder. I had already done this in my other jobs, so I am relaxed."

ESTABLISHES A SYNAGOGUE IN BROOKLYN

Ellen Lippmann
FROM LIBRARIAN TO COMMUNITY ACTIVIST TO RABBI

In 1972, when Ellen Lippmann graduated with an English and literature major from Boston University, American Judaism reached a milestone. A woman named Sally Priesand completed rabbinical training at the Hebrew Union College in New York and became the first ordained female rabbi.

Lippmann, who turned 50 in 2001, didn't closely identify with Jewish life during college or immediately thereafter. Even so, she was thrilled by Priesand's accomplishment, and joining the rabbinate became her goal and personal guide in future years when she was considering becoming a rabbi.

After college, Lippmann got a job in public libraries in the Boston area and, four years later, she earned a master's degree in library science from Simmons College, also in Boston. Even as she was entering the library profession, however, she was seeking something different. "I started considering whether I wanted to become a rabbi, but after five years of college and library school, I was not ready for five more years of school at the time."

In the early 1980s Lippmann left Boston and public libraries, and moved to New York City to run the clearinghouse at the National Commission on Resources for Youth and the Literary Assistance Centers, organizations where she once again used her library skills.

But the idea of becoming a rabbi persisted. If Sally Priesand and an increasing number of women within the reform Jewish movement could do it, then why not Ellen Lippmann?

"Finally, in my mid 30s, I reconsidered the idea. It seemed it was the time to

> "After five years of college and library school, I was not ready for five more years of school at the time."

do it, or I would never do it."

Although men and women within the Jewish religion do not have a "calling," as in the Christian faith, Lippmann said that her recurring thought about becom-ing a rabbi was something akin to a calling. Her parents, actively involved Jews, were in shock when she made her announcement. "They thought I was going through another wacky phase of life, but after a while they came to accept, and later fully support, my career change."

When she entered the Hebrew Union College–Jewish Institute of Religion in 1986, Lippmann was not, as she suspected she might be, the oldest student in her class. Others also were in their late 30s and 40s; they included some lawyers and government adminis-trators. Lippmann's lack of fluency in Hebrew was no obstacle at the time, because all students spend their first year off campus in Israel, learning Hebrew and studying about Israel and Jewish traditions.

It had been ten years since Lippmann had been a student, and it took awhile to get back into the academic routine. "My first day in school, I brought a single notebook with me. I forgot that I needed a different notebook for each class." But she realized that being in rabbinic school was where she should be.

To pay for her education and expenses, Lippmann took out student loans, worked in several communities as a student rabbi, and did some teaching. A long-time community activist, she also started the HUC's Feeding the Homeless Program.

After she was ordained in 1991, she was hired as the East Coast director of Mazon, which in Hebrew means food or sustenance. The Mazon movement asks Jews to donate 3% of the cost of a wedding or a bar or bat mitzvah to Mazon to feed hungry or under-nourished people. Lippmann's job required promoting the Mazon concept among rabbis and Jewish organizations in the eastern U.S.

But Lippmann soon realized that she longed for her own congregation. After leaving Mazon, Lippman supplemented her income by working several

days a week at a Jewish community center in Manhattan, as director of its Jewish Women's Program and founder of a small library. In 1993, she founded and became rabbi of Kolot Chayeinu/ Voices of Our Lives, a nontraditional congregation, unaffiliated with any Jewish movements, in the Park Slope section of Brooklyn.

"We are a progressive congregation in many ways, while still adhering to Jewish traditions. We serve a diverse community of both gay and straight

"Interestingly, all my careers focus on helping people find what they need — whether information, learning, or Judaism."

members, and our congregation includes many interracial families, with members who are African Americans and Asians." The congregation also provides an outlet for community activism.

Kolot Chayeinu has grown since its founding, but it remains a congregation with only about 150 members. Seven years after Kolot Chayeinu was started, the congregation became able to employ Lippmann full-time and she left the community center. "Interestingly, all my careers focus on helping people find what they need—whether information, learning, or Judaism. Nothing is lost, since I continued to use my library training and skills."

Even with a full-time job as a rabbi and continuing work, when possible, as a community activist with groups like New York Jews for Racial and Economic Justice and the Women's Rabbinic Network, Lippmann and her partner take off in the month of July to relax. They have a house in Dutchess County, 120 miles north of New York City, which they are renovating themselves. It's a chance to concentrate on spackling and painting, and a break with the other 11 months, when Lippmann adheres to an urban and people-centered lifestyle. "If at all possible, I feel that everyone should take time off. For me, this time is invaluable to being the kind of rabbi I try to be."

RELATES BUSINESS TO PARISHIONERS' NEEDS

David Hutchins

THERE'S A HIGHER CALLING THAN COMMERCIAL BANKING

"I wonder what I'll do when I grow up." That's the way that David Hutchins, in his mid 30s, summed up his job as a midlevel bank manager.

Born in North Carolina, Hutchins lived as a youngster in Texas and went to Texas A&M. "I was an indifferent college student; it took me six years to graduate. I changed majors several times. I eventually became a journalism major, and my goal was to work for a nonprofit organization. Above all, I wanted to market a service that I could believe in."

Meanwhile, Hutchins married a young nurse whom he had met when she was taking care of his grandmother, who had been hospitalized in North Carolina. After graduation, Hutchins returned with his wife to North Carolina to look for work. While opening an account at Wachovia Bank, Hutchins's wife asked if the bank was hiring recent graduates. It was, and Hutchins got his introduction to banking.

Banking and Hutchins, however, were never a good fit, and soon he began looking for new opportunities. He thought about running a youth shelter or doing some other community work, and he started attending church more regularly.

During this period of uncertainty, Hutchins's wife's uncle, a Methodist minister, was dying. His peaceful death affected Hutchins deeply and inspired him spiritually. Hutchins told the story of the uncle's death at Sunday school, then at a Wednesday evening Bible study; the minister asked him to relate his experience at a Sunday worship service. The retelling of his experience moved Hutchins toward the ministry, but by then he had one child. There were

"Above all, I wanted to market a service that I could believe in."

financial issues to be considered if I quit work and changed careers. I decided to stay in banking until I found something I liked." Hutchins's wife continued in nursing, and they had a second child.

Then, in the mid 1990s, as the result of an administrative problem at the Wachovia bank, Hutchins left his job. "It was actually a blessing in disguise," he says. "It forced me out of a job that I didn't like. Otherwise, I might have stayed at the bank the rest of my career, because the job was safe."

Out of work and waiting to enter Duke Divinity School the next year, Hutchins got a part-time job as a lay pastor for a small and rural Methodist church. About the only training the church provided for this position is what Hutchins calls "preacher boot camp," two weeks in which candidates learn the basics of their new trade. Besides the experience, a small salary comes with the job.

When Hutchins started at Duke in the fall of 1996, he was told that because of his poor college record he would have to prove himself academically by the end of the first year. His limited financial resources became even more precarious when they moved to Durham and his wife gave up nursing. Because they had two young children and his hours as a student would be irregular, they felt it would be best for Lynn to stay home with the children.

To offset college and family expenses, Hutchins was assigned as a student pastor at the United Methodist church at Bynum, a rural town about 40 minutes from Duke.

The church has fewer than 200 members, about 60 of whom regularly attend Sunday services. It paid Hutchins about two-thirds of a pastor's normal salary, plus a housing allowance. In theory, his pastoral duties required only about 20 hours of work a week plus time to prepare sermons and other assignments relative to his church work. Fulfilling the Bynum assignment meant that Hutchins would complete his studies in four years rather than three.

Besides the pay and allowances, a student pastor gets the chance to work on a year-around basis with parishioners. Hutchins found that he had many of the same personal problems as his congregation.

"I know what it's like to pay a mortgage or to be a father of young children. The things you learn at class can be applied at church, and what you learn at church proves useful in the classroom. From this busy lifestyle, I learned how to juggle family life, the church and my studies. I was also committed to being a good dad and spending time with Jonathan and Elizabeth before they went to bed. I often started to study at 10 P.M." His grades averaged about 3.0, somewhat

"I know what it's like to pay a mortgage or to be a father of young children."

better than at Texas A&M, reflecting his new focus. Moreover, Hutchins, though an unhappy banker, actually finds that his banking back-ground is useful in the ministry.

"At Wachovia, I did lots of business with churches that needed loans to finance a new roof or to buy furniture. I also saw church members, who had little knowledge of money, handling the church's finances. Banking and my college degree in journalism taught me how to ask questions and listen for answers, traits necessary in dealing with parishioners."

After graduating from Duke, Hutchins moved his family back to eastern North Carolina, where he is now the associate pastor at the Greenville United Methodist Church, which has about 1,500 regular Sunday worshipers. Paid in the low $30s, plus a housing allowance, Hutchins supervises the church's eight-person professional staff, teaches in the Sunday school, and preaches in the minister's absence. Lynn, who put nursing on hold while Hutchins was a divinity student, is completing a few prerequisite undergraduate classes before being formally accepted into the University of North Carolina's graduate nursing program in Chapel Hill with the goal of becoming a psychiatric nurse or counselor.

Hutchins accumulated substantial debt at Duke. "I'll be paying off $40,000 in $300 monthly installments for the next 30 years. By then, I'll be near retirement age, but it's worth $3,600 a year to do the work you want to do."

WILL BECOME A MINISTER AT 45

Carter Askren

DIVINITY SCHOOL PUBLICIST GOES TO DIVINITY SCHOOL

Carter Askren, in his early 40s, entered divinity school in July 2001. Before he committed to a four-year academic process leading to a master's of divinity degree and ordination as a Lutheran minister, Askren spent nearly 18 months preparing for the career switch.

When Askren was growing up in Georgia, he wanted to become either a chef or a food-services manager, and he considered bypassing college altogether. But his parents encouraged him to get a college degree, and so he majored in food management at the University of Georgia's School of Home Economics. After graduating in 1983, Askren spent the next year in Atlanta working for a Marriott food-service operation that ran corporate dining facilities. Each month, as part of the Marriott training program, he was moved to a different facility.

"I was considering going to divinity school, but I knew I would never get a recommendation from a minister unless I had some community roots and ties with a church." Soon after Marriott moved him from Atlanta to Durham, he left Marriott to be a food-services manager at Duke. He was eager to settle down, sink some roots into the community, and plan to become a seminarian.

After managing a student cafeteria for 30 months, Askren enrolled at Duke Divinity School to get a master of theo-logical studies degree—an academic prelude before applying for admission to divinity school. "At the time, I was an Episcopalian, and the church wouldn't accept me as a divinity student unless I also spent at least one year doing church-related work." During this period, Askren freelanced as a writer for several

> **"I couldn't do the things I wanted to do as a lay minister or volunteer. My goal was to preach, and to celebrate the sacraments."**

local newspapers and magazines, and worked as a student assistant in the communications office at Duke Divinity School.

In 1987, he was called by an official at Duke Divinity School who told him that the director of communications had left the school and someone was needed to fill in on a temporary basis. Askren took the job and the next year he was named director. He held that job for 12 years, during which he received his master's of theology degree.

"All the while, gnawing away at me was a feeling of guilt for dropping out of the divinity program, but I also perceived an inner message in the call to head communications. The more I worked at Duke, and the more I got involved as a church volunteer, the more I wanted to be more actively involved in the church as a minister. I couldn't do the things I wanted to do as a lay minister or volunteer. My goal was to preach, and to celebrate the sacraments. The work I was doing at Duke was interesting, but it was somewhat impersonal. I wanted the personal relationship that a minister has with a congregation."

Askren's aim to help others was part of his personal development, and consistent with the spirit he found during this period when he read Daniel Levinson's *The Seasons of a Man's Life* (Ballentine, 1986). Watching others prepare for the ministry also made Askren all the more eager to become personally, not tangentially, involved as a minister. He did not want to postpone his decision on theology school any longer.

"At Duke, I had many good experiences. I worked with different department heads, faculty members, and administrators. When I become a minister, this experience, I'm sure, will prove invaluable. I know how to work with people, and to serve their different wants and needs."

His call to action came while he was producing his third video, interviewing a faculty member and looking for lively sound bites. He asked one instructor why people leave jobs with six-figure salaries to be ministers. "His

answer: 'This is a calling to do things you once thought impossible.' This hit me. I was too secure. Perhaps I had been at Duke too long."

As Askren moved toward the ministry, he left the Episcopal Church, and in 1994 he became a Lutheran, the church his parents had been married in and where he felt that his commitment to the ministry would be expressed more strongly.

Askren, who had been married for several years and was divorced in 1993,

"I wanted the personal relationship that a minister has with a congregation."

remarried in July 1999. His new wife, Susan Howard, a Duke development officer, had also been married before. Having been instrumental in supporting Askren's decision to switch careers, Howard understood the financial sacrifices involved.

In December 1999, Askren took a four-month educational leave from his job at the divinity school; it was important to maintain his fringe-benefit relationship with Duke because his wife would soon become an at-home mother and would lose her Duke health care coverage. After a 16-week, unpaid clinical pastoral education internship at Duke Hospital, Askren started a one-year paid residency in the same specialty area.

Askren resigned from the internship

after a few months to become a part-time lay Duke student chaplain. "I essentially do what a pastor would, except that I can't celebrate the Eucharist, marry, or bury people. I'm supervised by one of the pastors on the Lutheran Campus Ministry Council."

There are other benefits in his new job. "My wife returned to Duke, also as a part-timer, and since I have what is essentially a late afternoon and evening job, I stay at home during the day with our daughter."

Askren begins work on his master's of divinity at the Lutheran Theological Southern Seminary in Columbia, S.C., in the summer of 2001; he anticipates finishing divinity school and being ordained in 2005. Unlike some seminaries, this one requires students to spend an extra year in a church-related assignment before getting their degree.

"With the baby born in June, it seemed too demanding at the time to complete the paperwork, prepare for and attend interviews, and do the other things needed to get into the seminary in 2000. And, I also wanted to test the waters before I was ready to dive in the deep end."

It's Never Too Late to Be a Lawyer

THE FIRST THING WE DO, LET'S KILL ALL THE LAWYERS," said Dick the butcher in Henry IV. More than 400 years after Shakespeare wrote this commentary on lawyers, the merits of the legal profession are still controversial. Depending on who is asked, lawyers are deemed a force to be reckoned with or the bane of society. Witness the revolving-door nature of the profession: As lawyers in their 30s and 40s call it quits, an equal number of men and women of the same age are leaving other careers to enter law school.

It's no secret that a large percentage of practicing lawyers want to do something else or blend their legal experience with another career. Peter Travis (profiled in chapter 2) draws upon his litigation know-how as an executive search consultant, and David Deiss (profiled in chapter 3) is a small-press publisher who uses his legal training to prepare contracts for authors.

Lawyers leave active practice frustrated by long hours, tedious assignments, and a workplace environment that fails to match their law school dream of being the next Clarence Darrow. "Some lawyers find themselves underemployed and undercompensated," said Paul Carrington, professor and a former dean of Duke's law school. "Others find the work pace burdensome or are attracted by vast financial incentives in business. It is also a factor that many entering students are chiefly attracted to the status of the profession, not the work or the role of the lawyer."

While the pool of potential career-switching lawyers is high, *Federal Reports* (www.attorneyjobsonline.com), which monitors lawyer employment trends, noted that "very few lawyers totally drop out of the law, that is, move to Vermont and open a bed-and-breakfast inn." In "Landing a Non-Traditional Legal Job," the *Federal Reports* guide pointed out that there are more than 600 things one can do with a law degree other than practice law, including becoming an FBI special agent, a corporate secretary, a supervisor of public trust accounts, and an affirmative action/equal opportunity officer.

The Job Market

Employment opportunities for lawyers are starting to level off, and the job market will not soon see anything like the dramatic spurt in the number of job openings that were available during the 1970s and 1980s. Even so, the Bureau of Labor Statistics expects that job opportunities for lawyers should rise through 2008 about as fast as those for physicians, veterinarians, and the clergy.

Law schools now produce nearly 40,000 lawyers a year, two-and-one-half times the number in 1970, and about 10% higher than the 1990 rate. The American Bar Association (www.abanet.org) reported in 1999 that about 1 million lawyers were actively practicing in the U.S.

Given that the supply of lawyers exceeds demand, it's a good thing that not all law-school graduates intend to practice law. In 1998, about 11% of law school graduates took a different career path—business, graduate school, and investment banking.

More than 70% of Fordham University Law School's class of 1999 (www.fordham.edu) work in law firms (nearly 65% in firms with 100 or more lawyers), and the rest work as judicial clerks, prosecutors, or public-interest lawyers, or in legal and nonlegal jobs in business.

For career changers, getting the first job needn't be tricky, said one law-school career counselor. "I always advise older students to prepare for the likelihood that during the screening interview, most likely the first stage, they are probably going to be interviewed by someone younger than themselves. I tell them that if age isn't mentioned by the interviewer, it is in the air, and they should make it clear that they know that they are starting out and realize that they have a lot to learn."

As a law school graduate in his late 30s, Steven Sawyer, a former naval aviator (profiled later in this chapter), did not find that age was an obstacle. "I was fortunate to get offers from almost all the firms where I interviewed. If there was any preference, it was a preference in favor of older, nontraditional law-school graduates like myself." And, as a lawyer, he has even found some similarities between practicing law and piloting a Navy helicopter.

> **The quality that nontraditional law students bring with them is the specific knowledge of another field.**

"While I don't doubt that some firms prefer younger men and women in their 20s, I found that many firms placed a premium on workplace experience. The quality that nontraditional law students bring with them is the specific knowledge of another field. I frequently call upon my experiences as a bellhop, dishwasher, busboy, lifeguard, department store manager, factory worker, naval officer and helicopter pilot."

High Entry-Level Salaries

The National Association for Law Placement (www.nalp.org), which, as its name implies, tracks the job market for lawyers, describes the current salary situation in law as the "Gunderson Effect," named after a California law firm with the unwieldy name of Gunderson, Dettmer, Stough, Villeneuve, Franklin, & Hachigian. In late 1999, this firm announced pay raises for associates that assured them of a $125,000 salary, a guaranteed bonus of $25,000, and the possibility of another $5,000 in a discretionary bonus to make sure that staffers did not jump ship for jobs with dot-com companies. Other large, metro-center law firms also responded with pay increases and significant signing bonuses.

The situation is akin to that in professional sports when free-agent athletes start a bidding war among the franchises for their services. And just as for franchises in smaller markets, it taxes the ability of law firms in smaller markets to match such salaries to hire and to retain staffers. As a result, the NALP pointed out, lawyers will be cashing fat checks, upping their standard of living, but laboring longer hours. Big-league salaries have also trickled down to summer interns, with some West Coast law firms paying student interns $2,400 a week.

NALP cautions against euphoria and recalls, "The 1990–91 recession hit the profession with the same suddenness as the 1988–89 pay raises, and, as it did, associates were laid off in droves."

Even with skyrocketing salaries in some markets, NALP noted that the median salary for all entry-level lawyers six months after graduating from law school in 1998 was $45,000. Lawyers earned $60,000 in private practice; in corporate jobs, $50,000; in academia, $38,000; in the judiciary, $37,500; in government, $36,000; and in the public-interest sector, $31,000.

Getting Into Law School

The law-school entrance process is flexible—and much simpler than getting into medical school, with its slew of required pre-med courses.

Law-school applicants are judged on their college academic records and LSAT (Law School Admission Test) results. Career changers can add one more credential, namely, their previous jobs and the value of this experience. Law-school hopefuls include musicians, writers, and engineers, as well as representatives from nearly every professional, business, and crafts skill.

The LSAT (www.lsat.org), a half-day exam given four times a year, is designed to measure whether the applicant has an aptitude for the law. The LSAT tests the ability to think and reason logically, to analyze information, and to write accurately. In 1999, the Law School Admission Council administered 104,000 exams.

With so much riding on the test results, applicants frequently take an LSAT cram course to help prepare themselves. The cram-course operators, of course, say that attendees raise their scores. Cram courses do give career changers—many of whom have not taken an aptitude test, or any kind of academic test, for 10 or 20 years—a chance to warm up before the big game.

The volume of applicants varies from school to school. In 2000, Yale University Law School received nearly 3,200 applications and admitted 259 students, about an 8% acceptance rate. Pepperdine University accepted 48% of more than 2,600 applications; the University of Pennsylvania, 29% of 3,422 applications; Ohio Northern University, 49% of 1,115 applications; and Case Western Reserve, 60% of 883 applications.

In addition to the 183 law schools approved by the American Bar Association, another 30 to 40 (most of them are in California) are nonaccredited schools. A few of those have been started too recently to be eligible for accreditation. Others fail to meet ABA standards, say, because their ratio of full- to part-time faculty is out of balance or because their libraries are inadequate.

It's important to compare the national law schools with the majority of law schools, which have a regional and local orientation.

Harvard, Yale, Stanford, Chicago and Michigan, along with another 15 to 20 other law schools, are called "national" law schools because their graduates usually seek jobs outside the school's local or regional area. What's more, their curriculums rarely focus on state or local law. That's not to say that a graduate of the University of Oregon law school is unwelcome in a Chicago law firm, but there's a better chance that an Oregon alumnus will work in the Pacific Northwest. Most New York Law School students are from the metropolitan New York area, and in 1988, over 90% of its graduates found their first jobs in New York, New Jersey, and Pennsylvania. So it's important to compare the national law schools with the majority of law schools, which have a regional and local orientation.

Guides published by Barron's Educational Series (www.barronseduc.com) and Peterson's Guides (www.petersons.com) are a good starting point for familiarizing yourself with the different types of law schools. Both series provide an easy way to compare curriculums, tuition, scholarship funding, and entrance requirements, and to study sample LSATs.

Curriculums are standard through the first year to the first year and a half of law school. All students are required to take a series of core courses in contracts, torts, civil procedure, environmental and constitutional law, and legal writing. They are then free to take electives in corporate, intellectual property, labor or tax law, or to focus on state and local law.

Forty percent of the ABA-accredited schools conduct four-year evening programs, compared with the three years that it takes day students.

No two schools have the same tuition, but of course private law schools get top dollar. Tuition, books, and fees approach $30,000 a year at some private law schools, but the figure is considerably less at state-supported and local schools. It is not unusual for law-school graduates to accrue tens of thousands of dollars of debt to pay for their professional education.

Career changers should consider the pros and cons of evening school. One out of every ten law students is a part-timer, and approximately 40% of the ABA-accredited schools conduct four-year evening programs, compared with the three years that it takes day students. Night students often use their law degree in occupations such as real estate broker, bank trust officer, or an engineer practicing patent law. This is not to say, however, that entry-level jobs are not available in law firms or as judicial clerks.

One educational option has practically vanished. Only seven states allow students to "sit for the bar" as lawyers like Abraham Lincoln learned their law. Nowadays "reading the law" is done in conjunction with some law-school training. And California is the only state that accepts a correspondence law degree.

After graduating from law school, regardless of the school, and often just as they begin their new careers, fledgling lawyers will take another national exam. Although there is no official, national bar examination, 47 states (excluding Indiana, Louisiana, and Washington) require applicants to take the National Conference of Bar Examiners' Multistate Bar Examination, developed by the National Conference of Bar

Examiners, along with state bar exams in the states in which they wish to practice.

Related Careers

For the past five years, Robert Smith, assistant dean for career services at Duke University's Law School, has taught a four-week workshop on alternative careers for lawyers at Duke University's continuing education program. Smith finds that many of the students are unsure of their future direction. They want to continue being lawyers, but they also want to change direction in their careers. Some want to do something different within the law and others seek a new professional identity. Most would-be career-changing lawyers understand that dropouts from the profession lose their identity. No longer will they be known as "lawyer Bob."

Smith helps his students to realize that they can find happiness in jobs that directly or indirectly use their legal skills. Smith is more than a classroom adviser. He has the personal credentials to support his approach to alternative careers. A lawyer himself, he took a two-year break in his career to be a scuba-diving instructor in the Virgin Islands. Smith then switched from litigation into executive search, and recently to his present work in career services.

Short of finding an adviser like Smith, you can consult the following books, which present the facts and discuss alternative careers for lawyers: The American Bar Association published *Changing Jobs for Lawyers,* and Deborah Arron, a lawyer turned career counselor, wrote, *What Can You Do With a Law Degree?* (Niche Press, fourth edition, 1999). For lawyers not intending to practice law but wishing to use their legal training, there is "Landing a Non-Traditional Legal Job," published by Federal Reports, mentioned earlier. The guide lists more than 600 careers open to lawyers in such areas as civil rights, international trade, labor relations, media and entertainment, and legislative and regulatory affairs. Another resource is Kim Walton's *America's Greatest Places to Work with a Law Degree* (Harcourt Brace, 1999).

Joint degree programs in law and another area of expertise

are common on most university campuses. Engineering, medical, environmental, and education students attend law school with the goal of combining two different academic disciplines into a single career. At the University of North Carolina's law school, about ten to 20 students in each class are pursuing joint degrees, said Kimberly Reed, who was until recently director of career services. Students may pool a master's or even doctoral degree in business, regional planning, or public health with a law degree.

The American Intellectual Property Law Association (www.aipla.org) represents over 10,000 attorneys who specialize in law relating to patents, trademarks, copyrights, and unfair competition. Not surprisingly, many intellectual property lawyers are also engineers and scientists. They work as in-house attorneys, often clustered in high-tech centers like Silicon Valley, Route 128 near Boston, or Washington, D.C., the home of the Patent & Trademark Office and the Copyright Office. Others work for intellectual-property law firms, where the pay is higher than that typically paid by corporate patent departments or government agencies.

POINTS TO REMEMBER

- **Law schools** produce 40,000 attorneys a year, 10% more than in 1990.
- **Only half of all lawyers** work in law firms.
- **Taking "cram" courses** is advised before taking the LSATs.
- **It is important to understand** the difference between a national and a regional law school.
- **Age 30-plus** is no obstacle to getting a good legal job.

- **Most lawyers** make a good, but not an exorbitant, salary.
- **Salaries** for entry-level lawyers at the very large law firms have soared. But remember that economic dips have tended to slow down recruitment, along with job opportunities.
- **Lawyers who leave** the practice of law find that their skills are in demand in many other fields.

Hybrid legal specialties are on the rise. The American Association of Nurse Attorneys (www.taana.org) has a membership of 500 practicing attorneys who are also registered nurses. Shirley Pruitt, who is profiled later in this chapter, is a former intensive care pediatric nurse with a specialty in pediatric malpractice law.

Some People Who Made the Change

Law seems to be a "love it or hate it" profession. Law schools attract some of the most talented college graduates—excellent students, campus leaders and the like. They compete vigorously at law school, graduate and get their first job, and after six or seven years, they're either on track or they've become disillusioned. Whereas plenty of people in other fields also become disillusioned, unhappy lawyers don't stick to a job they dislike. They jump ship. Their skills are in demand elsewhere. But, as mentioned earlier, disillusioned lawyers in their 30s and early 40s are being replaced by career changers of the same age. This chapter discusses several lawyers in their 30s, 40s, and even one in his very early 50s who are enthusiastic about their new profession. Three of these lawyers are associates with midsize firms, another works as a medical malpractice specialist, and the other plans to blend investment banking and law when he completes law school.

TRADED IN SCRIPTS FOR CASE LAW

Tim O'Neal Lorah
ACTOR HAS A NEW ROLE AS A LAWYER

At his law-school graduation party, Tim O'Neal Lorah's father toasted his son by saying that he had just grabbed the merry-go-round of life. Hold onto the brass ring, he said, since one rarely gets another chance. Lorah knew the meaning of his father's challenge, having given up a successful career in acting and restaurant management to become a lawyer.

The road that Lorah, now in his early 40s, took to become a lawyer was somewhat unconventional. As a teenager in Pennsylvania, he read and took note of stories in the local newspaper about trials and judges. He thought about being a lawyer but dismissed the idea in favor of acting, starting with high school productions and later majoring in theater at Pennsylvania State University. By the time he graduated from Penn State, he had an Actors' Equity union card and an even keener interest in perfecting his theatrical skills. Lorah sharpened them in a two-year master's program at Florida State University's Osolo Conservatory, which mixes classroom studies with practical stage experience in drama, comedy, and musicals.

To achieve in the theater means but one thing to actors—New York City. In 1984, Lorah moved to New York, and for the next four years he acted in off-Broadway productions, road companies, and television commercials. Except for one year, he made enough money to support himself without the need for a part-time supplemental job.

"But I was living my life out of a suitcase, and I wanted to set down roots. I wanted to make money by acting in New York shows, not by traveling." Like so many other actors, Lorah became a

> ## "I gave her all the reasons not to go to law school— I'm too old, I hadn't been in school in many years, and I would fail once I got into law school."

waiter. He found a job at the Landmark Tavern, an upscale Irish-style bar and restaurant on the West Side of New York, a few blocks from the theater district. He could leave the job for a month or so when he was acting.

"After a year I was promoted, and it seemed an end to my theatrical dream because the Landmark's owners wanted me to make a commitment. I took the job as the assistant manager, and they sent me to wine tasting and food school to learn the tricks of the trade. The general manager stepped down, and I was asked to take his place. I remember telling the owners that I didn't think

I was their man. They felt differently, and I became general manager.

"I liked being manager. My job responsibilities expanded. When I had financial questions, I'd call my brothers, both CPAs, and ask them to explain things. And I enjoyed working with the waiters, many of whom were actors."

A year or so later, Lorah found that the job was getting rather routine, and he began discussing options with his friends, including Maria, the fiancée of his former roommate at Florida State University and a lawyer with one of the leading New York law firms. "She said that I should go to law school, and I gave her all the reasons not to—I'm too old, I hadn't been in school in many years, and I would fail once I got into law school. She was persistent. She sent me articles from the *New York Law Journal* to read."

Lorah was slow to follow up on his friend's prodding. He talked to career changers and to lawyers, but that's about as far as his investigation went. He felt comfortable working at the Landmark, and his income was good.
Why take a risk?

By 1992, Lorah felt that he had delayed his decision on law school long enough. He obtained brochures from several local law schools. The next step was to take the LSAT.

"By then, I had been out of school eight years. I took a Kaplan cram course. My days were rather hectic. I worked a few hours at the Landmark, and literally sneaked off to the Kaplan classes, went back to work, and then in the evening

after work, I'd cram some more. I did okay on the LSAT. NYU and Columbia turned me down, I was wait-listed at Fordham, but I got into Brooklyn and New York law schools."

Before he made his final decision to enter New York Law School, Lorah monitored a few law-school classes. Lorah was still concerned about being a career changer and being an older student, but several of the instructors persuaded him to think more positively.

Lorah had another choice to make:

"I drove myself at law school, and I drove my friends berserk. I wanted the dream, and I didn't want to fail."

whether to be a full-time student or a part-time evening student, so that he could continue to work. The hours were too long at the Landmark to work, go to school, and study in any one day. So that he wouldn't have to work, Lorah saved sufficient money to support himself for three years, and prepared to take out student loans to pay for his tuition, but he ended up receiving a scholarship.

While he was working at the Landmark, Lorah had appeared in some off-Broadway shows and television commercials. Before he entered law school, he made his final stage performance with a summer staging of *Funny Girl.*

It was his swan song: goodbye to one dream, and hello to another one.

"At law school orientation, I felt that I had made the biggest mistake in my life. As I looked around the room, the students looked so young and so eager. Then I met a woman in her mid 50s and we talked it out about being older students. It helped ease my mind."

Lorah did very well at law school, graduating sixth in a class of 238. By then, he had overcome his initial academic shyness, and his early impression in class that the other students were so much brighter because they had been trained as paralegals, had parents who were lawyers, or had college majors that were more related to law than the theater.

"I drove myself at law school. I immersed myself in my studies, and I drove my friends berserk. I had them drill and quiz me before tests. I wanted the dream, and I didn't want to fail. As an actor, I had an ability to memorize, and I was good on my feet in oral arguments." Lorah briefly considered entertainment law. He had a number of friends who practice in this field, but he decided to explore other legal specialties.

Lorah's high standing in his law-school class attracted the attention of Howard Levine, an associate judge with the New York Court of Appeals, the state's highest court, who selected him as a law clerk. "This was an incredible experience. I saw firsthand the fundamental part that law plays in our society, and law as a profession."

In 1998, with two years' clerking experience, Lorah became an associate at Schulte, Roth & Zabel, a New York law firm that employs approximately 275 lawyers. Because he is single and still lives in a one-bedroom, rent-controlled

Lorah did very well at law school, graduating sixth in a class of 238.

apartment, Lorah has been able to pay off his student debt in two years.

Lorah is assigned to his firm's litigation department as part of a team of lawyers representing financial institutions before a number of bank regulatory agencies. Like most law associates, he puts in long hours. In 1999, he billed clients for 2,900 hours of work; in 2000, he cut back to about 2,500 hours, which, in practical terms, often means 13-hour-plus workdays.

USES A PILOT'S CHECKLIST TO NAVIGATE IN LAW

Steven Sawyer
NAVAL AVIATOR SWITCHES TO CORPORATE LAW

As an associate at Quarles & Brady, one of Milwaukee's larger law firms, Steve Sawyer, in his early 40s, has an office that overlooks Lake Michigan. The last time he had such a good view was from the cockpit of a Navy helicopter.

"When I graduated from high school in Milwaukee, I went to the University of Michigan as a premed student. I would have become the fifth generation in my family to go to medical school. Things didn't work out that way. Both my parents were seriously ill my freshman year, I hurt my foot so I couldn't try out for the swimming team, and my grades were terrible. I left Michigan at the end of the year."

After several tries at two other colleges, Sawyer went to work with a temp agency, where he worked for a variety of companies. The next year, he entered Colorado State University as a freshman. Four years later, he graduated with a degree in business, but, as Sawyer puts it, an undistinguished academic record.

In the back of his mind was the thought of becoming a lawyer. "I have always liked to debate issues with other people, and I felt that the skills that I learned at home while growing up, regarding being precise with language, would help me if I were a lawyer."

In his senior year, Sawyer had a number of interviews with corporate and other recruiters. "When the Navy recruiter came, I thought about a Navy career. My brother-in-law was a Navy flyer, and my grandfather had been a naval flight surgeon during World War II. I took the aptitude test and did very well. At the same time, I was wined and dined

Sawyer decided that the peripatetic lifestyle of a naval officer didn't fit with his idea of raising a family.

by a retail chain in Sacramento, Cal." Sawyer took the retail job, went through its training program, worked in several clothing departments in one of the stores, and then was assigned to its Reno, Nev., branch store. "I began to realize that a retail career was not for me, and I left the chain a year to the day after coming to work."

Back in Milwaukee, Sawyer applied to the Navy, was accepted, and was sent to Pensacola, Fla., to officers candidate school. From there, Sawyer was commissioned as an ensign and trained as a land-based helicopter pilot.

About this time, Sawyer married Kathy, an elementary school teacher whom he had met in high school. Sawyer spent the next eight and a half years in the Navy on search and rescue missions, disaster relief, and VIP transport duties.

When the opportunity came to broaden his career as a naval officer, he volunteered to attend Naval Justice School in Newport, R.I. He completed the seven-week course with honors, and, in addition to his duties as a pilot, he was assigned as the legal officer handling all military and administrative legal matters for a squadron with over 300 people. This assignment whetted his interest in the law as a career option if he were to leave the Navy.

In 1990, Sawyer's wife became pregnant and Sawyer, then 32, decided that the peripatetic lifestyle of a naval officer didn't fit with his idea of raising a family. "If I ever was to consider going to law school, I better think of it now."

With poor college grades, Sawyer needed to do well on the LSAT if he was to apply to law school. "I took the Kaplan course, and threw myself into it. Every night for six weeks I would go to the library at Old Dominion College to study for four hours. On the day I took the LSAT, I thought a silent prayer, 'If this is what I'm intended to do, give me some sign.' I felt good about the tests." In fact, he scored at the 99% level.

The next step was a two-hour drive to Charlottesville and the University of Virginia.

"I sweet-talked my way past a secretary and walked into the office of the head of the admissions committee. I said that I wanted his opinion, not about whether I would be accepted at UVA,

but what my chances were of getting into a decent law school. He looked at my Colorado transcript and my LSAT score and said that one canceled out the other. If I was serious about going to law school, I should get a master's degree to prove that I was a good student."

When the Navy transferred him to Key West, in addition to performing his naval duties he became a weekend student at Troy State University. Two years later, Sawyer completed his naval commitments, as well as his master's

> ## "I have always liked to debate issues with other people, and I felt that the skills that I learned at home, regarding being precise with language, would help me if I were a lawyer."

degree in management, with a 4.0 academic average.

"I submitted applications to 15 top law schools in cities where Kathy and I felt we could live. I eliminated law schools in New York City, but I did apply to Harvard and was turned down."

When Sawyer applied to Notre Dame, a retired Navy captain happened to be on the admissions committee and his appreciation of how the Navy had helped to turn Sawyer's life around helped assure Sawyer's acceptance there.

"At law school, I found the Navy had taught me self-discipline. I also had learned how to work when you're tired."

The Sawyers had a second child during Sawyer's third year at Notre Dame. Throughout this period, Sawyer's wife taught school in South Bend. Although the pay was low, her job came with health care benefits. Besides collecting income from the G.I. Bill, which paid the rent and some living expenses, Sawyer took out student loans, which he expects to pay off before their final due date in 2006.

Graduating with honors, Sawyer dropped the idea of becoming an aviation legal specialist, which he had once thought would be a good use of his flight experience, because he found the field much too specialized for his taste. With two degrees in business, he opted for business and corporate law.

"Kathy and I both wanted to stay in the Midwest. Our roots and family are here. We both come from Milwaukee." He worked as a summer law clerk at Foley & Lardner, Wisconsin's oldest and largest law firm, and then joined the firm as an associate after graduation. Thirty months later, a Foley client, Case Corp., a farm equipment company, asked him to join its in-house legal staff. Five weeks after he went to work at Case, the company merged with a Dutch Company, New Holland, N.V.

Ever since he had gone to work for Foley & Lardner, search firms had called Sawyer regularly. "Over the years, I must have had 25 calls, but none of these openings had ever interested me. By now I was ready to change." Sawyer's wife, who was teaching school a few blocks from home, had little interest in moving again. When the headhunter called with an opening at his level at Quarles & Brady in Milwaukee, however, Sawyer said yes. The entire job search process took less than five weeks. Sawyer joined Quarles in May 2000 as a corporate lawyer with the seniority of an associate who had gone to work in the firm in 1996.

Sawyer has even found a connection between pilot training and corporate law.

"I came to the point in a complex legal transaction, on a bank transaction involving $500 million, where I was not totally sure what I should be doing," he says. "My gut reaction was to go forward, and handle the task at hand. Then I went back in my mind to the time in the Navy when I was about to solo as a pilot, and we were told that if we got lost we should go through a checklist to help us land safely. The process starts with a confession to yourself that you are lost. Years later, I was lost as a lawyer. I didn't have a legal checklist. I went to the partner on this case, asked a number of questions, and within 15 minutes I had a clear understanding of what I needed to do."

SAME LANGUAGE, DIFFERENT FORUM

Shirley Pruitt
NEONATAL–NURSING SPECIALIST DOES MALPRACTICE LAW

Early in her nursing career, Shirley Pruitt, now in her late 30s, wanted adventure. Recently divorced from a post-high school marriage, she left a hospital nursing job in her hometown, Battle Creek, Mich., and relocated to Charleston, S.C. "I wanted to have a different lifestyle, and to live near the ocean."

Pruitt got a job in the intensive-care nursery that handles the most serious cases at the Medical University of South Carolina. Her job was to accompany seriously ill newborns by helicopter from throughout the state to the hospital for treatment. As the only medically trained person on the helicopter, Pruitt was in a position to make critical, life-saving decisions on each trip.

Although she came to realize that many aspects of nursing were exciting, much of the job was routine. She also wanted a career that had an element of autonomy that was unavailable in nursing.

"I knew that I wanted to eventually do something other than nursing. I thought about medical school, but, after working with doctors and residents, I found that the physician's life was too hard for me. Somehow, I knew the answer was law. My sister-in-law, who is a lawyer, encouraged me. Otherwise, I knew nothing about the law, or how to become a lawyer."

Moreover, Pruitt faced numerous hurdles if she was to change from nursing to the law. Her nursing certification was based on only two years' training at Kellogg Community College in Michigan. "I could have gotten an academic degree at the College of Charleston, but if I didn't get into law school or the law

> **Much of nursing was routine, and Pruitt wanted a career that had an element of autonomy that was unavailable in nursing.**

didn't work out, I would no longer have any tangible skills." The alternative to a liberal arts degree requiring four years of school was to get a nursing degree in two years from the Medical School of South Carolina, where she worked. So she went to nursing school while working at her job as a neonatal nurse.

Then she applied to five law schools. She was wait-listed at the University of North Carolina's law school, her first choice, which, after establishing residency in the state, would have been cheaper than Wake Forest University, in Winston-Salem, her second choice. Because she did not want to delay entering law school, however, she started at Wake Forest. "While a Wake Forest law student, I worked as a nurse on a need basis. When Baptist Hospital needed me, they'd call. Nursing paid some of my living expenses. I did not want to be a student who lived at the poverty level." Pruitt also took out loans, which should be paid off in 2002, ten years after graduation.

"Law school was different than I expected. There were no small quizzes during the semester. You study some cases all term, and then, at the end, there is a test. You can assimilate information as you go. I liked this process, and I graduated in the top 20% of my class."

Pruitt's professors advised her to go into general practice law, but Pruitt knew exactly what she wanted to do. If she couldn't get a job working in medical malpractice, she'd work for a hospital doing risk management law, in which she would help the hospital assess whether to settle potential lawsuits or defend itself in court.

Nursing got Pruitt prompt job interviews, except with the Navy's Judge Advocate General Corps, one of her job preferences. "One morning, after much delay, JAG finally called to say that I was accepted for training as a naval officer. I was rather annoyed, since several of my male law-school classmates, who were not as good students, had been accepted by JAG weeks earlier."

The same afternoon Pruitt also received a call from Yates, McLamb & Weyher, a law firm in Raleigh that specialized in malpractice law. When Pruitt joined the firm in 1992, it had 15 lawyers, and it has doubled in size over the past eight years. "What I liked is that I didn't have to get involved in general law, and I could specialize in malpractice work from the start." Pruitt defended physicians and hospitals, not patients, nearly exclusively in birth-related cases. About 90% of the cases are child brain-damage suits. Her nursing experience had persuaded her that many families bringing suit are not blameless in the negative outcomes over which they bring suit.

"I liked that I didn't have to get involved in general law, and I could specialize in malpractice work from the start."

"I like malpractice law because it relates to medicine. I enjoy reading medical journals and interviewing doctors. I understand medical records and charts. I can speak to doctors in a medical language they use, which is an asset when you have to tell them about their legal risks and the possible financial liabilities they face." Her cases, if they go to trial, may take up to three years, but many are settled before trial in one-third the time.

Pruitt's life has changed in other ways, too. She married a self-employed inspector and building contractor, and when their daughter was born in late 1998, she stayed home for three months. Her husband, whose office is at home, provided half the child care. When she became pregnant with their second child, she took an extended leave from the law firm and is still undecided when she'll return to work.

"I am still officially on 'indefinite leave.' I suspect that when I'm ready to work again, it will be first as a consultant, doing work from home.

"When I completed three months' maternity leave after Caroline was born, I did a thorough budget analysis including a spreadsheet on our income and expenses. We could live on a single income, namely, Pete's, if we lived within our means, and that would give Pete more time to expand his business. We know how to keep our expenses low. We considered moving to a more expensive house, but we decided against it. We also bought and drove used cars."

Now that her youngest child is nearly one year old, she plans to start consulting for a few hours a week. "Nothing exciting," she says, "just reviewing and analyzing medical records for cases." It's her first step toward returning to the job market in a few years.

GRAY HAIRS AND EXPERIENCE

Columbus Coleman, Jr.
A BANK VICE PRESIDENT GOES TO LAW SCHOOL

Columbus Coleman is at an age (early 50s) when many of his contemporaries are considering early retirement. Coleman, however, is a full-time law-school student getting ready for the next phase of his career.

Coleman graduated from the University of Texas in 1970 with a degree in electrical engineering. He spent the next two years in the Army, and then had a brief stint as a Shell Oil Co. engineer. "Engineering is great, the people were great, but business interested me even more than engineering."

Two years later, Coleman, majoring in corporate finance, received an MBA from the University of North Carolina, in Chapel Hill, and accepted a job with Wells Fargo, which recruited him for its San Francisco headquarters.

Four years later, the bank transferred him to New York as vice-president and general manager of Wells Fargo Securities, an operation that provided financial and investment services to Fortune 1000 companies. When Wells Fargo merged with Crocker National Bank, the company wanted him to return to San Francisco, but Coleman, now a confirmed New Yorker, decided not to relocate.

In 1982, Time, Inc., which was one of Coleman's Wells Fargo customers, hired him as a financial adviser. Time,

then was a much smaller organization, published *Time, Fortune, People* and *Sports Illustrated* and books; its lone nonpublishing venture was Home Box Office. Coleman, primarily a corporate strategic planner, helped develop a plan that led to Time's becoming a media-entertainment conglomerate.

"I was always working with lawyers, and I was frustrated that I wasn't a lawyer. I missed good opportunities when they affected or delayed my work."

Six years later Coleman was ready for a new corporate finance challenge. It came from Canadian Imperial Bank, one of the largest banks in Canada. For the next 11 years, Coleman managed a $500-million portfolio and advised bank customers on capital structures, financial strategies, and acquisition opportunities. "But I became bored with the job. I found that I was always working with lawyers, and I was frustrated that I wasn't a lawyer. I missed good opportunities when lawyers affected or delayed the work that I was doing."

On the theory that, if you can't lick

them, join them, Coleman decided to go to law school. Coleman didn't intend to work for a law firm or a corporate law department, but to combine law with his existing business skills and his training as an engineer.

"I was nearly 50 years old. I thought, if I don't go to law school now, I'll never do it. I didn't want to change my lifestyle; I wanted to maintain my standard of living. I was too old for that, and I had no desire to struggle. Going to evening school didn't make much sense either. At my level, I couldn't work for a bank and also go to law school. My job was much too demanding."

Not wanting to leave New York or the brownstone house he owned, Coleman applied only to local law schools. Although he was accepted by New York Law School, he found that many of the schools to which he applied discouraged older students, particularly those his age and older.

For a brief period after beginning law school, Coleman worked at the bank, mostly completing assignments and passing the workload to his successors. During this period, he attended school Monday through Thursday and worked at the bank on Friday and weekends. "The first few weeks were quite a challenge. I had always liked school; it took about three weeks to get comfor-table in classes. There are lots of gray hairs in the class. We don't ask ages. When a student, knowing I'm an older student, says, You

must be 42, I say, 'Yes.'" Then, in 1999, Coleman severed his ties with the Canadian Imperial Bank, and became a full-time student.

Coleman found that his business and life experiences give him an edge in his studies. "It's fun to see the 23-year-olds discussing issues where they have so little experience. Unlike them, I can see how technology has changed things. All this experience is helpful in making legal decisions."

Unlike most other law-school

> **"It's fun to see the 23-year-olds discussing issues where they have so little experience. Unlike them, I can see how technology has changed things."**

students, Coleman, who is single, will graduate debt-free. He attended the University of Texas as a National Merit scholar and UNC on a scholarship and the G.I. Bill.

It's too early to tell what direction Coleman's career will take when he receives his law degree in May 2002. He may return to Texas. He's also considering working for a technology company or doing venture-capital financing, and he'll have a law degree to help accelerate the business deals.

JOURNALISM PROVIDES A CRITICAL EDGE

Jay Johnston
A NEWSPAPER EDITOR SWITCHES TO CORPORATE LAW

For two years, when he was in his 30s, Jay Johnston, now in his early 40s, averaged less than six hours of sleep a night. He worked at the time as a news editor on the *Asbury Park Press,* one of New Jersey's largest dailies, went to law school during the day, and commuted to law school and the job by car, averaging 170 miles a day. Johnston's dizzy pace meant that his wife, Irene, an intensive-care pediatric nurse, and his young children had an absentee husband and father during that time.

After a less than distinguished academic record at the College of William & Mary, Johnston had trans-ferred to Rider College in Trenton, N.J., for a degree in journalism, which he earned in 1984. In his senior year, the *Asbury Park Press* hired him as a municipal reporter, and over the next seven years, he covered local and state news, including three years as a state-house reporter in the *Press*'s Trenton state government bureau.

"It was now time to find how sausage is made. Up to then, as a reporter, I had been an outsider, but I wanted to see how government actually worked as an insider, not as an observer, and I became public affairs director in the New Jersey Department of Community Affairs. My tour was cut short with a change in the state's political leadership, and it

was time to look for another job."

While a state employee, he enrolled as an evening student at Temple University Law School, in Philadelphia.

Attending law school was consistent with Johnston's long-term professional goals. "Going to Temple was part of an earlier dream deferred. In high school,

Johnston has been able to meld his news and legal know-how with clients involved in media technology and Web-based operations.

I had thought about being a lawyer, but I had also thought about being a news-paper reporter." And working as a reporter on the *Asbury Park Press* seemed a more exciting opportunity right out of college than attending law school. Later, he discovered that the news field has its limitations, while the law appeared to have broader career horizons. Fortunately, Johnston's wife shared his view. He intended to practice law, not just to obtain an additional background skill.

The Johnstons had two children (a third was born in 1997), but they were still a two-income family, so they could pay his tuition from their cash flow. Later on, when his wife opted to stay home and their finances changed, Johnston borrowed to pay for law school. This situation meant dwindling disposable income for several years.

Johnston decided to return to journalism to provide income while he completed law school. He persuaded the *Press* to rehire him, this time as a news editor in its main offices in Neptune, N.J., which is on the Jersey shore near Asbury Park. "I had to persuade management that it might be a good idea to have someone like me with some legal training around."

The *Press* at that time was an independently owned newspaper, and its management felt that they needed someone on the newsroom floor who understood the paper's legal needs. Johnston was hired for a shift that started in the early afternoon and ended in mid evening. He drove from his home in Yardley, Pa., to Philadelphia, about 30 miles away, to attend Temple as a daytime student and then had a 75-minute drive to work. During the school year, he arrived at Temple two hours early so that he could study before class. Johnston and his wife agreed on certain limits to his schedule during his two-year grind as editor, student, commuter, and family man. "My agreement with Irene meant that the summers were sacred— no law school, and I tried to avoid studying on weekends. The time was reserved for the family."

Expecting to complete law school in

1997, Johnston felt his dual skills as a lawyer and newsman would meld. However, when the *Press* was acquired by Gannett in late 1997, legal matters were moved to Gannett's executive offices. For one year before ownership was transferred, Johnston was the *Press*'s newsroom counsel, on such editorial issues as potential libel.

Once Johnston decided to leave the *Press* for a full-time legal job, he found the search process somewhat daunting. His area of interest was in intellectual-

"Law firms were not enthralled. I had not done any clerkships, I was in my late 30s, an unknown quantity and I didn't fit into the first-year associate mold."

property law, a specialty that focuses on trademark, licensing, and copyright issues. "Law firms were not enthralled with my background, since I had not done any clerkships, I was in my late 30s, an unknown quantity and I didn't fit into the first-year associate mold." Nor were they impressed with his experience as a reporter, an editor, and a government public affairs officer nor with his ranking in the top 5% of his law school class.

In October 1999 Johnston was hired as an associate by a Philadelphia law firm, Dechert, Price & Rhoades, which merged eight months later with a British-based firm with an equal number of names on the door. The new firm emerged as Dechert, with an international staff of 600 lawyers. As a member of the Intellectual-Property department, Johnston has fortunately been able to meld his news and legal know-how with clients involved in media technology and Web-based operations, areas of familiarity from his work with the *Press*.

Even though hostility between lawyers and reporters is assumed to exist, Johnston finds that the "differences in the disciplines are largely matters of degree. Lawyers and journalists are paid to analyze issues, then harmonize and crystallize those issues in writing. For journalists, it's a news story; for lawyers, a memo or contract, motion or appellate brief. The principal difference is the rigor of the analysis and the depth and precision of the writing."

Journalism provides Johnston with an edge in his new career. Knowing how to how to write clearly and being able to listen allows Johnston to separate what's really important in telling the story from what is unnecessary and distracting. While interviewing for stories and in supervising reporters and editors, Johnston also developed good inter-personal skills.

Johnston now commutes to work by train, but his workday starts at 8:30 A.M. and ends with his return home 12 hours later.

Entering Medicine: Not for the Faint of Heart

WHY MEDICINE? IN THE PREVIOUS CHAPTER, CAREER changers described the epiphany that spirited them to prepare for a career in the ministry. A similar spiritual calling is the motivator in medicine. The decisions by the career changers in this chapter to go to medical school were not made overnight, considering that they had family responsibilities. Each of them had reached a point in their lives when it was "now or never."

Whether the goal is to practice medicine, dentistry or nursing, or to use the dozens of scientific and technical skills needed to meet current health care needs, career changers will find no shortage of jobs in the health care field. This chapter focuses on medicine and nursing. From the standpoint of career changing, medicine should have been excluded, considering that only 7,000 men and women over age 28 apply each year to medical school and that less than 30% are accepted. Even so, I have focused on how to switch careers into medicine because this career path represents a particular challenge. There are no shortcuts into medicine. A career changer embarks on an 8- to 12-year program, depending on the number of years it takes to complete premed courses and the duration of the residency. Taking this route requires dedication and determination.

Entry into nursing requires a specific course of study lasting

2 to 4 years. Like physicians, nurses are vital throughout the health care field, from surgery to hospital administration.

Medicine

Medical school is hard, don't let anyone tell you otherwise," says Amy Dryer, a former teacher who will graduate from Columbia University's School of Physicians and Surgeons in 2003. Advising "older" premed students via an online newsletter produced by Columbia's postbaccalaureate premed program, Dryer told them that the road that lies ahead is filled with "lots of academic information and vocabulary I've never heard, and more reading that I can carry, much less read.... If you consider what our privileges and responsibilities will be in four years, our training should be hard."

Dryer is part of a comparatively small yet slowly growing number of "nontraditional students," as medical schools refer to those who enter medical school later in life, usually in their late 20s and 30s, but occasionally even at 45 plus.

The Job Market

The Bureau of Labor Statistics is bullish about the future job market for physicians. A growing and aging population creates a greater need for health care services.

There are two main categories of medical doctors—approximately 740,000 doctors of medicine and 44,000 doctors of osteopathic medicine. They use nearly identical medical or surgical procedures, including drugs and surgery. Doctors of osteopathic medicine, however, place special emphasis on the skeletal system, and on preventive and holistic medicine. More than half of doctors of osteopathy practice primary medicine, a third more than medical doctors.

The solo medical practitioner, even in primary medical care, is a vanishing breed, having been replaced by physicians who are employed by group practices or as staffers at hospitals, clinics, health maintenance organizations, and government health care and public health agencies.

If a large income is a goal, it's better to consider investment banking. Physicians do well financially, but by today's standards in corporate America they're hardly overpaid. According to the American Medical Association (www.ama-assn.org), pediatricians, psychiatrists, and general and family practitioners have a median net income after expenses of between $120,000 and $150,000 a year, while specialists (such as obstetrician/gynecologists, radiologists, anesthesiologists, and surgeons) have median net incomes of between $200,000 and $270,000. First-year residents start their medical careers earning about $34,000.

Getting Into Medical School

Compared with teachers, lawyers, and the clergy, relatively few career changers age 30-plus choose to become physicians. The main obstacle is the long gestation period to complete premed studies, medical school, and a residency—along with the accumulation of considerable debt. Many possible older applicants are discouraged by the long trial-by-fire apprenticeship. And getting into medical school remains difficult. A review of a 1998–99 report on medical-school applications by the American Association of Medical Colleges (www.aamc.org) shows the following:

ALL APPLICANTS

AGE	NUMBER APPLYING	PERCENT APPLYING	NUMBER ACCEPTED	PERCENT ACCEPTED
20 and under	361	0.9%	259	71.7%
21–23	19,892	48.5	10,266	51.6
24–27	13,767	33.6	4,792	34.8
28–31	4,150	10.5	1,321	31.8
32–34	1,119	2.9	375	31.5
35–37	752	1.8	189	21.5
38 and older	883	2.2	177	20.0
TOTAL	**41,004**	**100.0%**	**17,379**	**42.4%**

As the table shows, nearly 7,000 people age 28 or older applied to medical school, and substantially less than one-third of them entered medical school the following fall. Those are hardly good betting odds, but they're still an improvement from a generation ago, when nontraditional students, especially those age 35 or older, were a medical-school rarity.

It's difficult enough for college seniors and very recent graduates to meet medical-school entrance requirements, but would-be applicants in their late 20s or older are in for a shock. The career-changing path is filled with booby traps that were put there not so much to dissuade older students but as a standard to assure that all applicants have met similar premed academic qualifications. A career changer's workplace and life experiences are considered an invaluable part of the candidate's portfolio, so long as all other requirements have been met.

Career changers are required to take premed courses that they may have avoided as undergraduate students.

This situation presents a challenge to older medical school hopefuls. Many have not taken a science course since high school, or they had college majors as diverse as business administration, music, history, or English literature. A premed course is not for everyone. Medical school is difficult enough, but the one to three years necessary to prepare for it can frustrate a 35-year-old career changer who is making the transition to the classroom after working for a number of years. Moreover, they're required to take premed courses that they may have *avoided* as undergraduate students, or if they took the courses ten or more years ago, chances are they'll have to retake them.

The nation's 125 accredited medical and 19 osteopathic schools have no preference as to a specific college undergraduate major, just so long as the applicant has completed one year each of biology, physics, and English and two years of chemistry. Some schools add calculus to their prerequisite list.

Depending on the scope of the program, completing a premed course means spending one to three years in the science classroom, with laboratory instruction. About 50 colleges have packaged the required premed courses into postbaccalaureate programs. These programs are designed for career-changing osteopathic, dental, and nursing school candidates.

Many postbaccalaureate premed courses are scheduled in the early afternoon, evening, and on weekends to enable students to work during the transition period. But Goucher College, in Baltimore, runs a full-time program that starts in June and continues for an entire academic year, which prepares students to apply to medical school after just one year.

Not everyone lives in an area that offers a specific premed program for older students. The best approach is to enroll at any accredited college or university that accepts nondegree students, and take the required premed courses. Medical-school literature or Web sites should indicate the premed courses that are required of applicants.

Packaged premed programs offer extra value by counseling their students on medical school protocols.

The packaged premed programs, however, offer extra value by counseling their students on medical-school protocols, an admission process that can take up to 15 months. They also guide them to apply to schools with higher-than-average acceptance rates for older students, conduct practice MCAT sessions, and explain the differences in medical-school curricula that are not always discussed in "how to get into medical school" guides.

Before applying to a postbaccalaureate premed program, do some basic research that goes beyond Internet resources and how-to books. A checklist should include a preliminary visit to a few medical schools, which offers you a chance to chat informally with admissions people. This doesn't mean that you're obligated or even want to apply to the school. If they are asked, chances are they'll provide the names of some current older students or recent graduates to contact—another item recommended for your checklist.

How can you discover the attitude of a school toward older applicants? While federal law bans medical schools from discriminating on age in making their admission decisions, the average age in the entering medical school class, according to the commentary given to Columbia's premed students, is likely to be higher at schools that value life experiences.

Medical schools encourage applicants to volunteer in a

hospital or clinic to learn directly about health care challenges. Michael Stern, whose profile appears later in this chapter, spent 18 months volunteering in the emergency room at St. Luke's/Roosevelt Hospital while he was a postbaccalaureate premed student at Columbia. Volunteering serves another useful purpose: It introduces students to health care professionals who can serve as mentors, guide them in selecting a medical school, and may even become medical-school references.

> **An interview is definitely not the time to say that a TV medical show was a primary inspiration for a pending career switch.**

An interview is a mandatory part of the admission process. One goal is to eliminate romantics, and not just among career changers. Medical schools are alert to students who, regardless of age, have been drawn to medicine for what the schools have determined to be the wrong reasons. An interview is definitely not the time to say that a TV medical show was a primary inspiration for a pending career switch. When nontraditional students change careers, admissions interviewers may question whether the applicants have the stamina needed to succeed in medical school. Then again, why would a 35-year-old want to spend up to three years taking premed courses and another 4 years in medical school and a residency just to have bragging rights to a medical degree?

The University of Arizona's medical school uses a selection formula that is similar to the process at other schools: Admission is based on college grades, MCAT scores, a personal statement, letters of recommendations, evaluations of personal interviews, and patient-related volunteer or paid work. High college grades alone are not enough to qualify for admission. Equally important is improvement in the applicant's grades each year. The medical school wants to see progress, not just how each candidate performed at the end of the race.

The Internet offers medical-school candidates a single application form that the American Medical College Application Service (www.aamc.org; click on "students and applicants") forwards to each school that the candidate designates. Not all members of the Association of American Medical Colleges use this service; in such cases applicants apply individually to each medical school. With a single application, however, the student has the advantage of preparing a single academic summary and a personal statement, which provide sufficient information for medical schools to screen applicants. Then the medical schools request more information, called secondaries, which usually consists of several essays. Personal interviews are the third stage of the process. As in all college applications, there are expenses. AAMC charges $380 to process applications to 15 medical schools. And, depending on the medical school, students pay additional fees for the secondaries.

Similar single-source routing systems are available to candidates for programs in osteopathy (American Association of Colleges of Osteopathic Medicine; www.aacom.org) and dentisry (American Dental Education Association, formerly the American Association of Dental Schools; www.aads.jhu.edu).

Statistically, the deck may be stacked against the acceptance of applicants over age 30 into medical school, but once accepted, such students often feel that they have an edge. Having had experience in the workplace, they have few misconceptions about realistic workloads. They're no longer strangers to the classroom; premed studies got them back into the study groove. And age can be a positive factor when dealing with patients. The physician with a few gray hairs and, in many instances, better "people skills" helps to put patients at ease.

The Importance of the MCAT

The Medical College Admission Test is the litmus test for medical school applicants, as are similar tests taken by osteopathic and dental school candidates. An outstanding college transcript and relevant workplace experiences notwithstanding, an applicant's future stands or falls with these exams.

Some older applicants may be exempt from taking the MCAT if they have taken them previously, say, as undergraduates. Each school sets its own rules. Some medical schools accept test results "forever," and others require retesting after a lapse of three to five years between taking them and applying to med school.

The test is given twice a year, in April and August. It's not the type of test for which a cram course will do anything more than sharpen test-taking skills. The MCAT consists of three multiple-choice sections, covering biological and physical sciences and verbal reasoning, plus two essays. Tests are graded by the MCAT's sponsor, the Association of American Medical Colleges, on a scale of 1 to 15. Columbia University warns test takers that a score of 8 or below on any part will most likely eliminate them from admission to an American or Canadian medical school.

The Cost

Going to medical school at any age is expensive, but it's indirectly more costly for older students who have left a paid job to make little or no money for four years at medical school and spend three to six or more years in a low-paying residency. At the same time, they are incurring household expenses that most 22-year-old medical students normally don't have. Medical schools advise all students to get their finances in order, a task that may cause an applicant to delay medical school for a year in order to prepare financially for seven to nine years of little or no income. Excess debt otherwise translates into family strain, a problem that older medical school students want to avoid.

More than half of the nearly 125 American medical colleges are state-owned and financially supported with lower tuition and fees than private medical schools. State schools are mandated to accept a high percentage of in-state residents, which means that geographical decisions come into play. It's little wonder that applicants often relocate to a state and declare their residency if they intend to apply to the medical schools in that state. Arizona University (www.ahsc.arizona.edu) issues a blunt warning to prospective medical school applicants that they must be residents of Arizona, or of Montana or Wyoming, which pay Arizona to provide medical school education to their residents.

Weill Medical College of Cornell University (www.med .cornell.edu), a private medical school on New York's East Side, provides incoming students with a financial-aid handbook that estimates four-year costs at $108,000 for tuition and another $71,000 to cover fees, books, equipment, food, rent, health insurance, and personal expenses in 2000. Married students and those with children have proportionately larger expenses.

The University of Colorado School of Medicine (www.uchsc .edu) in Denver, unlike Cornell, is a state medical school; Colorado residents pay tuition and fees that amount to an estimated $49,000 for four years, compared with nonresident fees of nearly $206,000 for the same education.

For most students, debt is part of a medical education. Cornell noted that the debt for its 1999 graduates ranged from $10,000 to $159,000, and nationally it averages nearly $91,000.

With debt comes the issue of repayment. Some loan agreements have a grace period of several months to several years after graduation, after which repayment must begin. At 8% simple interest, a student with $50,000 in debt will make

POINTS TO REMEMBER

- **A growing and an aging population** are fueling a need for more health care workers.
- **Solo practitioners** are rapidly disappearing.
- **Primary care physicians** earn about half the income of physicians in some specialties.
- **Candidates** for medical school who are 30 years old or older face admissions hurdles.
- **Regardless of age and workplace experience,** all candidates must take basic science courses.
- **The MCATs** is a critical entrance barometer.
- **Costs** are considerably higher at private medical schools than at state-supported medical schools.
- **Some medical schools** favor in-state residents.
- **Grants, scholarships, and loans** go hand in hand as a means of financing medical education.
- **The number of students** in nursing school is slipping.
- **The nursing profession** is accepting older career changers.
- **Nursing salaries** are on the rise.

loan payments of $607 each month for ten years; $478 for 15 years or $418 for 20 years.

Scholarships and grants are available from medical schools, the state, the federal government, and private foundations. Some students qualify for G.I. Bill educational benefits. All students qualify for a Federal Direct Stafford Loan, which provides $8,500 a year in loan benefits.

The military services and the National Health Service will pay education costs in exchange for medical service.

The Army (www.goarmy.com), the Navy (www.navyjobs.com), and the Air Force (www.airforce.com) all pay education costs for students at medical, osteopathic, and dental schools in exchange for military medical service. Philip Berran (profiled in chapter 3), divorced with one child, found a way to avoid any additional financial headaches. He was commissioned as a U.S. Army 2nd Lieutenant in his first year of medical school. For the next four years he received free tuition, books, and equipment along with a personal stipend of $1,000 a month. His military obligation, depending on the length of residency, is a minimum of five years of active duty as a medical officer, starting with the rank of captain. The longer the residency, the more years of active duty that will be required.

The National Health Service Corps (http://.bphc.hrsa.gov -nhsc) has a civilian version of the military program. Recipients are required to provide primary-care medicine either in private practice or to a government agency in areas where there is a physician shortage, most likely rural America. The payback is one year of service for each year of free tuition.

Some People Who Made the Change

Don't let anyone tell you otherwise: It takes perseverance and determination at age 30 or older to prepare for and then attend medical school. Ten years later, if everything goes smoothly, the career changer should be practicing medicine. The years between will be spent taking the required premed courses and medical school, followed by three to five years of residency.

The people described in this chapter made that commitment. For some it was not a solo decision; spouses also had to make personal sacrifices and alter their lifestyles. To become physicians, these people most likely assumed additional debt that will take years to pay off. To add to the challenge, these 30- and 40-year-olds were competing with medical-school students ten to 20 years younger.

Jamie Lovdal, a biologist for nearly 20 years, was motivated by a personal experience in dealing with her infant daughter's health problems. Stephen Galper's route was somewhat more circuitous; he fulfilled his high school dream after he had earned an MBA, worked as an accountant, attended law school, and operated his own law firm. Michael Stern, the son of a psychiatrist, was, like Galper, not prepared emotionally as a college student to make a commitment to medicine. Instead, he became an artist. In chapter 3, Philip Berran describes his odyssey from New York City cop and lawyer into medicine. Law school made him aware of opportunities as a pathologist and medical examiner. Catherine Ray's motivation is somewhat different. A dental hygienist for more than ten years, she needed more of a professional challenge. She decided on dentistry when her job as a hygienist became routine.

STARTS MEDICAL SCHOOL IN HER EARLY 40s

Jamie Lovdal
A LONG ROAD TO BECOME A PHYSICIAN

When Jamie Lovdal decided to become a physician in the early 1990s, she was nearly 40. The daughter of a foreign-service officer, Lovdal spent 15 of her first 19 years living in Europe and Africa. At the University of New Hampshire, she was a zoology major, graduating magna cum laude, and a member of Phi Beta Kappa. A few years later, she received a master's degree in marine biology from the University of Miami. No question about it, Lovdal was a dedicated science researcher.

Lovdal moved to North Carolina in the early 1980s when her husband, Philip, a land surveyor, was hired by a Raleigh-based engineering firm. Jamie Lovdal found a series of jobs, as a research technician and a research-laboratory manager at the University of North Carolina, North Carolina State University and the U. S. Department of Agriculture's Food Fermentation Lab in Raleigh.

"Up to the time that Kari was born in 1986, I had very little interest in being a doctor. Biological science was my field. But when she was a baby, Kari had health problems. We visited doctors and hospitals regularly to see about her eyes. I gained greater respect for medicine and physicians. And for the first time I began to think about becoming a doctor."

In 1993, after weighing what it would be like to spend the next eight to ten years training for a new profession and how it would affect her personal and family life, Lovdal decided to apply to medical school.

Philip agreed totally with her decision on medical school. Fortunately, she had completed nearly all the required academic coursework and her application

Few schools were interested despite her distinguished academic record and work as a scientist for nearly 20 years.

was further strengthened by her years of related education and work experience. As a state employee, she incurred minimal expense to attend North Carolina State University to take organic chemistry and physics courses, the only ones missing from her premed-course portfolio.

Snags surfaced when she applied to the four medical schools in North Carolina, and a few outside the state. She took her MCAT but "didn't ace them." Although one or two of the schools seemed interested in her academic record and her related workplace skills, several discouraged her from the outset of the application cycle. One medical school even went so far as to intimate that she should not waste her time in applying. Lovdal was amazed by how few schools were interested, considering that she had a distinguished undergraduate academic record and that she had worked as a scientist for nearly 20 years.

Fortunately for Lovdal, the University of Rochester's School of Medicine and Dentistry had a more open policy about admitting students over age 30 and accepted her. Lovdal could not attend immediately because her second child had just been born, and so turned down the offer and planned to reapply for admission the following year. Relocation of her family to Rochester also was out of the question; it would be difficult for Philip to find work as a surveyor because Rochester was somewhat depressed economically and there was less need for his skill there.

She reapplied the following year to Rochester and several other schools. Duke Medical School, which had turned her down a year earlier, placed her on a waiting list. "They said something interesting to me: 'In two years, if things don't work out in Rochester we'll reconsider you for admission in your third year.'"

In the end, Lovdal's family stayed in Raleigh and she went to Rochester.

"I commuted home for a long weekend once a month. Philip ran the house and took care of the two children. To spend more time with Kara, then eight, and Espen, under two, Philip no

longer worked overtime. Looking back, I was glad in some ways that I was alone in Rochester, since my studies would have kept me apart from them even if I was living at home.

"My class had about 100 students. Although I was the oldest, there were about ten other students who were 30 or older. Rochester was used to older students. They found they made good doctors. It was rough my first year. It had been awhile since I had been in a classroom with so many high achievers,

"My studies would have kept me apart from my family even if I was living at home."

most of whom had just graduated from college. Before the end of my second year, I reapplied to schools nearer to home.

"I had never heard back from Duke, so I finally called them to see why I had not at least been called for an interview. I was told that I had already been accepted."

The acceptance letter, it seemed, had been lost in the mail. She transferred to Duke as a third-year student in July 1996.

To pay for medical school, Lovdal cashed in $40,000 in retirement funds from her North Carolina pension plan. The money lasted about two years, but she took student loans to cover expenses at Duke for the third and fourth years. "I received a $9,000 grant each year as a state resident," said Lovdal. "We also consolidated our personal loans, and took out a second mortgage on our home. By the time I graduated from Duke in 1998, I had about $70,000 in student loans."

Her medical training has been hard on her two children, especially Kari, now a teenager, who had additional health and personal problems. Nearing graduation from Duke, Lovdal found that she was rejected for her medical specialty, emergency-room medicine followed by family medicine, with a hospital residency at Duke, because the hospital makes the selection on the basis of an application submitted online with the National Residency Matching Program (http://nrmp.aamc.org/nrmp) and she didn't make the match. After all those years of dealing successfully with challenges to get into and remain in medical school, Lovdal was told that the program judged that she wouldn't be able to make the necessary sacrifices to work in emergency room medicine. She was matched, however, in family medicine, and in May 2001 she will have completed a three-year Duke Hospital residency.

"I have reduced my options to working in the Raleigh area, relocating to southern Massachusetts to be closer to my husband's family, or perhaps overseas as a civilian working for the military.

"When I start practicing, Philip, who is a few years older, expects to retire as a surveyor, change careers and become a buyer and seller of paintings, something that he had been doing as a sideline for many years. I have few regrets other than the time that I was separated from my

By the time Lovdal graduated, she had about $70,000 in student loans.

family while I was in Rochester. I sometimes feel sorry for the younger medical school students. I don't really wish I was their age. Most of them have never had the time to travel or to take it easy. Before I ever settled down, I was a waitress and a tutor and I did odd jobs. In this respect, I feel that I have an edge over them by having had so many personal experiences beforehand."

AT 50, NEW DOCTOR BUYS TIME WITH PSYCHIATRY

Steven Galper
A PHYSICIAN VIA MANAGEMENT AND LAW

Steven Galper, now in his mid 40s, got tired of high school and dropped out, hardly an auspicious start for a future lawyer and physician. "I got my high school diploma by exchanging work for school credits. I mostly parked cars in a shopping center, and did odd jobs." Even with a negligible academic record, Galper's high school dream was medicine. No family pressures moved him in this direction. His father, a butcher, died when he was nine, and no other family members were doctors.

On the day in 1972 that he was accepted into Wayne State University, in Detroit, Galper was also inducted into the Army as part of a huge Vietnam War military buildup. Galper didn't go to Vietnam, but instead was sent as a medical corpsman to Fort Lewis in Washington State. While in the Army, Galper took college courses conducted at Fort Lewis.

"After my discharge, I went to the University of Washington with the intention of being a premed student. I could do most of the work, but organic chemistry was an obstacle. I wasn't a disciplined student. I spent a semester at the nursing school, but I soon realized that if you want to be a doctor, you don't want to be a nurse." With a checkered academic background, Galper became a psychology major.

A medical career now seemed remote. Galper took the GMAT with little intention of going to business school. He scored well, changed his mind on business school, and attended the University of Michigan's College of Business Administration in Ann Arbor. Two years later, he had an MBA degree

> "Sometimes I ask myself why I didn't become a doctor earlier in my life. I guess the answer is I wasn't dissatisfied enough, and I did not know that I could do it."

with a major in accounting. "I went to work for General Motors as a tax analyst. I was making more money than I deserved. My mother thought I had the ultimate job, working for General Motors. To her, I was a salaried man."

Despite his success, Galper didn't take long to decide that corporate life was not for him. Being a self-employed lawyer seemed more to his liking. Galper moved to Arizona to enter law school and take advantage of its cheap tuition for state residents—just $300 per year in the early 1980s. The first year, he paid out-of-state tuition rates; the next two years he qualified as a state resident.

During law school, he worked as a tax accountant for Ernst & Whinney's Tucson office. "When I graduated in 1981, I wanted to be self-employed, so I started my own firm and literally did tax returns for people who lived in trailer parks." From his trailer-park debut, Galper made the transition into a general commercial practice that employed a few lawyers.

"I was never really enamored with being a lawyer. Eating at me was why I had never gone to med school. The answer was simple. I didn't have the credentials to apply. I had to take premed courses and exams. Since I had taken science in college, premed courses had changed. I was advised to take them at the University of Arizona and not at a community college, so that I would be challenged to get good grades. I did, and I took the MCAT review courses twice."

At his medical-school interviews, admissions staff were skeptical. After reviewing Galper's accumulation of degrees, they wanted to be assured that he was not shopping for another degree. His response? He went to work as a volunteer in the local Veterans Administration hospital.

Galper was accepted by the University of Arizona's College of Medicine as the last student on its eligibility list. He also was accepted at Northwestern University, in Chicago, but to go there would have taken every dime he had. Complicating matters, Galper was living with Carol, whom he would marry in his third year of medical school. Going

to Northwestern would have meant commuting regularly from Chicago to Tucson to see Carol, along with accumulating considerably more debt.

Galper was fortunate in other ways to attend Arizona's medical school. It had a reputation for student diversity, including a proportionately high number of older students. In his late 30s, he was the one of oldest in his class. His grades were good, considering he couldn't memorize facts as easily as the younger students, but he found that his people

After reviewing Galper's accumulation of degrees, admissions staff wanted to be assured that he was not shopping for another degree.

skills were better. He first learned about the needs of patients as an Army corpsman, and his work as a lawyer had taught him how to relate to all kinds of people.

"Cliques exist at medical school. My closest friend for two years, and now an internist in Phoenix, was 23. He was broke, so I kidded him that he needed me to buy his lunch. I did his taxes. He had raw brain power, while I had practical experience relating to medicine. We needed each other."

Galper graduated from medical school in 1998. Initially interested in either geriatrics or internal medicine, he selected a joint residency in neurology and psychiatry in Tucson that he'll complete in June 2004. If he had been 15 years younger, Galper might have become a neurosurgeon, but this specialty would take several more years to complete. Psychiatry also buys him time, because psychiatrists retire later than other physicians. Even so, Galper will complete his residency when he's 50.

Galper finds that he continually uses his accounting and legal experience. "When I receive a financial statement on a patient's health care reimbursement from the medical department or insurance company, I can read and interpret

it. Other doctors disregard them.

"As a lawyer, I know how to deal with HMOs when they tell patients about their legal rights. I flip into my lawyer mode, and call the HMO case manager. I can be either subtle or not so subtle. One case manager jokingly asked me when and where I got my law degree. I replied from the University of Arizona in 1982.

"Sometimes I ask myself why I didn't go ahead and become a doctor earlier in my life. I guess the answer is, I wasn't dissatisfied enough, and I did not know that I could do it."

OPTS FOR EMERGENCY MEDICINE

Michael Stern
AN ABSTRACT PAINTER IS NOW A PHYSICIAN

Michael Stern, in his mid 30s, started at Brown University as a premed student. Stern took a number of the required premed math and science courses, but he found that he was not ready to commit himself to a medical career. He switched majors to study art history and studio art, concentrating on painting, his primary interest since childhood.

Graduating in 1986, he returned to New York to launch a career as a painter of abstract art. To supplement his income, he worked as an art installer at the Guggenheim Museum and the Museum of Modern Art, and he did carpentry.

"But I had never totally abandoned the idea of being a doctor. Even though I originally thought that I'd be painting for the rest of my life, there were parts of painting professionally that I did not like." In particular, he was concerned whether he would be satisfied in later years with being an artist.

In the early 1990s Stern once again considered going to medical school, but he recognized that he did not have the academic prerequisites to get in. After three years' delay, he finally acted on the materials he had received from Columbia University's postbaccalaureate premed program.

Career changing took on further complexities. Now married, Stern had to consider his wife and soon-to-be family as part of any career-switching plans. On his first day of class at Columbia, in September 1994, his wife, Gail, brought their first child home from the hospital. (The second was born during his first year in medical school.) Considering that he was no longer a full-

> "Frankly, I had a great story to tell." Interviewers saw that he had been a dedicated artist with the drive to succeed in a difficult field.

time painter, Stern knew that there was a lot riding on completing the premed program and getting into medical school.

Stern was a full-time student in a three-year program that consisted of a heavy dose of science courses. Columbia represented a shift in his approach to problem solving. "Up to then, I had spent the bulk of my time, by myself, thinking and working as an abstract painter." Because his courses required practical, not abstract, solutions, it meant a change in the way he thought and solved problems.

Because he was over 30, Stern was classified as a nontraditional medical-school applicant, which, in practical terms, meant fewer medical-school openings. So he decided to spotlight what made him different from other highly qualified applications. He discovered that having been an artist for ten years was a huge plus in medical-school interviews. Stern was questioned about his career as an artist. "It seemed that my application and my background were somewhat different. Frankly, I had a great story to tell; it made the difference." Interviewers saw that he had been a dedicated artist with the drive to succeed in a difficult field.

Stern had been advised to apply to a large number of schools, since most schools normally accept only about 5% of their applicants. He applied to 15 schools, and was accepted by nine, including five in the New York area.

Stern picked Cornell University's Medical College in New York City. He and his wife decided that they wanted to remain in an apartment near Columbia, where Gail was studying for a master's degree in English while freelancing as a writer and editor.

"As a medical school student, I soon realized that I knew how to deal with older people better than many of the younger students. And from my premed work, I knew how to apply myself to my studies. On the downside, my energy level was age 32, somewhat lower than that of the 22-year-olds, but I was in good shape from the physical work needed in painting and furniture making." So staying in shape became a concern.

Rather than taking mass transportation from his West Side New York apartment to Cornell on the East Side, Stern biked the three and a half miles to class in 15 minutes, weather permitting. In early 2001, the Sterns moved to Palisades, in Rockland County, about 20 miles north of New York City. No longer a bike rider, he commuted by car to Cornell for his final semester.

His background in art provided an additional asset. "I find some of my classes easier than others, because I think

As a painter, he lived in his head and through his eyes, while as a medical student, he engages in a more external process.

of things in three-dimensional terms. I automatically see the heart as a three-dimensional organ, and I easily visualize how the various parts function."

His old and new professions differ particularly in one regard. As a painter, he lived in his head and through his eyes, while as a medical student, he engages in a more external process—hearing, examining, and interacting with patients.

Stern graduated from Cornell on May 24, 2001, eight days after his wife received her master's degree in creative writing from Columbia. On July 1, he started a four-year residency in emergency medicine at Bellevue/NYU Medical Center.

By the time he graduated from Cornell, Stern had accumulated considerable debt. He financed his education primarily from savings, the sale of his paintings, parental help, and sizable Cornell loans.

Lifestyle is important to him. "I might have become a surgeon, but I don't want to go through a five- to six-year residency. I might have become a psychiatrist, like my father, but I like using my hands." Stern, however, likes the variety of medical skills involved in emergency medicine, the work schedule, often three days at work and three days off, and an opportunity to have time to continue painting and to spend time with his family.

While medicine is his primary professional focus, Stern can't totally escape painting. "I am always thinking about painting, and have many ideas swirling around in my head. It is now on the backburner, but it is definitely something I will return to in a mean-ingful way at some future point in my medical career."

WELL-PREPARED FOR DENTIST-PATIENT RELATIONSHIP

Catherine Ray
FROM HYGIENIST TO DENTIST

Growing up in Waynesville, a small city in western North Carolina, Catherine Ray had a role model. "She was my dentist's hygienist. She was a nifty lady who also drove an orange Porsche."

It's easy to see why Ray, who is now in her mid 40s, first took the two-year dental hygienist course at the University of North Carolina's School of Dentistry. Going the next step at that time and becoming a dentist was not in the cards. Her boyfriend, Kevin, who joined the Army rather than be drafted, was transferred to a military base near Stuttgart, Germany. In 1975 Ray joined Kevin in Germany. No sooner had she arrived in Stuttgart than her training as a dental hygienist earned her a job at the Army base.

When he completed his overseas duty, the couple returned home and got married, and her new husband went to college to get an accounting degree. After one year, he dropped out of college to become an air traffic controller. When he was sent to Oklahoma for training, Ray went along, and once again her skill was in demand.

"When Kevin completed training, we moved to Kentucky, where he was assigned to the Lexington airport. I got a job in a dental office. I also was active in the state hygienists association. At the time, we were trying to get the

legislature to permit hygienists to open their own offices, independent of a dental practice."

Kevin lost his job and his career in 1981 when he and thousands of other air traffic controllers were fired by President Reagan for going on strike. He went to the University of Kentucky to

> ## "One of the deciding factors was that I never felt that I received the recognition that I deserved."

complete his accounting degree.

Ray found that her work as a hygienist had become routine, like so many jobs and careers that plateau. "I got to know some women dentists, and decided that I wanted to switch careers. One of the deciding factors was that I never felt that I received the recognition that I deserved. I passed the dental aptitude tests, and even got credit for the biology and chemistry courses that I had taken at UNC."

No relocation from Lexington was necessary because the University of Kentucky had a dental school. "I was able to get all types of loans [12 years later they're just about paid off]. That made it easier to go to school for four years, even if it meant living on a single income."

About one-third of her class of 60 students were women, and six in the class were over 30. "I worked very hard at school. Even though I was an experienced hygienist, I was attending school with very bright students who found classwork to be lots easier than I did."

After graduating in 1988 as a doctor of medical dentistry, Ray and her husband returned to Chapel Hill where she had trained as a hygienist. She was selected for a two-year residency that was geared to associate dentistry more closely with general medicine. This meant that, like a medical resident, Ray made hospital rounds to attend to patients who had multiple illnesses that included dental problems.

"When I completed my residency, I wanted to open a practice where patients were generally healthy and did not need dental attention that had to be done in a hospital. My goal was to be more in control of my practice—the hours I would work and the types of patients I would care for."

Having been a hygienist was good grounding for the dentist-to-patient relationship. By the time she became a dentist, Ray estimates that she had already given 20,000 soft-tissue exams of the mouth, throat, and neck. Ray set up her practice in Durham, and as is true of newcomers in any field, her workday was long—often 11 hours a day, five days a week. When she set up her practice, Ray didn't realize that she would be operating a small business that hires employees, has a payroll, pays taxes, and buys equipment and supplies. Fortunately, her husband stepped in to handle the accounting and financial records on his computer.

"Then came a big surprise. Kevin and I had been married about 14 years. By then, we didn't expect any children, but I became pregnant. This changed the nature of my practice." Beginning with her son's birth in 1993, Ray altered her work hours. She opened her office about 11 A.M. so she could spend the early morning hours with her child. She saw her last patient at about 5:30 P.M., completed some professional paperwork, and was home 90 minutes later. Her schedule complemented Kevin's work schedule as an accountant with the county's Water and Sewer Authority, which permitted him to be home with their child in the late afternoon.

A few years later, Ray took a key step to further accommodate her role as a dentist and mother by altering her office hours even further. A 9 A.M. to 3 P.M. workday enables her to be home in the late afternoon, now that her son is an elementary-school student. She's not the only one in the office with a reduced workweek. Both her office manager and hygienist are mothers with similar work and home schedules.

Ray admits that if she worked longer hours she would earn about 25% more money. With a shortened workweek, she still doesn't have an orange Porsche.

Nursing

The future looks good for nursing. The job market is expected to grow over the next eight to ten years. The question: With groups like the American Association of Colleges of Nursing (www.aacn.nche.edu) and the National Student Nurses' Association (www.nsna.org) talking about a dwindling supply of new nurses as nursing-school enrollments continue to decline, how will the pipeline be filled?

When hospitals downsized and cut staffs beginning in the early 1990s, nursing was no longer considered an attractive and secure career. Nurses seeking better working hours and more pay found new outlets for their skills in industry and government. What's more, many of yesterday's nursing-school candidates are instead finding careers as physicians and in other health care specialties.

Even with its recruitment problems, nursing is the largest health care profession, with more than 2 million registered nurses. About 60% of nurses work in hospitals, or inpatient or outpatient clinics; the rest work in nursing homes, medical offices, and government health care facilities. This situation, too, is changing, with the shift of health care delivery from inpatient hospital to outpatient ambulatory and community facilities. Yet the demand for trained nurses continues. A growing elderly population, for example, with more acute medical problems translates into a need for many more nurses.

Getting Into Nursing

Depending on the academic approach they choose, career changers can make the transition into nursing in less than two years. The decision hinges on how much time you want to spend to qualify as a registered nurse.

There are several different ways to become a registered nurse. More than 2,000 schools offer a four- or five-year baccalaureate degree. The two-year hospital-based diploma program, once the most popular route into nursing, is being replaced by associate-degree programs at 1,000 community colleges. Both programs aim to get graduates into the job market in two years.

The key decision for career changers is whether they want or need another undergraduate degree to enter the job market. A four-year program, a natural career route for students directly out of high school, makes less sense for older career changers, whose goal is to get to work in the new career as quickly as possible.

Acquiring a four-year nursing degree means greater opportunity for promotion and a way to qualify for higher-paying careers.

A two-year program was once the academic end of the road for most nurses, but not so now. The American Association of Colleges of Nursing reported that, in 2001, nearly one-third of the nation's 104,000 students enrolled in bachelor's-degree nursing programs were nurses who were returning to school in what's termed an RN-to-baccalaureate program. Acquiring a four-year degree means greater opportunity for promotion and a way to qualify for such higher-paying careers as clinical nurse specialist, nurse practitioner, nurse-midwife, or anesthetist.

Older students are not a nursing-school oddity. Peggy Baker, director of the Watts School of Nursing, an affiliate of Durham Regional Hospital, finds that many students over age 30 wanted to become nurses when they were younger, but they took a different career route. About 50% of the Watts students already have a college degree.

Nursing as a second career also attracts men. About 6% of the nation's nurses are men. Comparatively few men considered nursing when they were younger. Fast-forward about ten to 15 years, and firemen and emergency medical-service technicians, trained in lifesaving techniques, find nursing compatible with their skills and experience. They now represent a small, yet steady, source of new nurses.

Nursing school tuitions vary. Similar to medical schools, private-university nursing schools are more expensive than state-college, community-college, and hospital-based schools.

Nursing salaries are rising, but registered nurses are still leaving the profession for better pay elsewhere. The median salary is approximately $42,000. The lowest paid earn $29,000 a year, while the highest paid 10% of all nurses earn more than

$69,000. In regions with shortages of nurses, higher salaries and signup bonuses are used to recruit staffs. Specialty nurses and those with master's degrees are at the top of the pay scale.

Some People Who Made the Change

Carol Beebee and Travis Skinner each had diverse careers before deciding to attend nursing school. Both considered becoming physicians when they were younger, but at the time, they lacked sufficient focus. Nonetheless, they never lost their interest in health care. Beebee acted upon her dream in her late 30s, and Skinner embarked upon his nursing career in his 40s.

FINDING THE RIGHT PATH

Carol Beebee
FROM A SERIES OF ODD JOBS INTO NURSING

As a student, Carol Beebee, now in her late 30s, was a high achiever, valedictorian of her high school class in Half Moon, Cal., and Phi Beta Kappa as a biology major at the University of California at Santa Cruz, graduating in 1985. As she drifted for the next 15 years in search of a career, her work accomplishments rarely matched her academic achievements.

"At college, I knew I wanted to do something in the health care profession, and for a short time I was a premed student. I was a classic stress-case student, always nervous about grades. The day of an exam, I would call my mother, tell her I would fail the test, and then get an A. I made the high grades to get into medical school, but when the time came, I didn't have the energy or interest to jump straight into medical school and start the pressure all over again.

"After graduation, I wanted some time off; no more school. I joined the Peace Corps and was sent for two years to Western Samoa, where I taught biology to high school students."

Returning home, Beebee decided she'd be a teacher. "I got my credentials to teach in California, but I couldn't find a job in a school where I wanted to work." It also was a bad time to be looking for a teaching job in the San Francisco Bay

area because a number of schools were reducing staffs. As an alternative to a permanent job, Beebee worked as a substitute math and biology teacher.

"I even got some long-term teaching jobs substituting for teachers on maternity leave," Beebee said. "But, frankly, I wasn't a very good teacher.

"Though I sometimes worry that I didn't get into health care years earlier, it's better in your late 30s than never at all."

The kids walked all over me."

So Beebee did temporary office work and was a legal secretary. But she had a problem: She had little direction.

During this indecisive period, she met Martin, a few years younger than she and also lacking direction. He had been an uninspired high school graduate who never went to college. Encouraged by Beebee, with whom he shared enthusiasm for the outdoors, he developed an interest in biology that took him to college, where he got his degree in biology and set his goal to teach college.

Beebee's disjointed 12-year career as Peace Corps volunteer, part-time teacher, office administrator, and secretary began to take a different direction once Martin, now her husband, was accepted into Duke University's doctoral program. When they moved to Durham, they were particularly excited about the North Carolina housing market. Houses were affordable, even for a graduate student, compared with California's high-priced homes.

"Buying a house was a turning point in my life. There was a house that I wanted, but didn't buy, because we were told that the house was in an area where road construction would be a problem for the next two years. Up to now, I had been a classic drifter, but if I was willing to consider buying a house in an unsuitable area, why wouldn't I consider going back to college and doing something real, rather than worrying about a house? That's when I decided I'd be a nurse and put my biology education to work."

Beebee became a Duke employee in August 1998, knowing that a year later she would become eligible for its college reimbursement program, available to students preparing for occupations in which Duke needs employees. Nursing is one of those areas. Because Duke no longer offers an undergraduate nursing degree, the school for pays Beebee's tuition, lab expenses, and books at the University of North Carolina School of Nursing in nearby Chapel Hill. In turn, Beebee has a 20-hour-a-week job at Duke, but she's paid at a 40-hour- a-week rate and receives benefits. Moreover,

Duke guarantees her a nursing job when she graduates. Meanwhile, Beebee works at the Duke Diet and Fitness Center, doing what she calls "brainless" work, compiling patient medical summaries. She purposely doesn't want a more stressful job, because nursing school is her primary responsibility and it is stressful enough.

"When I get my degree in May 2001, all I owe them is two years of work as a nurse at Duke Hospital. But we'll be here anyway since Martin will not be getting

As an older student, Beebee trusts herself more. "Instead of panicking if I don't get an A, I'm content to get As and Bs."

his doctorate until 2003 at the earliest."

After an absence of 13 years from the classroom, Beebee, one of the older UNC nursing students, approaches her studies differently from the way she did when she was younger. "I'm no longer a stress case. I trust myself more. Instead of panicking if I don't get an A, I'm content to get As and Bs. Before, if I got less than a 95, I considered myself a failure."

For her first job, Beebee is still considering different nursing specialties, from working on a medical-surgical floor to pediatrics. She is also interested in women's health issues and possibly in becoming a family health practitioner.

Beebee expects eventually to return to California, and perhaps to even become a mother. "Though I sometimes worry that I didn't get into health care years earlier, it's better in your late 30s than never at all. I can't regret the paths I took in the past, but it's good to be on the right path now."

MADE A PRACTICAL CHOICE

Travis Skinner
A PHARMACOLOGIST, ENTREPRENEUR, AND STOCKBROKER BECOMES A NURSE

Travis Skinner, in his early 50s, had a career that took many twists and turns, including a stab at getting into medical school, before he decided after nearly 25 years of working to become a nurse.

As a high school student in Durham, N.C., Skinner wanted to be a test pilot. This dream was scuttled when, as an aeronautical engineering student at North Carolina State University, he hurt his back. Skinner transferred to the University of North Carolina to study chemistry, where he found a good way to pay his expenses: In return for free room and board, he worked 20 hours a week as a lab clerk at the Veteran's Administration Hospital in Durham.

One year into his UNC studies, Skinner got married and moved to Boston. Once again he paid for his own education. "I went to Boston University, worked full- or part-time, and got an interdisciplinary degree in science." Following a divorce in the late 1970s, he returned to Durham, planning to go to medical school, but his college grades were abysmal. "To prove that I was for real and a good student, I got a master's from UNC's School of Pharmacology." Skinner liked the various scientific disciplines represented in the field.

About this time, Skinner met Barbara, who would eventually become his second wife. A doctor's daughter, she didn't like a doctor's lifestyle. Growing up, she never saw her father, and she did little to encourage Skinner to be a doctor. "I applied to medical school twice, and on both tries I was wait-listed. I told her I'd try one more time; then I would do something else. On the third try I was once again wait-listed, so that was it."

He preferred the nurse practitioner program, because it called for less training and, at his age, he wanted to get going.

Skinner was hired to set up a psycho-pharmacology lab at Duke, which he ran for five years. In his third year, his supervisor went on temporary assignment elsewhere, leaving Skinner in charge. But Skinner found that being the head of a lab in name only was disconcerting.

In 1985, he left Duke for Siler City, about 40 miles west of Durham, where he bought two pieces of property, a few miles apart, along with a herd of 125 head of cattle. Although he had no ranching know-how, he said breeding cattle was not difficult. During the mid 1980s, however, he made a critical error and bought calves at a high price. A year later, at about the time the cattle would have gone to market, cattle prices declined.

He was out of the cattle business in two years. Using cash from stock-market profits, he bought a wholesale poultry business. In two years, the business had grown to the point that it was bought by a Charlotte company, which wanted to expand its operations.

Skinner liked the stock market, and he became a registered representative for Wheat Securities, which was subsequently acquired by First Union Corp. Instead of concentrating exclusively on retail sales, Skinner made three small IPOs (initial public offerings) worth several million dollars each, which paid off nicely, as his commission was 1.5% of the offering. Skinner left the company when he was told to restrict his work to retail sales.

One of the companies that he had helped to finance was Touch Scientific, which had perfected a method of measuring the amount of tears produced by the eyes, something that ophthalmologists find useful in studying their patients' eyes. Skinner joined Touch in 1991 as sales manager, but left in 1995.

Divorced again, with no kids and no house, Skinner wondered, what's next? He still had a desire to be a doctor, so he returned to UNC, took some premed courses, did well in his classes and well enough on his MCAT. He also worked at Durham Regional Hospital as a health care technician "mostly doing scut work" as a way to get recommendations from doctors.

Then, on two occasions in a single week, Skinner stayed up for nearly 24 hours. He realized that, as an older student—he was nearing 50—sleep deprivation is an occupational hazard for medical-school students and residents. Age had taken its toll. Skinner stopped thinking of a medical career.

But the health care field was not closed. He wondered about becoming a physicians assistant or a nurse practitioner, two relatively new professional jobs in modern health care. He preferred the nurse practitioner program,

Skinner has some ideal nursing jobs in mind: in an embassy overseas or on a cruise ship.

because it called for less training and, at his age, he wanted to get going. As a nurse practitioner, he would be able to write prescriptions, diagnose patients, and handle many other routine medical procedures. The prerequisite to becoming a nurse practitioner is certification as a registered nurse. Skinner became a nursing student at Watts School of Nursing, an affiliate of Durham Regional Hospital. Because he didn't need another college degree, the Watts program was a shortcut to a nursing career.

It took less than two years to complete his nurse's training. In July 1999, Skinner went to work as an emergency-room nurse at Durham Regional, and the next year he entered UNC's two-year nurse practitioner program. As a UNC student and state resident, he receives $6,000 to cover tuition. He has also shifted his part-time weekend work from Durham Regional Hospital to a medical center in Raleigh, where he finds the higher ratio of nurses to patients more to his liking.

"UNC's new dean of nursing is leading the transition in our nursing education to an Internet-based platform. Our early courses encourage us to use the Net to gather information for classes and to communicate within the class. When I complete the program, I will have developed a library of information sites that will aid me in caring for patients, regardless of how far removed I am from a major medical library."

After he passes a national certification test, Skinner should initially earn between $45,000 and $55,000 a year. Three years later, the pay increases to more than $75,000.

Skinner has some ideal nursing jobs in mind: in an embassy overseas or on a cruise ship. "It's a good way to see the world, make a good salary, and save some money."

Teaching: The Classroom Is Calling

YOU NEED A REPORT CARD TO KNOW WHAT'S TAKING place in education. At first glance, it would seem that there is a healthy supply of educators entering the workforce, sufficient to man the nation's classrooms. Schools of education are producing record numbers of teachers: more than 200,000 a year, up 49% from the mid 1980s.

But even more teachers are needed to serve 53 million students from pre-kindergarten through high school, a population that has grown since 1990 by 14% (or 6.6 million students). The U.S. Department of Education (www.ed.gov) predicts that up to 1 million teachers will retire in the next five or six years. Teachers who are retiring at age 60 or older account for nearly two-thirds of the turnover.

The annual classroom turnover rate for teachers ages 30 to 50 is about 12%. Half of those teachers leave the profession altogether, while the rest transfer to other schools. These teachers need to be replaced. Suburban communities have less trouble attracting and retaining teachers than do inner-city and rural schools, from which new and experienced teachers have been fleeing. Not surprisingly, teachers of science, math, English as a second language (ESL), and special education are most in demand in inner cities and rural areas.

College education majors don't necessarily take teaching

positions when they graduate. Some never teach and some decide after a year or two in the classroom that teaching is not for them because they find the work too difficult, don't perform very well in the classroom, decide on a different career, or want to make more money.

In short, schools have a retention problem.

If this were a financial profit-and-loss statement, the numbers on one side of the ledger would show strong sales (the increase in the number of prospective teachers) outweighed by a failure to retain new and experienced teachers and to replace teachers leaving the classroom. But there is a solution: Career changers—men and women who seek to use or adapt their current skills in a job where they believe they can make an important contribution to society—represent an untapped source for new teachers.

The First Steps Toward the Classroom

Teaching should not be considered as a fallback second career for downsized or disgruntled managers and professionals. Prospective teaching candidates can measure their affinity for teaching in the following ways:

- **Find out how good you are with students,** keeping in mind that your own children won't provide a fair measurement. Work a few hours a week (perhaps at lunchtime to avoid a workplace conflict) reading to second graders or mentoring high school students. The "Y," Junior Achievement, Boys and Girls Clubs, scouting, and Little League provide other ways to test your skill with youngsters.
- **Better yet, ask yourself,** Do I really want to spend eight hours a day, five days a week, with first-graders or with high school seniors?
- **Your first teaching job** will probably be in an urban or rural school. Consider how comfortable you are or would be in such an environment.
- **Second-career teachers,** like many other new teachers, have trouble handling classroom discipline. Don't be surprised if the methods you've used in business, a profession, or the mil-

itary fail to carry over into the classroom.
- **Speak to second-career teachers.** What route did they take into the classroom?
- **Visit your local board of education** to learn about teacher employment opportunities and requirements.
- **Use the Internet** to access a state's department of education Web site. Here you will find posted traditional and alternative certification requirements.
- **Do another Web search** to learn which colleges offer the courses that are needed to qualify for state certification.

Earnings in the Classroom

Don't bother comparing entry-level salaries of teachers with the starting pay for computer programmers and investment bankers. The minimum average starting salary for a public-school teacher is $26,639. Alaska leads the pack at nearly $33,000. One-third of the states pay newcomers several thousand dollars below the national average. (See the table on the following page.)

Pay gets somewhat better for teachers with ten or more years on the job. In its latest survey, the American Federation of Teachers noted that New Jersey teachers averaged nearly $52,000 in 1999, or $23,000 more than average pay for South Dakota teachers with this much experience.

Salaries are fixed by either the state, the county, or the community. How soon a teacher will achieve the maximum salary possible differs by state and by the number of advanced degrees the teacher has.

A Shortcut to Teaching

It took a projected shortage of teachers in the early 1980s to create the alternative teacher certification movement. The goal at the time was to attract engineers and scientists who would become math and science teachers, and to get them ready for the classroom as rapidly as possible. Shortcuts were needed to permit these career changers to be licensed as teachers without going through several years of teacher training.

Even though educators were reluctant to hire unseasoned teachers, they had little choice, considering the need for science and math teachers.

Teach for America (www.teachforamerica.org), begun in 1990, places May and June college graduates, few of whom were education majors, in inner-city or rural schools after six weeks of training. In 2000, it placed nearly 2,000 recent graduates. Paid an entry-level salary, according to the region,

WHAT TEACHERS EARN

Here's how the states compared in terms of average and beginning teacher salaries in 1998–1999. States are ranked from highest average salary to lowest, according to the American Federation of Teachers.

STATE	AVERAGE SALARY	BEGINNING SALARY	STATE	AVERAGE SALARY	BEGINNING SALARY
New Jersey	$51,692	$29,112	Vermont	$36,697	$25,435
Connecticut	50,277	31,391	Florida	35,916	24,402
New York	49,686	30,808	Alabama	35,820	29,092
Michigan	48,711	27,822	Tennessee	35,490	22,645
Pennsylvania	48,457	29,793	Kentucky	35,383	24,387
District of Columbia	48,275	30,000	Iowa	35,007	24,333
Alaska	48,275	32,884	Maine	34,906	24,962
California	46,326	29,105	Kansas	34,634	23,006
Rhode Island	46,286	26,237	Arizona	34,582	26,163
Illinois	45,286	28,954	South Carolina	34,506	23,827
Massachusetts	44,051	28,055	Texas	34,448	26,261
Oregon	43,789	28,589	West Virginia	34,248	23,316
Delaware	43,223	29,981	Idaho	34,062	20,814
Maryland	42,545	27,605	Utah	34,007	22,957
Nevada	42,528	28,482	Wyoming	33,480	22,836
Indiana	41,159	26,171	Missouri	33,463	25,164
Ohio	40,734	23,087	Nebraska	32,880	22,611
Hawaii	40,416	28,315	Arkansas	32,761	21,273
Minnesota	39,809	24,462	New Mexico	32,161	24,393
Wisconsin	39,374	24,839	Louisiana	32,000	23,500
Georgia	38,993	27,908	Montana	31,536	21,676
Washington	38,530	23,645	Oklahoma	31,107	25,258
Colorado	38,157	25,489	Mississippi	29,550	21,346
Virginia	37,709	25,777	North Dakota	29,002	19,136
New Hampshire	37,405	24,406	South Dakota	28,386	21,376
North Carolina	36,883	25,338	**Average**	**$40,574**	**$26,639**

they make a two-year commitment to stay on the job, during which they must take education courses to qualify for certification in the states where they are working. The program seems to pay off, given that 60% of Teach for America's alumni are still working full-time as teachers.

Not everyone supports on-the-job training. Schools of education and the teacher groups like the National Education Association and American Federation of Teachers want career changers to spend at least a year or more taking education methodology courses, and interning as student teachers.

Shortcut certification programs have been implemented in more than 40 states plus the District of Columbia, according to the National Center for Education Information research (www.ncei.com). The exceptions are Alaska, Indiana, Iowa, Kansas, Montana, Nevada, North Dakota, Rhode Island, and Vermont.

> **An estimated 115 second-career teacher education programs are sponsored by colleges, foundations, and the federal government.**

Each state approaches certification differently. For example, Pennsylvania puts alternative recruits through two weeks of methodology training before they enter the classroom. For the next 15 months, recruits must also earn their certification through a university program that focuses on methodology.

Alternative certification must be catching on because second-career teachers are no longer a classroom oddity. There are an estimated 115 second-career teacher-education programs sponsored by colleges, foundations, and the federal government, and more than 125,000 career-changing teachers are already in the classroom. With favorable teacher performance ratings, legislators, officials in higher education and local school districts are increasingly supporting such programs.

Three Alternative Certificate Programs

A search for alternative education fellowship programs aimed at people who have been in the workforce but not as teachers starts with the National Center for Education Information (www.ncei.com). NCEI has tracked alternative teacher preparation and state certification policies since 1980. Information can be obtained through the state education departments in the 41 states with alternative certification.

Peace Corps Fellows

Columbia University's Teachers College (www.tc.columbia .edu/pcfellow) sponsors an alternative certification program to train former Peace Corps volunteers to become teachers in New York City's public-school system. Its program began in 1985 in response to *A Nation at Risk*, a report warning that an entire generation of American children were growing up scientifically and technologically illiterate. In spotlighting the dearth in science education, educators and business leaders started to explore different remedies. Alternative teacher certification would attract science and technical professionals into teaching. One source was military personnel, many with engineering degrees, who could retire in their late 30s. Similarly, corporate managers were challenged to consider ways to solve the problem. If schools were not turning out technologically savvy students, how would business find educated workers? In response, companies formed partnerships with schools in their community.

Columbia's Teachers College then expanded from training only math and science teachers into preparing teachers for bilingual education, English as a second language, and special education, areas in which New York was experiencing a critical shortage of teachers. Twenty new fellows are accepted each year. (Two of them, Jane and Scott Hall, are profiled in this chapter.) Fellows attend a six-week course during the summer. In September they enter the classroom, where they will be monitored throughout the school year by Teachers College faculty members, and begin taking courses toward a master's degree in education. Participants earn their Teachers College degree at about the same time that they qualify for a New York State teaching license. About one-third of the 300 former fellows have continued to teach in New York City beyond their obligation to teach for two years after being licensed.

Stipends cover about 30% of the cost of the master's program, but other costs are partially offset by the salary and benefits of a full-time New York City teacher.

GATE: Golden Apple Teacher Education

The Golden Apple Teacher Education program (www.golden-apple.org), or GATE, works with the Chicago public schools and Northwestern University. To qualify for the program, applicants need an undergraduate degree and five years of work experience. Teacher preparation is divided into three phases: It starts with six weeks of summer school at Northwestern and student teaching in Chicago public schools. Interns are mentored their first year by experienced teachers from the Chicago public schools and by GATE staffers.

The next summer, interns return to Northwestern for three weeks; the university then recommends them for an Illinois state teacher's license. Twenty-eight men and women became 2000–2001 interns, up from the 17 career changers who launched the GATE program in 1998.

Like Teachers College, which is committed to training teachers for the New York City public schools, GATE has a similar tie with Chicago's public schools. Interns are paid the same salary as all other entry-level teachers, and they are required to teach in the Chicago school system for three years. The cost to participate in the 14-month program is $12,000. (John Shemwell, a GATE intern, is profiled in this chapter).

Troops to Teachers

The Department of Defense (DOD) began the Troops to Teachers (TTT) program (www.voled.doded.mil/dantes/ttt) in the early 1990s, when the armed forces were downsizing, to help former military personnel find jobs as teachers. The DOD also recognized the potential of military personnel who, then as now, were retiring with 20 years' service while only in their early 40s, or perhaps leaving the military at an even earlier age.

Troops to Teachers provides referral, job placement, and certification assistance through its offices in 20 states, usually in cooperation with each state's education department. For help in the other 30 states, TTT directs personnel to contact the state's department of education. Since 1994, 3,500 former members of the armed forces have become teachers. Tennessee, Georgia, North and South Carolina, Florida, Texas, California and Washington State have led the way, with each state employing more than 100 of these teachers.

Demand has been high for people with academic and workplace skills in math and science, as well as for those who can teach special education in inner-city and rural schools. About 55% of the new teachers work in elementary and middle schools, and the rest in high schools. Nearly 60% of the military career changers are between the ages of age 35 and 45.

Some 90% of the teachers are male, a sharp contrast to the 2-to-1 ratio of women-to-men teaching in public and independent schools. Moreover, 29% of the teachers are from a minority or an ethnic group, and one in four teaches in an inner-city

POINTS TO REMEMBER

- **A teacher shortage** continues, especially noticeable in inner-city and rural schools.
- **Science, math, special education, and English** as a Second Language (ESL) teachers are particularly needed.
- **Alternative certificate programs** are starting to bring increased numbers of career changers into the classroom.
- **Forty states** offer some form of alternative certification.
- **Schools are more** **welcoming** these days to teachers with alternative certification.
- **The timespan** between changing careers to the first day in the classroom can be quite short.
- **Independent schools** offer numerous advantages to career changers.
- **Prospective teachers** can start doing their homework while still working at another job.
- **The average starting salary** of public school teachers nationwide is $26,369.

school. The retention rate has averaged 70% after five years.

TTT no longer provides any financial incentives. It initially gave stipends of up to $5,000 to prospective teachers and grants of up to $50,000 to school districts as an incentive to hire former military personnel.

Independent Schools: Another Route Into the Classroom

Headmaster Ed Costello of Durham Academy, an independent school with nearly 1,200 students, pre-kindergarten through high school, has little interest in hiring a lawyer or any other manager or professional who has burned out and suddenly wants to be a teacher. "I'm looking for people at any age with knowledge in a field of study, and just as important, someone with a demonstrated ability to work with kids, and in the case of the older career changers, not just their own kids." Costello says it might be good idea for prospective teachers to take one or two courses in educational methods as nonmatriculated students at colleges with teacher-education curriculums before changing careers, but this is not critical.

Of the 115,000 schools in the U.S., about 25% are private. The National Association of Independent Schools (www .nais.org) represents more than 1,000 private schools with 473,000 students, 10,000 administrators, and 48,000 teachers— the same number of classroom teachers employed by Chicago and Detroit combined.

By public-school standards, independent schools are a small part of the employment market, but they're of particular interest to career changers because they usually do not require state certification. Independent schools offer smaller classes and a smaller student-to-teacher ratio (9 to 1 versus 17 to 1 in public schools), more opportunity to provide individual attention to students who need it, and less bureaucracy.

Salaries vary dramatically, ranging from $10,000 to $108,000. The median pay is $24,000 for starting teachers, and nearly $51,000 for experienced teachers. A flexible pay scale applies to entry-level as well as long-time teachers. Thus a chemist with a master's degree and ten years of related workplace experience normally receives a higher starting salary than a recent college graduate.

Western states tend to pay more than schools in the Southeast and Southwest; teachers in day schools earn more than teachers in boarding schools, which factor in on-campus faculty housing. Not all prospective teachers view on-campus housing as an attractive perk. When Murray Decock (profiled in chapter 12) was offered a teaching job at a New England prep school, he turned it down. "No way," he said, would he, his wife and young children live in a student dorm.

To investigate independent schools, start with Independent Education Services (www.ies-search.org), an affiliate of the National Association of Independent Schools, or apply directly to the schools. Another good resource is *Private Independent Schools,* published by Bunting and Lyon, available in many public libraries and online (www.buntingandlyon.com).The directory lists information about more than 1,000 American schools, including their Web sites and e-mail addresses.

Some People Who Made the Change

T he six profiles in this chapter represent a distinct cross section of teachers. Tom Bloch did what very few chief executives of a large public company have done: He relinquished his CEO title along with his high pay and benefits in the family's business, H&R Block, to teach in an inner-city school. His change differed in style, but not in spirit, from that of Cora Straight, whose interest and talents as a teacher might have been lost if it hadn't been for her personal drive and determination, military career, and assistance from the U.S. Army.

DOWNSCALED, BUT FULFILLED

John Shemwell
FROM NUCLEAR-SUBMARINE OFFICER TO HIGH SCHOOL PHYSICS TEACHER

Physics has proved to be the thread stitching together much of John Shemwell's undergraduate and graduate-school education and workplace experience.

Shemwell, now in his mid 30s, graduated second in his class from his Daytona Beach, Fla., high school. He wanted a competitive college environment and liked the glamour of naval life; the U.S. Naval Academy seemed like an ideal academic setting. Concentrating on physics at Annapolis, Shemwell selected duty in the nuclear Navy, one of the more demanding jobs. Before being assigned to the USS *Michigan,* a Trident nuclear-powered submarine, he earned a master's degree in physics from Johns Hopkins University. Even though Naval Academy graduates are required to serve only five years on active duty, Shemwell intended to make the Navy his career. One of his goals was to command a ship.

Several years after graduation, Shemwell began to find that the life of a naval officer left little personal time or opportunity to spend with his wife, Jenny, whom he married in 1991. His began planning to leave the Navy in 1994, when he was stationed in Portugal at NATO's regional headquarters. "That was a great experience, but it was not the best location to research a future career. In the back of my mind, I knew I wanted

to be a teacher. I thought the next step was to get a doctorate, not in physics, but in English. I applied to Columbia University, but I was not accepted. This was a godsend since I realized that science, not English, was my field."

Shemwell left the Navy after nearly seven years of active duty. He moved

"I found the interaction with kids uplifting. I normally finish each day on cloud nine."

to Chicago for a job in engineering management with General Electric. "Chicago was an ideal location, since Jenny and I are both city people. We live in a condo, and to this day we don't own a car."

The GE job broadened his management and technical experience, and Shemwell was given a lot of responsibility. The pay was good, but not as high as his pay in the Navy, where he, like most nuclear-trained officers, had received incentive pay as a way to retain them on active duty. By his second year at GE, Shemwell had started to explore career alternatives. The demands of his job conflicted with his idea of spending more time with his family and not having to travel on business. "I was making more money than we actually needed, and we had less time to spend it."

Shemwell's father-in-law, a college professor, encouraged him to become a teacher. Shemwell looked for ways to become certified in Illinois without spending two unpaid years in a teacher-training program.

In June 1998, 16 months after joining GE, Shemwell left. He was offered a job teaching physics in a private school, but instead he joined the Golden Apple Teacher (GATE) program, just established with Chicago as its base, a 14-month alternative route for career changers to obtain Illinois teacher certification. As described earlier, the GATE program was organized to attract career changers into the Chicago public schools as teachers.

The GATE requirements were simple. Shemwell spent each morning during the first summer as a student teacher; in the afternoon he took courses in educational methods at Northwestern University. He started teaching in the fall semester. His master's degree in physics increased his starting pay to $33,000 a year, slightly higher than what other new teachers without master's degrees earned.

During the rest of the academic year, Shemwell was coached by a GATE representative, also a teacher, on ways to improve his classroom techniques, and he attended evening classes at Northwestern. "These classes were geared toward our classroom experiences. Our homework was to do a certain type of teaching in our class,

videotape it, and then submit the tape along with our critique." The second summer he returned to Northwestern for additional coursework, and was recommended for an Illinois teaching license.

Shemwell teaches in an inner-city school that has all the social and academic problems associated with urban education. Physics is offered at only half of Chicago's 77 high schools. Shemwell teaches basic physics, as well as an advanced-placement physics class.

"You have to learn to motivate them. I was surprised to find how creative I could be."

The Navy taught Shemwell how to deal with people from different backgrounds, but he has found that teaching high school students differs from teaching sailors. As an instructor, Shemwell can't make the same demands on teenagers in a school with a 30% dropout rate that he could on sailors who are subject to military discipline.

"You have to learn how to motivate them. I was surprised to find how creative I could be. I liked being my own boss in the classroom. I found that I was well-suited to teach, skilled in dealing with people, and above all I found the interaction with kids uplifting. I normally finish each day on cloud nine."

Shemwell and his wife had set a goal: that their respective jobs would be interesting, above all, but not demanding to the point that it would sap their energy and restrict their life together. Until they had their first child, in July 2000, Jenny Shemwell was director of volunteers at St. Clement's Roman Catholic Church in Chicago. "We've been fortunate since I changed careers," said Shemwell. "We have not taken on any debt. We are not big consumers and we live in a condo, which we can afford. In short, we are prepared to live within our means."

Shemwell's agreement with GATE requires him to teach for three years in the Chicago public schools. Afterward, his aim is to continue to teach in Chicago or in another large city or small town.

ADMINISTRATOR SUBS FOR FUN

Ramona Ramirez
FROM THE ARMY TO THE CLASSROOM TO THE SCHOOL OFFICE

Ramona Ramirez, now in her late 40s, met her future husband in a sixth-grade classroom in Arizona, and they've been a team ever since. Ramona and Dale married after graduating from high school, and Ramona joined the Army one year after her husband did. The Army became their employer for more than 20 years. Four of their five children were born overseas.

For Ramona Ramirez, the Army provided the opportunity to obtain a college education and do the types of work that set the stage for a post-Army career in teaching and school admini-stration. Her transition began in Germany, where she was a student in the University of Maryland's overseas extension program. She earned a bachelor's degree in business manage-ment in 1986. Her classroom studies complemented many of her Army duties: inventory control, facilities management, office automation, and budget admini-stration. A college degree was followed by promotion to chief warrant officer and appointment as an administrator with the Judge Advocate General.

After nearly 20 years in the Army, eligible for early retirement, Ramirez was undecided on the direction of her civilian career. Her options were teaching, getting a law degree, or getting a job as a law-office administrator. One thing was

certain: She and her spouse would return to Arizona to be closer to their families. By the time Ramirez attended the Army's preretire-ment briefings, she had already decided to teach. She felt comfortable in a classroom, having done some teaching in the Army on a range of subjects, from using weapons to preparing and publish-

> **"I didn't want to be a classroom teacher for the rest of my career. I liked being a supervisor in the Army, and I wanted the same status in education."**

ing legal orders. Fortunately, her last Army assignment was in San Francisco, which was convenient for job interviews in Arizona.

Ramirez was an early recruit to the Troops to Teachers program. "I heard about this program when I was in Europe. While working in San Francisco, I went on leave to Arizona, and on one of my first interviews, I was offered a teaching job in the Isaac School District in Phoenix. But I had to tell the principal that I couldn't start work for another two months until I was discharged." The principal accepted the delay.

Troops to Teachers provided Ramirez with some tangible benefits. Besides planting the seed about teaching as a second career, it funded her future schooling with a $5,000 stipend, an amount that covered the cost of education courses at the University of Phoenix and enabled her to get certified as an Arizona teacher. Discharged from military service in 1994, she went to work that year as an English as a second Language (ESL) or bilingual (English and Spanish) teacher in the Isaac School District. Besides being supervised by teachers in her school, she took education courses at the University of Phoenix to meet Arizona certification standards.

Ramirez's husband, Dale, retired on 54% of his military pay; Ramona Ramirez receives slightly less because her military service was briefer. When they moved to Glendale, a Phoenix suburb and their first civilian home, Ramirez, in her early 40s, was pregnant with their fifth child.

Ramirez's first job was teaching elementary grades where her fluency in Spanish proved valuable. Her husband stayed at home during her workday, caring for the baby, and worked evenings as a sports referee. A year later, he was hired as a physical education teacher's assistant.

Ramirez's postmilitary career did not stop with being an elementary school teacher. "I love to teach and it is cool to see kids respond and do well. But I didn't want to be a classroom teacher for the rest of my career. I liked being a supervisor in the Army, and I wanted the same status in education." Ramirez's first step toward a supervisory job was to get a master's degree in education administration and supervision at Arizona State University and, in May 2001, a doctorate degree in the same subject.

After five years in the classroom, Ramirez got her first job in school management. In June 1999 she was appointed assistant principal in the Cartwright School District, at a school with 1,100 students and a 106 teachers and support staff. "Even though I'm now an administrator, I still miss working with kids and teaching. When a class needs a substitute for a few hours, I eagerly return to the classroom."

TAKING THEIR SKILLS OVERSEAS AND BACK AGAIN

Jane and Scott Hall
EDUCATION VIA A TRAVEL BUSINESS AND THE PEACE CORPS

Jane and Scott Hall, in their mid 40s, have been working partners for 20 years. They met on a trip to Europe; both were interested in tourism and both were from Wisconsin. He graduated from the University of Montana and she from the University of Wisconsin.

"We went to work in the travel business in Chicago," says Scott, "and for the next ten years, we were tour leaders, escorting corporate and alumni groups overseas and visiting about 50 different countries."

When the Halls decided to go out on their own, they moved to Madison, Wis. For eight years, during the spring and summer months, they conducted nearly 60 bike tours. In the beginning, they were Bike Wisconsin's only employees, but their staff grew to 20 tour leaders. During the off season, the Halls free-lanced as overseas tour directors. Eventually, they became eager to do something different. Jane Hall wanted a change from dealing with payroll, taxes, personnel, and administrative problems. By then in their late 30s, they sold their business, saved the money from the sale, and considered joining the Peace Corps for the experience and as the first step toward becoming teachers following their overseas tour.

At the time, the Peace Corps was looking for volunteers with skills in operating small businesses, and the Halls' credentials were impressive. The Peace Corps suggested that they work in eastern Europe, but the Halls preferred a warmer climate. Jane spoke Spanish fluently; Scott did not. He believed an assignment in Central or South America would give him the chance to learn

Having lived and worked in Central America, the Halls have an understanding of their students' community and family needs.

Spanish. They were sent to Jinotega, a coffee-growing region in the Nicaraguan mountains.

"In Jinotega, I worked in a cooperative, training men as metal workers and car mechanics," says Scott. "Many of the men had returned from military service, and they wanted to learn a civilian skill. I ran an apprentice program, so that they could qualify for a job, along with a separate program, sponsored by the Association for the Blind, to develop a sheltered workshop program for handicapped workers, and a third project teaching English to a group of physicians and to junior high school students." He also started some business classes for the owners of small businesses who wanted to learn English.

Jane had different assignments in the same community, including supervising a small business workshop and teaching the participants about marketing, promotion, and the other management chores that she had performed with Bike Wisconsin. "I also helped them create a children's room in the local library and get a grant to operate it.

Each spouse received a monthly salary of $190, out of which the couple had to pay all their expenses. The salary was considered good by local standards, equal to what a physician earned. The Peace Corps also put aside another $200 a month per person for each month of overseas service, as a form of savings, and paid their round-trip transportation to and from Central America.

When they completed their tour with the Peace Corps in late 1996, the Halls returned to the U.S. and spent the next six months conducting incentive travel tours to add to their savings.

The Peace Corps had furthered the Halls' interest in teaching. By living and working with the people of Nicaragua, they had acquired basic teaching skills that would carry over into a classroom in the U.S.

The Halls learned about the Peace Corps program, sponsored by Columbia University Teachers College in New York City, while exploring the Teachers College curriculum, and it seemed to provide a natural bridge into the classroom.

The Peace Corps paid half of their Teachers College tuition. The Halls went to work as full-time New York City teachers for $31,000 each a year, plus benefits and interim licenses. Teachers College is a key part of the Peace Corps package, which requires that participants be candidates for a master's degree in education. Two years later, both Halls received their master's degrees, as well as New York City and New York State certification as English as second language teachers.

All of their careers— travel, biking, business owners, Peace Corps, and teaching—have been oriented toward the customer.

The Halls initially worked at George Washington High School, near the bridge of that name, in the northern part of Manhattan. Most of their students are from the Dominican Republic. The school has low student test scores, a high dropout rate, and all the problems associated with inner-city education. The Halls' fluency in Spanish is helpful, and sometimes essential, when they are teaching and in dealing with their students' parents. Having lived and worked in Central America, they have an understanding of their students' community and family needs.

During the Halls' tenure, George

Washington was closed as a general high school and almost immediately reopened as a facility with several different specialty schools on the same campus. Scott taught international business, and Jane focused on media and communications. In the classroom, she drew upon her college journalism training and the promotional work she had done at Bike Wisconsin.

In June 2000 the Halls completed their four-year Peace Corps obligation and returned to the Midwest to be nearer their families. They selected St. Paul, Minn., a community with a diverse foreign population requiring ESL teachers. Jane teaches at Humbolt High School, a school with a high proportion of Hispanic students, and Scott works at Johnson High with students from Asia, Central America, Mexico, and Africa.

Both Halls find that there are similarities between their current and previous jobs. All of their careers—travel, biking, business owners, Peace Corps, and teaching—have been oriented toward the customer. "By the time we started teaching, we already knew how to deal with students and parents, whom we see as our customers," says Jane.

SPECIAL EDUCATION IS HER CAUSE

Cora Straight
MANY SACRIFICES TO BECOME A TEACHER

Nobody can say that Cora Straight's early life was a picnic. Born near the Gulf of Mexico in Ocean Springs, Miss., she was one of ten children. Both parents worked in nonskilled jobs.

At age 14, Straight, now in her early 40s, participated in a federally sponsored program that allowed teens to work while they attended school. "I got a job cleaning in an elementary school. I said to myself that someday I would be a teacher, and have my own classroom."

Within a few years, one of her brothers had been shot and another was in prison. "When my brother died in 1974, I would have quit school, but one of my teachers showed me how to get through my trials and tribulations." Straight again vowed to become a teacher.

After her brother left prison, he began working for a shipyard. "He taught me that even if you make a mistake in life you can still continue to march."

Straight was a good high school athlete, and when her softball team played in a tournament at Delta State University, in Cleveland, Miss., she became determined to go to college. She began her post–high school education at Jackson County Junior College, and completed her degree in physical education at Delta State.

"After college, I could not find a job.

I went back to cleaning schools. I worked at a shrimp market and a Burger King. I was fired when I saw my boss getting drugs out of a hiding place in the store." Frustrated at not being able to get a good job even with her college degree, Straight returned to junior college to take classes in business; then, in August 1982, she and her sister enlisted in the Army.

As a teen, she promised herself a career in teaching. After the Army and three degrees later, she got her classroom.

Straight spent 12 years in the Army; as a staff sergeant, her job was to stock supplies, order parts, take inventory, and keep records. In the mid 1990s, after serving in Desert Storm, Straight decided to leave the Army. Her sister, who had left the Army in 1993, was teaching school in El Paso, and their father had died in an accident in Mississippi. It was time to return home, but she needed a civilian job. She was also a single mother (her daughter is now 17). She read about the Troops to Teachers program in the *Army Times*. With her years in the Army, a college degree, and an honorable discharge, she met the qualifications for the program. She applied for and was offered a job in Starkville, Miss., teaching special education, but the program required her to attend school to obtain specific teaching skills. Straight earned her second bachelor's degree, in special education, from Mississippi State College, and followed it up in May 2000 with a master's degree in the same subject and state licenses in both education and physical education.

The only thing Straight misses about the Army is the cost-of-living allowance. She acknowledges that the Army taught her how to be punctual and work hard until the mission is completed, and how to teach people until they understand what is being taught.

Straight is not satisfied, however,

with her $27,000 salary as a special-education teacher in an alternative high school, which means living from payday to payday. At first, she cleaned houses to make extra money, but gave that up for a 20-hour-a-week job as a drug and alcohol prevention specialist. "I speak to church youth groups, and work with young men in a rehab treatment center and with juvenile delinquents."

When her daughter graduates from Starkville High School, where she's an honor student, Straight is considering leaving Mississippi to find a better-paying teaching job, this time armed with classroom experience and two degrees in special education. "But leaving won't be easy, because I love all the kids that I work with," she said.

UPGRADING INNER–CITY EDUCATION

Tom Bloch
A CORPORATE CEO FINDS HIS ANSWER IN TEACHING

Tom Bloch's 20-year career with H&R Block ended in 1995, when he resigned voluntarily as president and chief executive officer of H&R Block, a $2-billion-plus tax-preparation and computer-service firm started by his father and uncle in the 1950s. Tom Bloch, now in his mid 40s, had become a career changer, with the goals of teaching school and becoming a local advocate for better inner-city education.

By his early 40s, Bloch had found that the peripatetic lifestyle of a corporate executive grated on him. Since 1992, when he was elected company president, he had found the job all-consuming; he had had little time for himself or his family. "I was the type of executive who took business problems home with him. When one of my sons would ask me a question at dinner, it would go right over my head. I was thinking of something else."

The decision to leave corporate America for teaching was not a casual one, considering that he had a good relationship with his father and uncle and that he had worked at H&R Block ever since he graduated from Claremont McKenna College in 1976. "I discussed it and agonized over it with my wife, Mary, who is a lawyer, and my sounding board. Though it was my decision to make, I wanted her to participate in the process. Our two sons were youngsters and weren't involved." On one occasion during the hectic tax season, when he was ready to resign, Mary advised him to delay his announcement because his departure would be badly timed.

Giving up a job is never easy, especially when the job provides power,

It is rare for a 40-year-old whose family name is synonymous with his business to forgo high pay and prestige to teach school.

prestige, and an annual salary of more than $600,000. In Bloch's case, those considerations were negligible, compared with the significance of leaving the family business. Bloch was the only second-generation person in either his or his uncle's family who was working for the company. He was the obvious heir apparent.

"I finally had to tell my father of my plan. H&R Block was his baby. I didn't spring it on him. I agonized over it. Even after I told him, my father was confident that I would never leave.

"When I told some of the other people at Block, they had one of two reactions. One group said that I was nuts to walk away from a great salary, a great career, and great perks; the other said, 'Do I envy you.'"

The consequences of Bloch's decision were somewhat eased by the fact that he and Mary lived fairly modestly; in addition, he was assured of additional income from savings and personal invest-ments. To some observers, his departure might seem rash, but compared with the decision of some contemporaries who retire in their mid 40s, his decision to be active locally was consistent with the Bloch family's close community ties.

When Bloch officially resigned, the announcement became page-one business news. The resignation had to be made publicly, because the Securities and Exchange Commission and the New York Stock Exchange require that public companies disclose important corporate events, such as the resignation of its CEO. The news release resulted in headlines and prime-time television interviews. Leaving corporate America for a better job is one thing, but it is rare for a 40-year-old whose family name is synonymous with his business to forgo high pay and prestige to teach school.

Some speculated that Bloch would use his management acumen on the faculty of a university business school, but Bloch said he planned to teach in Kansas City. "I didn't want to teach in a white suburban school. They had enough good teachers, so I picked an inner-city school."

To qualify for certification to teach

elementary school in Missouri, Bloch took education courses at Rockhurst University in Kansas City. Bloch was no newcomer to the classroom. An economics major, he had taught French for a semester at a local elementary school when he was a college student, and he had frequently taught at H&R Block tax classes.

He started his search by visiting a number of inner-city Kansas City schools. St. Francis Xavier, a private Catholic middle school, caught his attention

"I didn't want to teach in a white suburban school. They had enough good teachers, so I picked an inner-city school."

because it served children of a downtrodden neighborhood and was aligned with Rockhurst University in some joint education programs. He chose private over public schools because he could start work before being certified as a Missouri teacher. He taught math, a subject that he had enjoyed as a college student, with an annual salary of $21,000 a year, about 3% of his former pay. His goal was to help make St. Francis into a model urban school. While also teaching an introductory education class at Rockhurst, he created a companion program that links each of his Rockhurst education students as a coach with a group of students at St. Francis Xavier.

Bloch has recently shifted his educational focus. While continuing to work one day a week at St. Francis Xavier, he has also started to teach middle-school math at University Academy, a charter school that he co-founded. The University of Missouri–Kansas City, one of the charter school's sponsors, pro-vides a number of resources. The academy rents space from the university, the academy's principal is a UMKC School of Education faculty member, and some of the university's students work at the school. University Academy, which opened in September 2000 with 200 students through the ninth grade, expects within the next few years to add grades 10 through 12. Its mission is to bring high-quality education to inner-city students.

"Sometimes kids ask me why they need to take or know math. They ask, 'How will studying math help me get a job?' I try to tell them that whatever they do, they'll need math to get or hold a job.

Reflecting on his experience in the classroom, Bloch says, "I find there is little relationship between the corporate boardroom and the classroom, since different skills are needed in each environment."

USES REPORTING SKILLS TO MAKE CAREER CHANGE

John Selix
A RADIO NEWS DIRECTOR IN THE CLASSROOM

John Selix, now in his early 40s, majored in journalism at the University of Oregon, in Eugene. After graduation in 1981, Selix stayed in Eugene to work at KEED, an AM country-music radio station that had a small but good news-desk. Two years later, he was hired as a reporter by a larger Eugene station, KUGN AM-FM, where he stayed for nine years.

Shortly after he became news director in 1989, he started to have ambivalent feelings about the job. Like many others who earn a promotion to management, Selix missed doing the hands-on work of his trade and didn't much enjoy the administrative headaches and paperwork. The job had become "less exciting and less fun." He told the owner that he planned to look for a job outside of Eugene in a larger market because "I realized that there were a limited number of job openings on good news radio stations on the West Coast." Since he was still single, relocating was a solo decision. Selix's boss, however, hadn't been idle.

"One day he said that he had found a news director, and I was looking for a job.

"When all this was happening, in the back of my mind, I was thinking about what other careers would interest me. As a reporter, I had become interested in teaching, because I covered a lot of

education issues and school-board meetings. I had lots of friends who were teachers. But what really drew me into teaching was coaching Little League teams. I felt comfortable with kids."

While Selix continued to look for another news job to support himself, he started to research different ways

Selix talked to teachers and school administrators, and double-checked his ideas with career counseling.

to become a teacher and to investigate whether teaching was the right choice for him. He used his reporting skills when talking to teachers about their work to assure himself that he would get the same adrenalin flow from teaching that he got from news reporting. He went to the University of Oregon's career placement center for career counseling. "I took the Myers-Briggs test, which told me that teaching was one of my strong skills, but not as high as social work or clergy. Teaching is related in many ways to these two fields, so I felt comfortable with my decision to change careers."

Selix also talked to school admini-strators, who advised him to get into a teacher's certification program close to where he planned to teach, so that he could tap into the local network for job hunting. The San Francisco area, his likely destination, had several certification programs.

Before making his final decision, Selix worked as a school volunteer to acquire some hands-on experience. In one school, he put his broadcasting know-how to use by helping students on a high school radio station, an experience that reinforced his decision to become a teacher.

The pay scale for teachers was not a major concern, because the pay scale in radio news in Oregon was not especially high. He reasoned that taking on similarly low teacher pay would not significantly alter his financial status.

Selix wanted to get started as soon as possible. A number of college pro-grams did not begin until the following August, nearly eight months away, but the University of San Francisco offered a one-year teacher certification program starting at mid year, in January 1993, that blended classroom instruction and student teaching. He applied and was accepted.

Even though he could have had a part-time paid job to defray expenses, Selix decided to focus on the certificate program. "I hadn't been a student in 12 years, but I enjoyed going to school, and I did much better in California than I did at Oregon." He found that he was a far more dedicated student in graduate school than he had been as a typical, 19-year-old undergraduate student. Selix

financed his education with proceeds from the sale of his house in Eugene and from savings.

In 1994 Selix received a K-12 (kindergarten through high school) certificate, and was hired as a substitute teacher of third- and fourth-grade LEP (limited English proficiency) and ESL students by the San Francisco school system. In one class, he had students who spoke ten different native languages.

Although Selix was essentially a full-time teacher, the school district classified

Before making his final decision, Selix worked as a school volunteer to acquire some hands-on experience.

all new, full-time teachers as "long-term substitutes," so that it could deny summer health benefits to new teachers until they moved up to probationary or tenured status. That was one reason for Selix's decision to find another job outside the San Francisco system.

Two years later he left for a full-time job as a third-grade teacher with the Mill Valley School District, just north of San Francisco in Marin County, ten miles from his home. By this time, Selix had married a San Francisco high school teacher who subsequently began teaching in another school district in Marin County. Despite some regret at leaving the needier city schools for a suburban school, Selix said, "It was in my own interest to have a job in a nicer setting—cleaner classrooms and a pleasant outdoor environment."

He finds that his radio-broadcasting experience continues to come in handy in the classroom.

"I have a good sense of timing. I know how to organize lessons to fit into a specific time period, and I'm used to working on deadline. I try to instill that idea in my students. It's important for kids to learn about deadlines and the need to meet them. From radio, I also have a sense of the audience. I know instinctively how to keep the attention of the kids and how to vary my delivery style."

Becoming Your Own Boss

TO BUSINESS OWNER BILL KEMPFFER (PROFILED LATER in this chapter), it doesn't seem as if ten years have passed since he left his job as a Merrill Lynch stockbroker to start Deep River Sport Clays and Shooting School, in Sanford, N.C. The school struggled for the first five years, but it now has more than 350 member families who shoot clay birds and small animals. While many of his contemporaries continue to struggle in corporate jobs, Kempffer has been able to combine a business venture with his favorite pastime, hunting.

Not everyone is as fortunate as Kempffer to be able to convert a long-time hobby into a business. For many career changers, self-employment is a goal in itself; for others, it's a means of achieving career-changing and lifestyle objectives. Many entrepreneurs are satisfied to operate smaller manufacturing, service, and retail businesses; others have ambitious dreams that read like a Hollywood script. Craftspeople and artists also become self-employed entrepreneurs, as Stephanie Greene, a children's book writer, and her husband, George Radwan, an architectural designer, relate in chapter 11. Both left secure careers with big-time New York City advertising agencies for riskier work as independent craftspeople.

The Numbers Speak for Themselves

The statistics on the number of start-ups are staggering. In 2000 the Small Business Administration (www.sba.gov) guaranteed loans as part of its Section 7(a) program to nearly 44,000 new and already established smaller businesses that do not qualify for more traditional financing.

Dun & Bradstreet (www.dnb.com) identified 62,549 start-ups from January through June 2000, a dip from 70,170 during the same period in 1999. More than half of the start-ups are retail and service businesses. D&B defines start-ups as newly opened businesses; it excludes firms that have changed owners or changed names.

In a companion report, D&B profiled the typical small U.S. business, which employs a median of three employees and has median annual revenues of $150,000 to $200,000. Small-business owners, though, pay a price for their independence. More than half of the owners surveyed by Dun & Bradstreet work more than 51 hours a week, 15 hours more than the hours worked on average by corporate employees.

Consider, too, the darker side on entrepreneurial life: The American Bankruptcy Institute (www.abiworld.org) reported 35,472 business bankruptcy filings in 2000, a dip of 6.4% from the previous year.

Why They Take the Plunge

People go into business for different reasons, ranging from a decision based on sound research to a knee-jerk reaction to being downsized. According to the National Federation of Women Business Owners (www.nfwbo.org) and Catalyst (www.catalystwomen.org), which tracks women in corporate America, 55% of women business owners and 65% of male entrepreneurs said that they became business owners through a gradual process. Both men and women said that they had a winning business idea or came to realize that they could do for themselves what they had been doing for an employer.

The primary incentive for self-employment is simple: It's better to be a captain, enjoying the excitement of running a business hands-on, than to be a first mate, always dependent on someone else's decisions. Still, every silver lining has its dark spots. What happens next year when the aura of opening day has passed? As a one-time corporate manager, will you become bored with the nuts-and-bolts job of running a company? Can you handle a heavy work schedule with only an occasional vacation? When there's a problem, can you survive without a support staff to run the business?

Outplacement consultant Challenger, Gray & Christmas (www.challengergray.com) notes a change in entrepreneurial expectations toward the more realistic. Their study shows that whereas 20% of discharged executives and downsized managers started businesses in 1989, only 7% did so in 1999. Along with the proliferation of dual-income families, the consultants noted, has come a sense of urgency when it comes to balancing work and family, and starting a business directly conflicts with the pursuit of more time with one's family.

> **The primary incentive for self-employment is simple: It's better to be a captain, than to be a first mate. Still, every silver lining has its dark spots.**

Although not documented statistically, economic downturns and business merger-acquisitions seem to stimulate new business ventures. If you've lost your job and don't want to look for another one because you've been downsized before, what's there to lose? Start a consultancy at home. It may be simply an interim activity until another desirable job comes along or it may be a new career.

Let's Get Started

Greg Owens, in his late 30s, owns two diners in Chapel Hill. Owens left Elon College after his sophomore year. A summer job as a bartender and cook whetted his appetite for a career in the kitchen. After completing a two-year culinary course, followed by a series of apprentice jobs doing grunt work in the kitchen as a cook, and by eight years as a chef and then executive chef at hotels and country clubs in a number of southern cities, Owens was ready to take the next step, opening the first Owens Diner in 1992.

Owens urges owners of smaller businesses to learn to grow in way that is consistent with their business and personal-life plans. Owens closes his restaurants on major holidays, when he wants to be at home with his family, and he feels that his employees should do the same.

Owens believes it is a good idea for employees to see that the owner does more than drive by to pick up cash and credit card receipts.

"The first commitment is to build a working relationship with a bank. This means paying monthly payments on time, and meeting all other financial obligations." Now that he's been in business for nine years, the banks are coming to him, which was hardly the case in his start-up days, when personal and family loans got him going. Owens demonstrated a point known by owners of most businesses: Banks want to see audited profit-and-loss statements. Show them performance, and they'll be your friend.

Owens offers some advice that is applicable to most start-ups:

• **Select a strong theme for the business.** Identifying a niche, or specialty, is critical to Owens and to most other entrepreneurs. Take a page from the Owens diners: His dinners stress a family-style menu with a southern flavor, such as grits, collards, and ribs at affordable prices, yet he also serves gourmet dishes to attract patrons with more sophisticated tastes.

• **Expect unforeseen problems that can delay the launch.** Owens encountered a delay of 17 months in opening his first restaurant in Chapel Hill when inspectors discovered a septic tank that they wanted removed. At the time, Owens was a novice at working with city building-department inspectors in the process of getting a certificate of occupancy. He learned from that experience, and he now knows how to negotiate with inspectors. In 1997, he opened a diner in Durham, taking just three months to receive a certificate of occupancy. Four years later, however, he was in the process of selling the Durham diner, because he found it too difficult to hire and retain a kitchen and wait staff.

• **Do your homework and know what you want.** Owens visited other diners, talked with their owners, and read anything he could read on diner operations.

- **Keep the operations simple.** Owens buys all his produce from one vendor. This practice helps to assure better pricing and good delivery, and it simplifies accounting, paying bills, and keeping financial records.
- **Have a realistic business plan that covers all bases.** Blue-sky plans might look impressive, but they rarely include allowances for contingencies.
- **Be patient.** Owens needed three years to break even with his first diner. However, that was only half the time he had cited in what proved to be a conservative business plan.
- **Don't be an absentee owner.** Owens still works 60 hours a week. He believes it is a good idea for employees to see that the owner does more than drive by to pick up cash and credit card receipts. He can also be seen working in the kitchen or waiting on tables.

A Word of Caution

Tony Kleese is a farmer, and he deals with another type of problem facing small farmers: how a husband and wife can start a farming business and still pay the household bills. Kleese's answer is simple and it applies to most small start-ups: One family member works the farm and the other continues to work in a job to earn a steady salary. The partner should keep the paying job until the business starts to make money.

As executive director of the Carolina Farm Stewardship Association (www.carolinafarmstewards.org), Kleese shepherds owners of small farms, eight to ten acres in size, on ways to start and operate a small farm that employs only organic-farming techniques.

A farmer and former director of a sustainable farming program at a local community college, Kleese deals with career changers, many in their 30s, who have bought a few acres and want to give up what they're doing to become more self-sufficient. They share a desire for a different lifestyle and the chance to do more physical work. Knowing the dangers, Kleese tries to keep the romantics out of farming.

Time to Do Some Homework

Jess McLamb is full of advice for wannabes and the owners of recent business start-ups. Besides running a consultancy (www.ropergroup.com) that concentrates on the management and marketing needs of small companies, McLamb speaks to a hundred small-business workshops each year in North Carolina. "Some of these folks don't have the slightest clue of what they want to do. I ask them whether they are risk takers, and how much money they can commit to supporting themselves and their businesses in their early days."

One way to minimize risk, says McLamb, a former bank and insurance-company manager, is to do plenty of research. She finds that too many people decide to start a business on a moment's notice. "They've spent little time doing their homework, know little about their potential competition, and have little to no experience in running a small business."

McLamb cautions against blue-sky business plans.

"A realistic plan should emphasize projected cash flow, not accounts payable, which are of little use until they become cash flow. I find that start-ups overproject revenues and under-project expenses. They should live by what I call the 'rule of two,' which indicates that businesses should think conservatively and divide their projected revenues by two."

The Do-It-Yourself Approach

Not every new business owner has an MBA, but it's not that difficult to learn the basics. Booksellers and libraries stock plenty of how-to books and workbook guides to starting and running a small business. Some even focus on starting and operating specific kinds of businesses, such as a restaurant, bed-and-breakfast inn, travel agency, or public relations firm. *Entrepreneur* magazine concentrates on articles for small-business owners. *Inc.*, which bills itself as the magazine for growing companies, found seven entrepreneurs who spent less than $1,000 in start-up capital to launch their businesses, but were able to gross $1 million plus in revenues in a just few years. They compensated for their lack of money by learning how to obtain free or low-cost assistance. One entrepreneur used college interns to help him market compact discs on college campuses. Another owner received free booth space at a trade show in exchange for making presentations. His talks helped land some new accounts.

The Service Corps of Retired Executives, known as SCORE (www.score.org), is sponsored and supported by the U.S. Small Business Administration. Operating in approximately 390 communities, SCORE offers start-ups free access to a menu of services, consisting of one-on-one and team counseling, and workshops in sales and marketing, manufacturing, and distribution. It counsels about 300,000 entrepreneurs annually, and reaches about a fifth of them via e-mail counseling sessions.

Community colleges provides small-business operators with free or low-cost workshops. Durham Technical Community College's Small Business Center, for example, sponsors a 14-part workshop series several times a year, with sessions titled "Making the Most of Your Marketing Style," "What You Really Need in a Business Plan," "Taxes for Small Businesses," "Strategic Planning," and "Basis Bookkeeping."

> **Too many people have spent little time doing their homework, know little about their potential competition, and have little to no experience in running a small business.**

What About Franchising?

Franchising is big business. According to the International Franchise Association (www.franchise.org), franchising accounts for more than 40% of all U.S. retail sales.

At best, a franchise represents an entrepreneurial compromise. Buyers receive what they hope are a proven business formula and a strong marketing image. In return, franchisers set the guidelines on fees, use of their logos, quality control, marketing, advertising, and purchasing.

Franchising goes well beyond fast-food restaurants and includes a diverse listing of companies, such as Mail Boxes Etc., Lawn Doctor, and Management Recruiters International. As a rule, storefront food franchises are more expensive to buy and launch than a home-based craft, interior design, catering, or home maintenance franchise.

Franchising is not for everyone. Career changers who want to be the boss should realize that they are sharing that title with the franchiser, who has an ongoing financial and marketing interest in the franchise. In some ways, it is like buying a home. The purchaser and the bank both have an investment in the property.

> **Career changers who want to be the boss should realize that they are sharing that title with the franchiser, who has an ongoing financial and marketing interest in the franchise.**

George Krasner owned a Huntington Learning Center franchise. Although he recognized the marketing edge that franchises often provide, he advises an already experienced chef, carpenter, teacher, or gardener not to take the franchise route in their area of expertise. Other than furnishing some operating and management techniques, a franchiser can teach a top-notch carpenter little about home improvement. As an alternative, Krasner suggests that the carpenter take the up-front money needed to buy a franchise and retain a consultant who knows the specialty field to write an operating and marketing plan, and to serve as a mentor. The money that would have been paid to the franchiser for national advertising can be diverted to local promotions.

There's more to franchising than being the owner of what is often a mom-and-pop business. Some owners leverage their investments by parlaying a single franchise unit into a regional chain, or they create conglomerates. Nearly 20% of franchise operators own more than one unit—sometimes with the same franchiser, other times in different fields to increase diversification and lower risk if one franchise concept turns sour.

Taking Over a Family Business

Not all career changing is voluntary, as some people discover when they are pushed by parents to leave their chosen careers to join a family business.

For many years, I patronized a well-known Italian restaurant in New York City. It had been family-owned for several generations until the early 1990s, when the owner, who was nearing retirement, asked his two sons to run it. One son was a computer software programmer and the other a corporate middle manager. They accepted the invitation, and the result was disastrous. Neither brother liked restaurant work, and within six years the restaurant was out of business.

President Jimmy Carter's career enjoyed a different twist. A Naval Academy graduate and nuclear engineering officer in the Navy, Carter left his chosen and preferred career to return to Plains, Ga., and run the family's peanut farm after his father died. Ironically, farming introduced Carter to local politics, and he began his climb up the political ladder.

"Family businesses do not enjoy a wonderful reputation in spite of all the good they do and their huge presence across the world's economy," says Neil Koenig, author of *You Can't Fire Me, I'm Your Father* (Kiplinger Books, 1999). Koenig's accountant told him that the worst businesses are family businesses. "They just can't get past all their family stuff." Accordingly, Koenig finds that family businesses can be categorized as follows:

- **One group operates as though their business matters more than anything else in life.** "The business dominates everything. It consumes them," said Koenig.
- **The next group of owners takes a family approach.** "Their business means family. Running the business like a business is not on the agenda."
- **The worst approach for a family businesses is one in which "neither the family nor the business is emphasized.** One is in shambles with the other on the verge of becoming so."

Looking at the transfer of executive power to the next generation, Koenig notes that "it is imperative for parents in family business to be certain that their children want to work in their family enterprise. They also need to be certain that their children are prepared to contribute to the success of the business."

The problems of family succession are not limited to small businesses. Alex Jones and Susan Tifft, a husband-and-wife writing team, have written two books that deal with succession in the newspaper industry. The first, *The Patriarch: The Rise and*

POINTS TO REMEMBER

- **Entrepreneurs work** at least 15 more hours a week than corporate employees do.
- **Owners often want to do for themselves** what they were doing for an employer. Don Mikush worked for a graphics firm before going out on his own in the same field.
- **A new business should have a strong theme,** like Bill Kempffer's sports shooting club.
- **Entrepreneurs should follow the "Rule of 2,"** that is, divide the income that you're estimating by two, in order to estimate more accurately what you'll really earn.
- **The boss needs to be there;** absentee ownership rarely works. Greg Owens says it's vital that the owner do more than drive by to pick up cash and credit card receipts.
- **Plenty of low-cost** or free resources exist to help start-ups.
- **Launching a business** differs from holding a job in corporate America. It requires lots of hands-on work with little staff assistance.

Fall of the Bingham Dynasty (Summit, 1991), focuses on the family that owned the *Louisville Courier-Journal* and *Louisville Times* for several generations until it sold out to Gannett. The other, *The Trust* (Little Brown, 1999), chronicles the family that continues to control the *New York Times*.

The Bingham family failed to find ways to bridge family infighting, while the *Times* succeeded by applying a Koenig-like approach in succession. As Jones and Tifft put it, "The family that owned the *Louisville Courier* and *Times* had imploded in a fiery feud of money and power, and put their distinguished papers on the auction block."

The *New York Times*, however, developed an orderly and practical way to train a family member to head the newspaper, although it did not always seem so apparent. It also created a stock plan and agreements within the family about the sale of large blocks of stock to nonfamily members, so that the *Times* can avoid a fate similar to the Louisville newspaper.

Some People Who Made the Change

Entrepreneurs range from the men and women who deliberately started businesses with limited growth potential to those who expect to expand their businesses into large publicly owned companies. The six business owners described in this chapter run small retail and service businesses. The largest is the Angus Barn, a restaurant with annual sales in the $10-million-plus range. These owners have a common bond: None of them want to be corporate employees; they enjoy the helm.

COMMUNICATION IS KEY

Don Mikush

OUT OF CHEMICAL SALES INTO A GRAPHICS DESIGN FIRM

Don Mikush, in his early 40s, is fortunate because his wife, Sandra, a college classmate, "saw in me things I didn't see. I always liked to draw and sketch, and she said I should do something with it."

Sandra actually knew something about career changing. Her father, early in his professional life, had switched careers. Now a retired university administrator, he started his career as a lawyer. When her father told his employer, the law firm's senior partner, that he would be leaving to teach, the partner told him that he sometimes wished that he had done the same thing.

Mikush is a Duke University graduate with a degree in mechanical engineering, a skill requiring an ability to draw, though not in the creative way he would need when he became a graphics designer. He transferred from liberal arts in his sophomore year, believing that he would find better job opportunities in engineering.

After graduating from Duke, he joined DuPont as a sales engineer in Dallas and was soon winning sales awards. It appeared that he was being groomed for a management position and an eventual transfer to the company's headquarters in Wilmington, Del. The move would have pleased him.

"We were getting tired of living in Dallas. We wanted to get back closer to family—and trees—in the East. I was about 27, and it became clear that DuPont could not quickly enough satisfy our need to move, so I looked elsewhere for work. I was hired by Jack Harvey & Associates, a large manufacturing representative firm, to open a sales office in the Raleigh-Durham area.

"Sales never suited me very well,

His skills help him to ensure that everyone on his team is working toward the desired result.

even though I was fairly successful at it. After I'd spent two years as a sales rep for Jack Harvey, Sandra challenged me to consider a career that would better utilize my creative talents. I took the Myers-Briggs test. If I recall correctly, the test results suggested that everything I was doing professionally didn't match my personality. I particularly remember that 'sales' didn't fit my personality/ capabilities profile as well as technical tasks did. I don't remember whether the results specifically mentioned graphic design."

After researching a number of different careers, including architecture, and even getting a real estate license (a possible career if he didn't return to school), Mikush was admitted to the graduate program at North Carolina State University's School of Design. "At that time, they accepted folks with no design experience who showed promise. I think that they were intrigued by my Duke engineering degree and my sales experience, which was an unusual combination for their applicants."

While Mikush was a NCSU student, Sandra, a Duke fund-raiser, paid the bills for the family, which now included two small children, one born the day after Mikush started school.

After his first year at graduate school, Mikush worked a summer internship with the Cassell Design Group, a small graphic-design firm in Durham. He never returned to college, but instead became a full-time Cassell employee. Over the next several years, Mikush helped owner Keith Cassell build the firm's client base and reputation doing just about everything—design, sales, and work with clients.

"In 1992, Sandra was offered a great position with a foundation in Winston-Salem. I persuaded Cassell to open a branch office, and we moved. After four years, Keith decided that he really wanted to focus on his clients in Durham, not Winston-Salem, so in exchange for my minority ownership in his firm, he helped me set up M Creative."

Mikush started his graphics firm at home. The plan, then and now, was to design brochures, alumni magazines, CD-ROMs, videos, and Web pages for colleges, hospitals, and other midsize to large organizations, many in the Winston-Salem and Greensboro area.

He discovered that being a boss is somewhat different from being a part-owner. Mikush had to learn how to hire and fire, pay taxes, and run a business. Like many business owners who want to control expenses, Mikush started out hiring freelancers, but as the workload grew, he began to build a staff of full-time designers.

Mikush worked at home for the first four years, even as his firm grew. "I hired graphics people. It eventually became apparent that it was time to get out

Although he is an engineer, Mikush admits that he's not very technical, and as a graphics designer, he's not very artistic.

and get an office. At one point, Sandra came home from work to find different meet-ings taking place in the kitchen, the dining room, and my office."

M Creative (www.mcreative.net) employs about eight full-time staffers. Much of the new business comes by word of mouth. Mikush finds that his past technical training carries over into graphics design, and that he uses a variety of different skills. Although he is an engineer, Mikush admits that he's not very technical, and as a graphics designer, he's not very artistic. He finds that it is more important to be able to formulate and communicate ideas. What he learned in engineering school is how to structure a project and how to think in a linear way. Above all, he's able to do nearly everything his business requires: sell services to clients, organize and manage projects, and act as a liaison with the client and his graphic designers. His skills help him to ensure that everyone is working toward the desired result.

Both Mikush and his wife are involved in nonprofit work. Most of his clients are nonprofit groups, and she is a foundation executive. "When I show her something we have done, she says, 'That's neat.' We have our own little joke: She works for a foundation that gives money away to worthy groups, and I work for a business that spends such funds."

LEAVING CORPORATE AMERICA PAYS OFF

Charlotte and Pat DiLeonardo
THEY LEAVE IBM FOR SELF–EMPLOYMENT

Charlotte and Pat DiLeonardo, both in their mid 40s, met at Carnegie Mellon University in Pittsburgh in the mid 1970s. She was studying graphics design, and he was majoring in industrial design. With their academic backgrounds, they were naturals for "big company" careers.

And so they went to work for IBM in Poughkeepsie, N.Y., Pat in 1978 and Charlotte in 1980. The were considered to be on a management fast track, Pat in technology and Charlotte in general management and human resources. In 1987 IBM transferred them to Raleigh, N.C. Five years later they took a company buyout and resigned, Pat after 14 years and Charlotte after 12.

The DiLeonardos actually had little reason to take the buyout and leave IBM. The money was good, and they had all of IBM's fringe benefits. Even though their future looked secure, they wanted more independence in their jobs. Even as a college student, Pat had wanted to own his own business. His father had worked for a steel mill, and when his mother retired from her job, she started what became a successful Italian restaurant in his hometown, Beaver Falls, Pa. Nonetheless, both sets of parents were upset that the DiLeonardos were giving up corporate security.

The DiLeonardos looked at different kinds of business opportunities. A franchise seemed a better route than starting their own business. They knew computer technology, but little about managing a small business. A franchise, they reasoned, would help them learn these necessary skills, and a printing franchise seemed like a logical step to take. It would permit them to use their

Even though their future looked secure, they wanted more independence in their jobs.

technical and marketing skills in a field that was being rapidly computerized.

In 1992 they bought an AlphaGraphics franchise, in Raleigh, and opened a small store that they would replace in 1997 with a much larger one. The company has since given them franchise rights for all future AlphaGraphics stores in the city. To broaden market penetration for AlphaGraphics' range of print and photocopy services, they have acquired contracts to provide companies with AlphaGraphics' services from onsite facilities. Accordingly, they opened an AlphaGraphics operation at GE Capital Mortgage Company's office in Raleigh, replacing GE's in-house printing facility; and they have a similar arrangement with Sonopress, a CD producer in Asheville, in western North Carolina.

The DiLeonardos purchased the AlphaGraphics franchise with a combination of savings, funds from their IBM buyout, and a second mortgage on their home. Five years later, with a successful track record, they found bank financing somewhat easier to obtain. Able to show a sound balance sheet within three years of their start-up, they received a tradi-tional commercial loan to purchase a second Raleigh store in 1996 from a previous AlphaGraphics franchisee, to move, double the size of the original store, and to acquire additional equipment.

IBM management training taught them a number of valuable lessons.

Says Charlotte, "We knew how to delegate work, not to try to do everything ourselves, trust other workers and not to micromanage. We now have employees who operate our stores and printing equipment. This allows me to concentrate on sales and marketing, and Pat to be the software and equipment expert. IBM showed us how to deal with and think like big-company employees. This gives us the confidence to work with our customers, who are mostly the owners or managers of businesses. Yet there are some disadvantages in leaving IBM; we have no peer groups of fellow employees to formally or informally bounce ideas off."

As franchisees, they must live by certain guidelines established by Alphagraphics. Still, says Pat, "While our contract indicates that we have to offer a basic number of services, after that we're free to offer any other printing-related services that we want. We are free to buy equipment from our own suppliers. In many ways, we operate on our own."

As the parents of a teenage son, Charlotte and Pat hoard their family time. They try to keep business out of their home as much as possible. Even so, the business is omnipresent.

Says Pat, "I can't fully extricate myself

> "IBM showed us how to deal with and think like big-company employees. This gives us the confidence to work with our customers."

from the business. Once my beeper went off when I was on the ski trail. I answered it, realizing that the call had already been filtered by our store manager, so I knew it was important. But even with this type of disruption, it beats a day in the office. I'd still rather be skiing, instead of looking at ski scenes on a computer screen in my office."

Lifestyle is important to the DiLeonardos. Fortunately, most of their customers are companies that operate on a Monday-through-Friday business week. For the first five years in business, the DiLeonardos did not take a vacation, but they have since made up for that.

In 1999 they were away from the office for eight weeks on ski trips and vacations in Cancun and Africa.

Over the years, they've considered whether they should sell their Alpha-Graphics franchise and do something as independent business owners. But Pat's meticulous records show that the return on their franchise purchase was well worth the price.

STARTS RESTAURANT AFTER LAW SCHOOL

Scott Maitland
DESERT STORM WAS HIS ROUTE TO BECOMING AN ENTREPRENEUR

When Scott Maitland, now in his mid 30s, graduated from West Point, he expected to be a career Army officer, and he couldn't imagine that anything would take him in a different direction. Maitland had had an excellent high school academic and athletic record, and West Point seemed to be a good place to get a good free education.

But Operation Desert Storm, where he served as a combat engineer, changed his mind about the Army as a career. "From this experience, I determined that I never again wanted to be supervised by some-one who is more stupid than me." At the time, the Army was down-sizing, and it lifted the five-year active duty requirement for West Point graduates. Maitland resigned from the Army 18 months earlier than would normally have been permitted. "I had several months of free time while my discharge papers were being processed, so I had plenty of opportunity to consider different careers."

He began the process by researching places to live. He had no intention of returning to his home base, in Whittier, Cal. Research showed that North Carolina's weather and business climate suited his personal needs.

Maitland's primary career objective was to be independent, not to work for anyone else. He decided that his first step would be to attend law rather than business school. "I felt that business schools were turning out people who wanted to work for Fortune 500 companies. A big-business career was not part of my plan. Anyway, I thought that the skills I would learn as a lawyer were closer to my goals of owning my own business."

Maitland compensated for his lack of restaurant experience by reading everything he could find on brew pubs.

Though Maitland had been near the top 10% of his West Point class academically, his grade-point average was not impressive, because there was no grade inflation. Thus, it was important for him to do well on the LSAT. Maitland received what he described as a respectable score of 160. His application to law schools was timely. "It was after Desert Storm and my accomplishments, as a returning combat officer, impressed law schools. I received a full scholarship to the University of North Carolina Law School; I was also accepted by Stanford, UCLA, and Michigan law schools."

Maitland's objective was a legal education but not a career as a lawyer.

His credentials—top 10% of his law school class and class president—impressed law-firm recruiters, but to no avail. Maitland had other plans. Smitten with Chapel Hill, he wanted to start some type of local business. At the time, TGIF planned to open a brew pub restaurant on the top floor of a four-story building soon to be completed at the intersection of two main Chapel Hill streets. The idea of a chain restaurant taking the space repulsed Maitland.

A year earlier, Maitland's father had died, bequeathing him $50,000 that he could use as seed money. When the TGIF deal fell through, he decided to start a restaurant in the same space. "I knew it would attract UNC under-graduate, law, business and medical students, alumni, and local residents. It took me about one year to write a business plan to raise money." His first plan failed to interest investors or commercial loans because Maitland had no previous food-service experience, but he had learned from his parents and West Point to set goals and be persistent. He compensated for this lack of restaurant experience by reading everything he could find on brew pubs.

Research led him to Daniel Bradford, publisher of *All About Beer Magazine*, and Joseph Smith, owner of a New York City restaurant. They agreed to support him and to assure possible investors that Maitland's project was sound. The revised business plan resulted in a $500,000 guaranteed Small Business Administration loan from the Centura Bank and an equal sum from 35 private investors.

Maitland's restaurant, Top of the Hill, which can serve 40 at the bar and 240 people in the restaurant and an outside terrace, opened in September 1996. Less than three years later, Maitland opened a second brew pub in Raleigh, 25 miles away, as an outlet for the excess Chapel Hill beer production.

Maitland is now changing the theme in the Raleigh restaurant. He plans to reopen in late 2001 after converting it into the Glenwood Cider House, which will brew several different hard ciders and serve regional cuisine. The restaurant

> ## "At first I tried not to run the Top of the Hill like an ex-Army officer. Then I realized that a more disciplined military style was needed."

in Chapel Hill has a $2 million payroll and 150 employees, many of whom are UNC students. "At first I tried not to run the Top of the Hill like an ex-Army officer. Then I realized that a more disciplined military style was needed. My employees know there are rules and that they need to follow them."

Although technically he's a rest-aurateur, unlike many such business owners, Maitland leaves the day-to-day decision making to his managers. On New Year's Eve in 1998, he married Rebecca, a trained restaurant and hotel administrator, who handles back-office administration. His wife's presence gives Maitland the time to explore new business ventures.

Maitland, who once spurned a legal career, is using his legal training to qualify as a certified financial planner.

"I tried to answer this question, 'How do you structure the financial dimensions of your life after you are successful? I found plenty of commissioned sales-people who wanted to handle my money, but I wanted unbiased, fully integrated estate and financial advice from someone who had made his own money, as well. I realized that I would have to become that person myself. I believe that many doors will open once I become a financial planner, especially when I combine that training with a law degree."

The experience of reinventing himself—from military officer, to law student, to entrepreneur—has made Maitland confident that he can achieve anything.

CAME TO APPRECIATE HER FATHER'S STYLE

Van Eure
FROM TEACHING IN KENYA TO HEADING A FAMILY BUSINESS

When Van Eure, now in her mid 40s, graduated from Rollins College as a physical-education major, she fled to avoid being tagged as a southern belle, a representative of a distinguished North Carolina political family, or an unwilling recruit in a successful family business. At 22, Eure, seeking a life of adventure and personal fulfillment, selected Kenya to launch her postcollege life. She started by teaching swimming, and then English, to youngsters. It gave her the confidence to start a Montessori school.

Once a year, at Christmas, she returned home. "I didn't like being back in the U.S. or in Raleigh. I would come home, spend some time with family and friends, and then return to Kenya. I found the U.S., unlike Kenya, to be crass, with too much hustle and too many rude drivers. I was depressed about American life."

During her fifth year in Kenya, she met and planned to marry an Australian. After bringing him home to meet her family, she broke off the engagement and reluctantly remained in America. In a rural area outside Raleigh, she found a rundown, dilapidated farmhouse, which she bought with her sister, Shelley, and she lived there for 14 years, even after Shelley married. "I took care of abused animals—horses, pigs, goats, birds, dogs, cats, and others. Over the years, I've rehabilitated more than 115 different animals. I find homes for most of them, but I have kept 11 animals."

Eure needed a job to keep busy and to support herself. She bartended at Darryl's, one of three restaurants then owned by her family, and she partied.

After the independence of living and

Learning the business meant hands-on experience in cleaning a bathroom, ordering supplies, selecting wine, waiting on tables, and cooking a steak.

working that she had enjoyed in Kenya, Eure did not find working in a family business dominated by her father to her liking. She and her father, though similar in many ways, grated on each other's nerves, hardly a good situation in a closely held enterprise. The Eure family eventually sold both the Darryl's restaurant and the 42nd Street Oyster Bar, but they kept the mainstay, the Angus Barn steakhouse, a local landmark since her father had opened it in 1960. "My father took me aside and asked if I wanted to work in the Angus Barn. Since no one else in the family wanted to work there, he said that he could keep it or sell it, but he wanted to give me the option before he considered the next step."

Eure reluctantly decided to give it a try, wishing all the time that she was back in Africa. "My father and I worked out an informal management-training program. He said I should work in each department until I knew it like the back of my hand." She spent the next six years learning the business, which to her father meant hands-on experience in cleaning a bathroom, ordering supplies, selecting wine, waiting on tables, and cooking a steak.

By 1988, although Eure was still not sure whether she wanted to work at the Angus Barn for the rest of her life, she was equally convinced that she did not want to see outsiders take it over. By then, she had begun to appreciate her father's style of management.

Then, in 1989, Eure's father was diagnosed with pancreatic cancer and died within a few months. Her mother returned to the Angus Barn as the behind-the-scenes partner until her death in 1997, while Eure became the working business partner. Today, the Angus Barn is a 11,000-square-foot, multistoried facility with 200 employees, a seating capacity of 650, and sales exceeding $10 million.

Eure had lots to learn about business management. Looking for new and creative ways to operate the Angus Barn, she read Kenneth Blanchard's *The One Minute Manager* (William Morrow, 1982), by then a business classic. Based on Blanchard's theories, Eure adopted a management style whereby the employees are empowered to have more control over their day-to-day functions. If, for example, customers do not like what they ordered, the wait staff makes the decision to either refund the money or serve another dish. No approval is needed from a manager.

Consistent with her approach to employee empowerment, all Angus Barn managers regularly rotate throughout the operation. "This way the cooks know

Consistent with Eure's approach to employee empowerment, all her managers regularly rotate throughout the operation.

what it is like to wait on tables, and the wait staff gets to know what kitchen life is all about. It applies to me as well. I might be assigned to the kitchen to cook steak on the grill."

Eure applies a number of the techniques that worked in her classes in Kenya to her orientation workshop for new employees. "I provide practical tips—how to shake hands, the importance of eye contact with customers, and how to graciously accept a compliment."

Eure's approach seems to work. Angus Barn's annual personnel turnover is less than 15%, versus a rate of 80% or higher at most restaurants.

In other ways, Eure is still not the typical 21st-Century manager. She personally rejects using a computer or e-mail to communicate with staff, suppliers, or customers; as her father would have done, she deals with everyone in person or by telephone.

Until the past few years, Eure worked 80 to 90 hours a week. But in her early 40s she married, and later, after suffering some signs of illness, learned that she was pregnant. Since becoming a mother, she has reduced her work week to 60 hours, spending the morning hours at home with her daughter.

RECYCLES A FAMILY BUSINESS

Michelle and David Lineberry
A NURSE AND A COP OWN A JEWELRY STORE

Michelle and David Lineberry, in their mid 30s, own an independent retail jewelry store, even though she is a registered nurse and he is a cop. Yet in many ways they have the ideal background to be retail jewelers.

Michelle's parents owned a small jewelry store in Durham, N.C., for 19 years. "The store was named after me. As an only child, I spent a lot of time in the store. It was a typical mom-and-pop store. My mother did the books and some selling, and my father was more interested in creating custom jewelry pieces, engraving, and bench-type work than retail sales. He taught me how to engrave and how to restring pearls, and I learned book-keeping from my mother."

Michelle's career plans, however, did not include retailing; nursing was her goal.

As a youngster, David wanted to be a cop, but it would be years before he would satisfy his boyhood dream. After graduating from high school in eastern North Carolina, David got a sales job in a jewelry store and then became a jewelry manufacturer's sales representative. On one sales call, he met Michelle at her parents' store, and they were married in 1988.

He was paid $22,000 a year in his first sales rep job, but he was required to pay for his car and traveling expenses. During the two years he worked in that job,

David also worked weekends at the Marriott to pay some of their home expenses.

"I worked for three years for another company, and the deal was somewhat better. I had a smaller territory—only Virginia, North Carolina and part of South Carolina—and I made $2,000

The Michelle name still retained considerable goodwill, and the opportunity to cash in on it was too good to pass up.

more a year, but this time the company gave me a bonus and a Volvo and paid my traveling expenses. Being on the road is not that much fun. I carried about a half-million dollars in jewelry. After I had checked into my hotel, I could not leave my room for the rest of the night."

In the mid 1990s, David quit working as a traveling sales rep to become a cop in Hillsborough, about eight miles west of Chapel Hill. Being a cop, David admits, represented a stage in his life, but he was also impatient; he didn't want to work for others for the rest of his life.

At the time, the last thing in Michelle's plan was to start a retail business.

Michelle liked being a registered nurse. By then, her father had died and her parents' store had been closed a number of years. "I know what it is like to be a retailer. Growing up, I only remember going to the beach with my parents twice. They were always in the store."

Even so, the idea of a family jewelry store persisted. The Lineberrys knew that Durham had only a few high-quality jewelers; moreover, the Michelle name still retained considerable goodwill, and the opportunity to cash in on it was too good to pass up.

The Lineberrys found an attractive store that had been occupied by an interior designer and required only slight renovation to meet their needs. "We used my name since it had good recognition in our market; many people knew me as a child hanging around in the store." The new Michelle's, three times the size of her parents' store, also takes a different sales approach. It focuses on retail jewelry sales, rather than the custom work for other retail jewelers that her parents preferred.

David's experience as a jewelry manufacturer's sales rep was a big plus. Jewelry manufacturers granted them lines of credit on the basis of his industry know-how and in anticipation of another retail outlet for their products. The Lineberrys financed their start-up by borrowing from family members and close friends. Michelle's opened in 1998, just a month before their second son was born; their other son was then 7 years old.

In his travels, David had called on many of the top jewelry stores in the Southeast. He knew what sold and what didn't. One jeweler he visited in Alabama sold quality jewelry along with nontraditional items, like Godiva chocolates; the owner had told him that people who buy expensive chocolate also buy good jewelry. Michelle's has taken a similar approach to the merchandise that it sells. Besides jewelry, watches, and other items identified with quality jewelers, Michelle's also sells Waterford

"There's more to running a store than being on the floor selling. It means dealing with manufacturers and taking care of paperwork."

crystal, Fabergé eggs, Reed and Barton silverware, and, of course, Godiva chocolates. The Lineberrys also plan to produce a catalog and start their own Web site.

Their business is open seven days a week, and the Lineberrys' working days are long. Michelle starts at 8 A.M. and leaves nine hours later. David gets in an hour earlier and works ten to 12 hours. But Michelle's has two full- and three part-time employees, too. Says Michelle, "We spend nearly every working hour together in the store or at home. I do the restringing and engraving, which I learned from my Daddy, and David deals with our sales people, manages the business, and buys merchandise. He also goes to the trade shows, since one of us needs to stay home with the boys and run the store.

"There's more to running a store than being on the floor selling. It means dealing with manufacturers, which David does, and taking care of paperwork, which I do at home on a laptop while David is still at the store. But we have certain rules. Most nights we have dinner together as a family, even if David has to return to work."

The Lineberrys also learned in other ways from her parents' experience. They close the store two weeks a year so they can go on vacation as a family.

The store is called Michelle's, but Michelle herself does not expect to be a lifelong retailer. "I plan to return to work as a nurse at least part-time."

A FAR CRY FROM SELLING BONDS

Bill Kempffer
BOYHOOD HUNTING GIVES BIRTH TO A BUSINESS

Bill Kempffer, in his mid 50s, remembers growing up on a farm in Belton, Missouri, south of Kansas City. Some of his fondest memories are of hunting with his father. Rather than taking up farming, however, Kempffer went to the University of Missouri, graduating with a degree in economics in 1966. Six years later, he left the Marine Corps after becoming a commissioned officer, training as a helicopter pilot, and serving in Vietnam. By then, his squadron was stationed in Jacksonville, N.C.

Kempffer spent a brief period as a commercial pilot before joining Merrill Lynch as a stockbroker in its Raleigh office. "It was a pressure-cooker type of job, with pressure to generate more sales and commissions each year. It created a 'what have you done for me lately?' relationship with some clients."

When Merrill Lynch moved some brokerage specialties from its head-quarters and regional offices to the branch level, Kempffer changed from being a general stockbroker to a commodity and currency specialist.

In the late 1980s, Kempffer read an article, "Hunting Without the Blood and Guts," in the *Wall Street Journal*. It described how, rather than killing small animals, hunters were shooting at clay rabbits, woodcocks, low-flying ducks, and teal. "After 16 years with Merrill Lynch,

I was beginning to think of doing some-thing else. Following the 1987 crash, Merrill Lynch wanted to decentralize the type of work I was doing. My wife, Mary, and I had no desire to relocate, nor did I want to be a general stock-broker. But if I left Merrill Lynch, I would be giving up a good income.

"I thought I would hire a manager to run the club. I was advised that this rarely works in a start-up, and that I was the guy who had to run it."

"I thought I'd open a sporting-clay club. First I approached the wildlife club where I was a member, but they had little interest in branching out into this type of hunting. Then I did a business plan on the premise that I would bring my father, who was retired in Florida, to North Carolina to run the club, while I continued working for Merrill Lynch. But I forgot one important detail: I didn't check with my father, who said that he had no desire to leave Florida. Then I thought I would hire a manager to run the club. I was advised that this type of approach rarely works in a start-up, and that I was the guy who had to run it."

The die was cast. Kempffer reviewed his business plan with Mary, who had recently gotten an MBA. "Mary's input was critical since I have a tendency to jump into something prematurely. Mary gave me her blessing."

Kempffer visited a few sporting-clay clubs in other parts of the country as part of his learning experience. At the time, there were fewer than 3,500 clubs. Compared with the more popular skeet shooting, the concept of shooting small clay animals and birds had not yet caught on in the U.S. The sport was developed in England in the early 1900s, became more popular as live-game hunting decreased and Parliament outlawed live-pigeon shooting in 1921. Clay shooting as a sport was imported to the U.S. about 60 years later. In the 1980s, many clubs were marginal or part-time operations; others had financial problems and would not survive. Over the past decade, however, membership in the National Sporting Clays Association (www.nssa-nsca.com) has quadrupled in size.

Kempffer compares certain aspects of clay shooting to golf. Just as a golfer moves from hole to hole, a clay shooter goes from one station on the course to another (there are even "golf" carts for oldsters and handicapped people). At each station, the shooter encounters a different kind of opportunity to shoot, which mirrors the wild game of the area. And, similar in spirit to sports fishing, where the catch is released after being netted, in clay shooting no animal is killed.

Kempffer was not discouraged by the lack of enthusiasm for a clay-shooting club. With Mary working at Nortel (she left the company in 1992 to take care of their baby daughter), he financed the club with savings, the sale of some stock, and a home-equity loan. In 1989 he bought 65 acres outside of Sanford, in rural Lee County, a 30- to 60-minute drive from the more populated Raleigh, Durham, and Chapel Hill area, and 30 minutes from the Pinehurst golf resort, and opened Deep River Sporting Clays

Kempffer uses his cold canvassing and prospecting skills to get companies to conduct outings or to sponsor events at the club.

and Shooting School (www.deepriver.net) in 1989.

"Deep River struggled for the first four or five years. By then I was able to pay myself a salary, and the concept caught on. People liked clay shooting as a family sport. It didn't take too much training to become proficient. And they liked the idea that animals or birds were not being killed."

Looking to expand its services, the club, with a membership of 350 families, has also expanded its pro shop with fly-fishing equipment, clothing, accessories, and fly-fishing clinics.

In his Merrill Lynch days, Kempffer

learned how to do cold canvassing and prospecting for new customers, and to sell on the telephone, a practice he now uses to get companies to conduct outings or to sponsor events at Deep River. "As a broker, I had to do lots of my own research. I still do this to find new customers and suppliers." As a result of Kempffer's marketing, such companies as Nortel, Cisco and Rhone-Poulenc give their employees the option of shooting clays instead of playing softball or golf at company outings.

No longer a one-person business, Deep River has four full-time and four part-time workers, and nine instructors. Although he works harder than he did at Merrill Lynch, Kempffer does not expect to make the money he made as a broker. "But I'm my own boss, and I'm working outdoors doing many of the things I learned and enjoyed growing up on a farm."

HE STILL WORKS THE PHONES

Bob Page

CPA TURNS HOBBY INTO A $70–MILLION NICHE OPERATION

Bob Page, now in his mid 50s, worked as an auditor with the state of North Carolina, but he devoted his spare time to collecting and selling old and often discarded china and glassware.

After several years in this dual lifestyle, Page surrendered job security and a steady paycheck in 1981 for the uncertainties of self-employment as the founder of Replacements, Ltd., which has evolved into the world's largest retailer of old and new china, crystal, silver, and collectibles. Page is the only person in his family to have gone to college, and his parents, tobacco farmers, were worried about his career change. Like so many entrepreneurs, he was confident that if he failed he could always get another job.

"I hated my 9-to-5 job. I read everything I could find on collectibles, and I lived for the weekends. I spent my weekends, evenings, and even lunch breaks at flea markets and antique fairs, learning all I could about china and glassware." He looked for all kinds of things. He took requests from people asking for tableware pieces, and when he found the items, he called them.

Before long, Page had a cluttered attic. A cardtable in his bedroom served as an at-home office, and he packed orders on the kitchen floor. Collecting was no longer a part-time hobby. In his mid 30s, he took the gamble, quit his job, and, with scant working capital, he rented a 600-square-foot storefront in Greensboro and set up Replacements. As a single man, he did not face the typical family pressures many other career changers do.

His first employee was a part-time

"I hated my 9-to-5 job. I read everything I could find on collectibles, and I lived for the weekends."

college student. Business picked up, and she got her two roommates to help out; then one of their boyfriends also became a part-timer. Page instinctively knew how to minimize expenses. He went to local dumpsters at night to retrieve discarded boxes, which he could then reuse to ship china and glassware.

Banks were less than enthusiastic about helping Replacements. "They laughed when I asked to borrow money. When I decided to buy a used van for $3,000 to carry goods from flea markets, I used my Toyota as collateral." Ever since, he has used his earnings to finance expansion, including the construction of a 225,000-square-foot showroom and warehouse.

Page's accounting experience proved

to be an asset in Replacements' early days. Although some entrepreneurs have plenty of passion for their business, they often do not understand the importance of sound money management and the need to keep meticulous and useful financial records. Page also did his own research on china and glassware.

Early on, Page maintained customer records on index cards; and in these precomputer days, product descriptions were available to collectors only in publications.

When sales rose from $150,000 in 1981 to nearly $4 million in 1984, it was time to convert to a computer-based system. Replacements now has more than 300 personal computers storing data on 7 million pieces of inventory in more than 145,000 patterns, and the buying habits of more than 3.5 million customers. Besides directories, Replacements has compiled its own proprietary database, which provides information on products available in its warehouse as well as U.S. and overseas suppliers.

In contrast to his appreciation of precise financial management, Page said, "I didn't even have a business plan. I give a talk each year to a business class at UNC. I shock them when I say that I still don't have a plan. I'm just out there doing it." Although Replacements has grown to international-market leadership, Page maintains full ownership of the company, which employs more than 700 full-time workers. Replacements' sales increase each year, but he doesn't want to see growth surpass customer service.

Page learned about china, glassware, and silver by reading, visiting retail venues, and filling orders. Replacements' employees do the same thing. Everyone is trained on the job, starting with Scott Fleming, executive vice-president, several other vice-presidents, and all the sales and warehouse employees. Most employees have had little or no related schooling or work experience.

When I was interviewing Page, the public-address system in his office

In contrast to his appreciation of precise financial management, Page said, "I didn't even have a business plan."

announced "Code 2," meaning there were customer telephone calls that were not being answered, a critical factor in a business that receives 26,000 requests weekly via telephone and the company's Web site (www.replacements.com), accounting for 90% of its $75 million in sales. When necessary, managers can work directly with customers using the company's computerized customer records and illustrated product descriptions. In January 2000, when Greensboro had its worst blizzard in nearly a century, Page made it into the office and personally handled 100 telephone calls in a day.

Replacements is a haven for other career changers. Page's companion, Dale

Frederiksen, taught math and coached middle and high school volleyball before joining the company ten years ago, and Dean Six, the company's glass expert, previously practiced law and worked for a nonprofit organization.

Pursuing Your Art and Your Craft

WHAT'S YOUR DREAM? WRITING POETRY, BUILDING furniture, or composing jazz—and making a living by doing it? Sounds ideal—downshifting to a less hectic pace while doing something you thoroughly enjoy. Jennie Keatts (profiled in chapter 2) was an up-and-coming marketing executive who cashed in the "good life" in corporate America and emerged as a jewelry designer. It's not an easy road, as the people described in this chapter will attest, but they have found satisfaction doing work with a creative bent, and in almost every instance, in being self-employed.

Career switchers can easily find out the specific entrance requirements for law, medicine, ministry, and education, which have defined career tracks. That's not true for painters, sculptors, potters, textile artists and the like. Craftspeople learn by doing, and enhance their skills with classes.

Author Jonathan Kellerman took a traditional approach in changing careers. A child psychologist, he became a full-time writer of psychological suspense stories. And like many other writers, he uses his occupation and personal experiences to provide the themes for his books.

Similarly, actors and actresses pursue no single career track. Many began performing in high school and college, honing their skills in school drama productions. Others attended specialized acting schools, and some never acquired any formal training.

Early in their careers, creative people use their other skills to help pay the bills. Harrison Ford, who was mentioned in Chapter 5, worked as a carpenter while trying to establish himself as a screen actor. His biographer, Garry Jenkins, in *Imperfect Hero* (Birch Lane Press Books, 1998), noted that Ford was so caring about the way he did carpentry that he wouldn't accept anything that wasn't perfect. If a customer suggested something that Ford thought was in bad taste, he would refuse to do it.

The Internet is the craftsperson's best friend, with chat rooms, online organizations, and publications dedicated to specific crafts.

To 30- and 40-year-olds, going to college for a degree in fine arts or music is often not affordable or practical. Yet there are a wealth of resources from which to learn, improve, and gain admission into a crafts field without spending years in school.

Want to learn glassblowing, weaving, spinning or woodworking? Begin by investigating what courses your local college or university or community college offers. Most midsize and large cities have an arts council or museum that sponsors workshops for beginners and more experienced craftpeople.

The Internet is the craftsperson's best friend, with chat rooms, online organizations, and publications dedicated to specific crafts. For example, to research career opportunities and salaries for musicians and actors, check out the Web sites of the American Federation of Musicians (www.afm.org), American Federation of Television and Radio Artists (www.aftra.org), Screen Actors Guild (www.sag.org), or the Actors' Equity Association (www.actorsequity.org)

And, of course, artisans should attend craft shows. Here's a chance to meet fellow craftspeople, share ideas, and see what's being produced.

Ultimately, there's the big decision that needs to be made. Do you continue making and selling craft products as a hobby or a sideline business, or do you convert it into a full-time occupation?

Another Perspective on Artisans

Many artisans fight success. Consultant Susan Inglis, who advises handicraft producers on ways to increase their marketing skills, finds that they often reject generally accepted business principles. "It is important that creative people think like business people. They need to remember, they are responsible for paying sales taxes, knowing the cost of materials that they use in their work, pricing what they make, and maintaining financial records."

In 1997, before she became a consultant, Inglis started Susan Sweaters to support herself and two children following a divorce. A few years later, Inglis evolved from just selling knit goods to associating with economic development agencies that aim to help small crafts businesses market their products. Based in Chapel Hill, N.C., Inglis has been retained by cooperative craft groups like Appalachian Design in West Virginia and craft organizations in Nepal and Latin America.

Inglis finds that many artisans cannot make a living from their work. To some, it is actually part of an overall plan to downscale in order to enjoy a simpler life. Even so, she tries to teach them to think like entrepreneurs—a message she drives home at the arts council and community-college workshops that she conducts. She tells craftspeople how to deal with consignment selling, and stresses the importance of agreements with retailers to cover damages on returned products.

"Learn what's taking place in your field. Visit stores and galleries, and see how other artisans present their wares. I suggest that craftspeople keep their full-time job during the transition period, unless they have a mate who is the bread-and-butter person."

Some performance careers are essentially off limits to career changers. One rarely finds classical musicians or composers who have had previous careers. Classical musicians normally launch their careers as comparative youngsters. Similarly, Elvis Presley and the Beatles were established stars in their 20s. Ballet dancers, like athletes, peak early and generally retire from performance by their late 30s, when they are likely to begin teaching or coaching in the same field.

In contrast to painting, sculpting, or poetry writing, the

cooking and news media fields are more structured, with certificate and degree programs that are being increasingly tailored for career changers.

How About a Career as a Chef?

Until the past 20 years, cooking or baking was a way to earn a living, but it was not considered to be a very glamorous, creative, or a desired career in the United States. Times change. Cooks have resurfaced as celebrity chefs, and cooking has been reborn as an art form.

Cooking or baking is a wonderful hobby, but let's be realistic when considering it as an option for career changers. It's one thing to prepare a dinner party at home and another matter to cook everyday for 100 or more customers. Get the facts before taking the plunge. Learn about life in the kitchen as a hospital kitchen volunteer or a restaurant apprentice. It will open your eyes to the practical side of being a chef or baker, where the 9-to-5 workday rarely exists. And forget about time off for holidays, weekends, and evenings. That's when the kitchen is often at its busiest. The work is also physically demanding. It calls for picking up 50-pound bags of sugar or flour, toting huge cooking pots, and working over a hot stove in a tight workspace. Most important, before you and your restaurant are profiled in *Gourmet,* expect to pay your dues in lower-level kitchen jobs.

"I wish I had a dollar for every well-meaning career changer who attended a six-month course and showed up to be an extern in my kitchen," writes Anthony Bourdain in *Kitchen Confidential* (Bloomsburg Publishing, 2000), in a tell-all book about restaurant kitchen life. Bourdain, the executive chef at Brasserie Les Halles, in New York City, wrote, "More often than not, one look at what they would really be spending their first few months doing, one look at what their schedule would be, and they ran away in terror."

Attending culinary or baking school is a good way to accelerate a career, but even here it pays to be cautious. A sensible approach is to attend the one-week exploratory course of the Culinary Institute of America (CIA; www.ciachef.edu), held several times a year at the CIA's Hyde Park, N.Y., campus.

For a few hundred dollars, you'll have an opportunity to sample the fare and see whether commercial cooking is for you.

The New England Culinary Institute (www.neculinary.com), in Montpelier, Vt., lists former college professors, computer programmers, farmers, bankers, and accountants among its students. Some older students are learning how to cook as the first step in opening a restaurant; others want to work on the line in a kitchen or bakery. New England Culinary recognizes physical fitness as a part of kitchen life; it requires students to participate in a sports and physical-fitness program.

> **It's one thing to prepare a dinner party at home and another matter to cook everyday for 100 or more customers.**

The Western Culinary Institute (www.westernculinary.com), in Portland, Ore., says that its "curriculum offers students an opportunity to acquire the attributes of a professional, entry-level chef. These qualities include stamina, dexterity, hand-eye coordination, ability to work with others, timing, and the artistry of good food presentation."

A 21-month program at the Culinary Institute costs about $30,000 for tuition and meals, but excludes lodging. CIA students, as well as students at other cooking schools, can offset academic costs with paid internships. An alternative is to work while going to school. Culinary schools and community colleges offer weekend and evening cooking and baking classes.

People who really want to start from ground zero can freelance in kitchens at night or weekends. One starts with scut, the dirty work in the kitchen, and moves on to prep work by cutting vegetables, lettuce, and meat. The work is hardly glamorous, but it does provide a chance to watch chefs in action. The next step is promotion to apprentice chef, followed by sous chef. Voila! You've gone up the ladder without going to a culinary school. This scenario, however, is actually more fitting to a 20-year-old than to a midlife career changer who attends cooking school as a shortcut into the kitchen.

Other than the owners and showcased chefs at the three- and four-star restaurants, kitchen personnel rarely become rich. The American Culinary Federation (www.acfchefs.com) notes that new chefs earn about $20,000 a year; five years later their pay increases an additional $11,000, and after ten years it is nearly $50,000. The National Restaurant Association (www.restaurant.org) reports that executive chefs earn about $60,000 a year. Celebrity chefs are paid at the superstar level for their talents divided between cooking and show business.

What About a Career in Journalism or Communications?

As admissions director at Columbia University's Graduate School of Journalism, Robert MacDonald defines an older student as being age 30-plus. About 50% of the "oldsters" are adding journalism to an already existing skill in a related field, 25% are late bloomers wanting to enter the field, and the rest are lawyers, physicians, and other professionals who want to blend journalism with their present work. The learning process comes with a price: Tuition alone is $33,000 for the two-year, part-time program, and $28,000 for one-year, full-time students.

The track for age-35-plus career changers is somewhat uncertain. Most midsize to large daily newspapers and television stations prefer to hire experienced news staffers. Entry-level jobs paying in the mid $20s, however, are available on smaller city newspapers and TV stations. Business and trade newspapers covering the diversity of American industry from advertising, automobiles and oil to computers or information technology need staffers who know these fields and can write. As such, a systems software engineer or software programmer is an ideal candidate to become a reporter or editor on a computer publication. The entry-level salary could range from $30,000 to $50,000.

Such skills also provide entrée to jobs producing Web-site content. Little is known about the career opportunities and pay in the dot-com media. Experienced reporters and editors, responding to the high-tech cache of new media, have been shifting to Internet newsgathering groups; newcomers have been bypassing traditional journalism altogether. The pay is usually higher than that for comparable newspaper and television reporting jobs.

During the dot-com shakeout in 2000, a number of online

publishers laid off staff members. According to the career-services office of Columbia Journalism School, alumni downsized by dot-com companies were already experienced print and broadcast journalists before they switched to this new medium. In reaction, they are returning to more traditional reporting and editing jobs.

The U.S. Department of Labor's Bureau of Labor Statistics (www.bls.gov) estimates that 60% of reporters work for newspapers, 30% in radio and TV broadcasting news, and rest for magazines and wire services. Newspaper mergers and consolidations, along with the general decline in newspaper readership and television news viewers, produce a somewhat stagnant, if not declining, job market.

A handful of TV anchors and syndicated newspaper columnists earn "major league" salaries. Most reporters and editors work at the other end of the pay scale. The top median wage for reporters after five years, according to a Newspaper Guild (www.newsguild.org) salary survey, is $1,384 a week at the *New York Times;* it declines to $387 at the *Observer Dispatch* in Utica, N.Y. Another 15 daily newspapers pay reporters with five

---

POINTS TO REMEMBER

- **The potential for making more money** is seldom the prime motivation of career changers.
- **Creative workers** often prefer independence in both their life and their work.
- **Creative skills** are learned at "school" and by doing them.
- **Chefs** are among today's media stars, but those "artists" are the exception.
- **Very few classical** and rock musicians are career changers. They tend to start young.
- **The news media,** old and new, generally require reporters and editors with previous reporting, writing, and editing experience.
- **Public relations** and advertising welcome trained journalists.
- **Career changers** who turn to an art or a craft for a livelihood are frequently pursuing their passion.

---

years' experience $1,000 a more a week, while reporters at 54 dailies earn between $700 and $1,000 weekly.

In comparison, reports the National Association of Broadcasters (www.nab.org), TV reporters average about $33,000 a year; radio reporters make slightly less. TV sports-casters and weather reporters are paid roughly $55,000.

Another option for career changers interested in journalism is advertising and public relations, fields that need trained writers and production specialists. A political reporter is an ideal candidate for a job with a governmental agency or lobbying firm, while airlines covet aviation writers. In most instances, the higher salaries are the attraction. The Public Relations Society of America (www.prsa.org) reported in its annual survey that the median public-relations salary exceeded $49,000, ranging from a low of nearly $23,000 to a $140,000 high.

Some People Who Made the Change

Other than Glenn Ruffenach, who works for the *Wall Street Journal*, and Lydia Gabor, a baker and innkeeper, the people described in this chapter are self-employed. Several worked for large organizations prior to making the break as designers, writers, and potters. One thing is certain: They did not make the change to earn more money. If anything, their choices entailed severe salary cuts, but they preferred the uncertainty of a craft occupation to the security of a corporate job.

COVERS THE 55–PLUS SET

Glenn Ruffenach
FROM THE ARMY TO JOURNALISM

At DePaul High School in northern New Jersey, Glenn Ruffenach, now in his late 40s, was a good enough track and cross-country runner to attract the attention of college recruiters. West Point showed an interest, and he became a cadet in 1970.

Ruffenach reflects that "no one is ready for West Point life, and neither was I." He completed the prescribed engineering and science program, graduated, and was commissioned as an Army second lieutenant in 1974.

West Point graduates have an obligatory five-year active-duty commitment. Some expect to leave the Army after five years, but Ruffenach was seriously con-sidering making the Army his career. He was assigned to the field artillery after completing both Airborne and Ranger training schools.

In 1978, at about the time he was due to be assigned to Korea, Ruffenach married. Army regulations would not permit him to take his wife, Karen, a teacher, and her two children with him. Not wanting to leave them behind, Ruffenach started to consider another career.

"While I was considering other career options, I read Richard Bolles's *What Color Is Your Parachute?* [Ten Speed Press, new edition each year]. The book provided good exercises in what I could do and what I enjoyed doing. I had always liked teaching and writing. As an officer, one does a lot of teaching. I wanted a career that combined my interests and skills. Journalism seemed to satisfy both interests. It was a chance to write, and, if readers read what you wrote, I was teaching them vicariously. And it seemed

"I had always liked teaching and writing. Journalism seemed to satisfy both interests."

you got feedback when readers praised or criticized your work."

Stationed at Fort Sill, Okla., Ruffenach concentrated his job search in the Midwest, visiting newspapers and television stations on weekends and leaves. "But I kept getting the same response: You don't have any experience; why don't you go to journalism school?" Thus, as he got closer to his resignation date in 1979, Ruffenach started looking at journalism schools. Because his wife was from St. Louis, he applied to the master's program at the University of Missouri's school of journalism, in Columbia, and was accepted.

Ruffenach found the transition from life as an Army captain to journalism not that difficult; his military experience had taught him self-discipline. Ruffenach took three rather than two years to complete the program, so that he and his family could remain in Missouri an additional year while his stepdaughter completed high school in Columbia.

Part of his tuition was paid by the G.I. Bill, and the rest from savings and part-time jobs at night and on the weekends, and a summer internship on the *Miami Herald*. The job provided the practical newsroom experience that employers seek when they recruit.

While he was at journalism school, he started reading the *Wall Street Journal*. "I liked what I read. But I really didn't have any thoughts about joining the paper. I had assumed that I would join a metro paper like the *St. Louis Post-Dispatch*."

In Ruffenach's last year at Missouri, a *Wall Street Journal* editor visited the campus to recruit reporters and copy-editors. "Thinking I had nothing to lose, I signed up for an interview. The interview didn't go very well, and I walked out thinking that I would never see the inside of the *Journal*." But it was noon time, and Ruffenach noticed that the visiting editor didn't seem to have lunch plans. Feeling that he had nothing to lose, Ruffenach asked him if he would like to join him for a sandwich. The editor agreed.

"Lunch, as it turned out, was more enjoyable. I was more relaxed, and he was no longer in an 'interview' mode. We talked about the paper, and our back-grounds and experiences. At the end of lunch, he asked me to send him some

clips. Several weeks later, I was invited to the *Journal's* New York office for a tryout on the copy desk, the final test before I was hired."

Over the next seven years, Ruffenach worked in New York as a copyeditor, features editor, and reporter. In 1989 he became deputy bureau chief of the *Journal's* Atlanta office, which is respon-sible for news coverage in nine south-eastern states.

Meanwhile, Ruffenach's interest in retirement issues was triggered by a

Feeling that he had nothing to lose, Ruffenach asked the *Journal* editor to lunch. It was a fateful invitation.

request from his mother, who was about to retire, to investigate medical benefits and social security for her. He looked for the answers, and found them trickier than he had assumed. After this experience, he volunterred to be the guest editor of a special *Journal* report on retirement. "From this assignment, I learned that retirees have all types of questions regarding health, retirement, finances, lifestyle, and other related issues. Besides editing the section, I wrote a number of the articles. Then I talked with my bosses about the possibility of making this a regularly published section that would appeal to Baby Boomers." In 1998 he was named editor of *Encore,* a quarterly newspaper supplement, based in Atlanta, which the *Journal* sends to several hundred thousand subscribers over age 55.

Looking back on his career and the 1982 *Journal* job interview, Ruffenach observes, "I guess that moment—deciding to ask the editor to lunch—changed my life."

APPLIES ART IN A DIFFERENT VENUE

George Radwan
AN ART DIRECTOR DESIGNS ARCHITECTURAL WOODWORK

As a teenager in Cleveland, Ohio, George Radwan, now in his early 50s, became interested in art. "I worked in a public library during high school, so I had access to all kinds of information about colleges. I wanted to be an artist. I found the Art Center College of Design in Los Angeles, sent for its catalog, and was blown away by what I saw."

A few years later, after brief stints taking classes at a local junior college and at Cleveland State University, Radwan applied to the Art Center, and to his surprise he was accepted. "My interest was advertising design. I liked the idea that the everyone on the faculty was a working professional."

Graduating in 1972 with a degree in fine arts, he was advised to go to New York City. Radwan's first job was with Ogilvy & Mather at $7,500 a year. He was an apprentice doing such grunt work as paste-ups of copyboards, a system that has nearly disappeared in the age of computer graphics.

Radwan was promoted to art director, and during this period he married Stephanie Greene, who was also employed at the agency (she's described in the next profile).

"We decided to work overseas for Ogilvy. I would have preferred to work for the agency's London office but there was a long line for this assignment. We were sent instead to Johannesburg on a two-year contract. Neither of us liked South African politics. After one year, we asked to be reassigned for the balance of our contract to the Hong Kong office. While we were overseas, we lived on my salary and banked Stephanie's."

After returning to the states,

As a commercial artist, Radwan had the drafting skills needed to create precision woodwork drawings.

Stephanie stayed with Ogilvy as a copywriter, while Radwan worked as an art director for several other New York agencies.

"We decided to relocate to New England as a joint writer/art director team. We were even interviewed as an advertising team by Ben & Jerry's. We both wanted to spend more time with our son. A job that Stephanie and I shared at a New Hampshire advertising agency paid us $75,000 a year, the salary that we were each making when we were in New York. But after a year, we decided that the agency was not very well run, so we quit."

By then, Radwan was enjoying making Shaker furniture, a skill he had learned from Stephanie's father. As a result, in 1988 he took a $7-an-hour job with a furniture company, working for a boss whom he thought had a somewhat erratic personality.

He left for a job with Henry Architectural Woodworking, in Winchester, N.H., about 20 miles from home, which was his introduction to architectural woodwork, a design and production function that includes exterior and interior woodwork. To do this work requires the creation of precise drawings, often from sketchy instructions, a knowledge of materials, and the ability to install custom wood-working in the décor of a college building, museum, or a corporate headquarters. Working with architects and general building contractors, the designer also specifies how to incorporate trim in desks, tables, and wallworks. As a commercial artist, Radwan had the artistic skills that eased his transition to preparing precision woodwork drawings.

"After four years as a draftsman and general manager making $15 an hour, it was time to move on. We chose Chapel Hill because Stephanie and I liked the weather and lifestyle. My boss pro-vided a safety net by letting me work for him in North Carolina. It made the move possible, but there was a hitch. He expected me to return to New Hampshire every week."

In 1995, after two years of commuting, Radwan decided to do the same type of work as an independent designer. "I was

on my own, and I had a number of clients. Even so, our income was dwindling. Out of the blue, my mother, not realizing that I was freelancing, sent me $5,000. She decided to give away some of her money while she was still alive. It kept us going for a while longer."

Radwan's career and income see-sawed. When business was floundering, he joined Cleora Sterling, a local custom architectural woodworking firm, as a project manager. His pay was $45,000, and his duties were similar to the work

"I can't afford any distraction or the slightest mistake. If that happens, designers and architects will never use me again."

he had been doing for the past six years. Then their lives suddenly took a detour. The couple decided to move to Bennington, Vt., which they felt would be a better place to raise and educate their son. Because they couldn't sell their house in Chapel Hill, they rented it to a retired couple who lived in it for a year while the couple waited for their own home to be built.

Radwan got a job working with a woodworking firm in Albany, N.Y., about one hour's drive from Bennington, which paid $60,000 a year. "I soon realized that the company's management left some-thing to be desired, so I left. Fortunately, we were free to leave since we were renting our home in Bennington."

They returned to Chapel Hill just as their renters were about to move into their own completed home. The move to Vermont and back had cost $18,000 in relocation expenses.

Radwan's employment saga continued. His former Chapel Hill employer wanted to reemploy him, but at the same salary as he had had a year earlier. Radwan decided to once again become an independent designer. His work is varied. Under contract from architects and general contractors, he prepares architectural woodworking designs for retail stores, college buildings, and corporate headquarters.

Sometimes there is more work than he can handle, and there are some drawbacks: waiting 30 to 60 days or more to get paid, and paying $20,000 a year to rent and operate his one-person office. Like many self-employed craftspeople, Radwan is subject to the whims of customers and the need to keep current customers and attract additional business.

"As an experienced art director, I have an eye for detail, but unlike advertising, where I worked as part of a team, I now work alone. In the past, I listened to the radio at work. No more. I can't afford any distraction or the slightest mistake. If that happens, designers and architects will never use me again.

"It sometimes feels that life is like a roller-coaster, but Stephanie has the confidence that I can do anything, and she never worries about money."

FOLLOWING A FAMILY TRADITION

Stephanie Greene

MADISON AVENUE COPYWRITER WRITES CHILDREN'S BOOKS

Nearly everyone in Stephanie Greene's family has worked in journalism or is in creative writing or magazine promotion. Her mother, Constance Greene, has published more than 40 children's books, and Stephanie's sister, Lucia Connolly (profiled in chapter 4), is a magazine writer.

After graduating from high school in Norwalk, Conn., Greene, now in her late 40s, went to the University of Connecticut , where she majored in French. After completing college, she got a clerical job at *Time,* a common entry-level position for journalism in the mid 1970s. Four months later, she decided that she wanted to work for a less structured organization. For two years Greene edited three weekly newspapers in Vermont; then came another two years as a reporter and feature writer for the *Norwalk Hour,* a daily newspaper.

In 1977, Greene left journalism for a job in New York City as an advertising copywriter with Ogilvy & Mather, where she met and married George Radwan (his profile precedes this one), who was an art director. Greene was assigned to write copy for American Express, TWA, General Foods, and Hershey. She left Ogilvy 12 years later when their son, Oliver, was born.

Greene, her husband, and Oliver relocated to Keene, N.H. Their objective was to get away from New York City, pursue a better lifestyle, and continue their advertising careers in a different environment. "George and I worked as creative directors of a small advertising agency where we shared jobs; he worked three days and I on the other two days. We were paid at the rate of

> # "I never stop thinking of plots and characters for my books. I think of ideas when I walk, drive, and shower."

a New York City advertising agency."

The job lasted about one year, when Radwan left to do something different. During this period, Radwan and Greene encouraged each other on ways to change careers. "At that time, I discovered Joseph Campbell's *Power of Myth* [Doubleday, 1988], which talks about getting back to the basics of life."

When Radwan got a job in Chapel Hill, N.C., the move helped to define a new career for Greene, too. Her long-time writing ambition extended beyond advertising copy. Her mother encouraged her daughter to persevere as a freelance writer.

"I kept trying to get my first book published. I had tons of rejection slips.

Before I ever sold my first book, I even went to Barnes & Noble to get a job selling books, but they only wanted to pay minimum wage. I talked to George about getting a paid job, and he said the same thing each time, 'Don't do it.' There are times when it would have been nice for one of us to have a well-paying job. But we try to live simply and not to buy things that would keep us in debt."

In 1993 Greene sold the first of her six books to date. She patterned her books and her main fictional characters on children her son's age. Hence, *Owen Foote, Frontiersman* (1996); *Owen Foote, Soccer Star* (1998); *Owen Foote, Second Grade Strongman* (1999); and *Owen Foote, Money Man* (2001), all published by Clarion Books. In 2000 came a non-Oliver book, *Just Another Moose,* published by Marshall Cavendish. Working on a newspaper, she says, taught her how to keep a sentence brief, and how to write a feature when the space is limited. "I never stop thinking of plots and characters for my books. I think of ideas when I walk, drive, and shower."

Greene works hard to produce a writing style and present facts in ways that appeal to her readers. To keep abreast of how children think, she reads to third-grade students on Friday afternoons. She listens to what they say, and how they say it. She does the same thing at home. "I often check a sentence or phrase with Oliver to make sure it's the way a youngster would say it."

Greene has her fans. One is Oliver, who wrote the following unsolicited comment for Amazon.com:

"I am the author's son, Oliver, who is meant to be the inspiration for her writing the Owen Foote series. I think that my mom is pretty good at understanding children like me. She does not know that I am writing this, but I

Greene listens to what kids say, and how they say it. She does the same thing at home.

hope someday she will see it. I remember the happy day when she sold her first book and I am proud of her. I think that all young soccer players will enjoy this book."

In the days when rejection slips were plentiful, Greene at times wanted to find another career. "I was flattered, when one of my editors was giving a talk to authors, that she told them, 'Never give up. I discovered Stephanie Greene in my slush pile of unsolicited manuscripts.'"

CONTRIBUTING HER WORK TO HELP OTHERS

Chris Schafale
A NEUROPSYCHOLOGIST MAKES POTTERY

When she was completing her post-doctoral studies in psychology, Chris Schafale, now in her late 30s, discovered that making pottery was a good way to unwind.

After graduating from the University of New Hampshire in 1984, Schafale left her home state for the University of North Carolina at Chapel Hill. In 1988 she married a biologist before completing her doctorate in clinical psychology in 1989. She spent a year working as a clinical psychologist before completing a two-year postdoctoral program in neuropsychology at UNC's Medical School.

"When I finished my postdoctoral work in the mid 1990s, I opened a private practice that focused on chronic illnesses. I took pottery classes at Pullen Art Center in Raleigh simply to unwind, and as a way to achieve self-expression." Because her practice did not keep her as busy as she had thought it would, Schafale ended up spending 20 hours a week at Pullen. At the time, she did not own pottery-making equipment.

"I was not the typical psychologist. I charged patients on a sliding scale, and I didn't do managed-care counseling. And unlike many other psychologists, I was not interested in working in a hospital or institution. Above all, I enjoyed my inde-pendence. While I saw patients, I would often daydream. I had trouble con-centrating on them and their problems. I found that I was not committed enough to my work. I closed my practice, and decided to spend more time as a potter."

Because Schafale's husband had a full-time job and benefits as a biologist with the state of North Carolina, she

"I took pottery classes simply to unwind, and as a way to achieve self-expression."

had the opportunity to reconsider her career options. Even with a working husband, however, Schafale believed it was important to contain costs when her goal was to become an independent artist, for whom a steady income would be doubtful.

While working as an independent potter, she discovered how physically taxing pottery can be. The potter needs to be able to lift 50-pound bags of clay as well as sit hunched over a pottery wheel for long periods of time.

Meanwhile, she also took up catering. "I've always liked to cook, something I learned from my mother. I started by volunteering to cater functions at a local retreat center, and for a brief period I was also the center's director. Catering and food preparation were great. It left me ample time to think and do pottery."

As Schafale discovered, however, catering, like pottery, is strenuous work. After three years of catering, she realized that she couldn't do two physically demanding jobs, catering and pottery.

"I also found that I didn't want to do catering forever. Was this what I wanted to be doing in 15 years? Yet catering is less stressful than psychology. In catering, the only real worry is serving a meal late. As a psychologist, a patient could commit suicide."

In 1998, Schafale moved to her present home in Fuqua-Varina, about 25 miles from Raleigh. Up to that time, she used the equipment and workspace at the Pullen Art Center. Now her basement is outfitted as a studio with a potter's wheel, an electric kiln, and a number of workbenches, costing less than $3,000.

It was one thing to become a potter, and another to make money at it. As a potter, Schafale makes pots, bowls, and decorative pieces which she sells at area craft stores and craft shows and through nonprofit charities. But like other artisans, Schafale found she could not earn a steady income from her art.

Schafale wanted to find a job that would permit her to spend the maximum time in developing her craft and not be physically taxing. Schafale searched for a job on the Internet, responded to an ad for a medical writer, and took a part-time job with a pharmaceutical researcher, editing and rewriting research reports.

Her doctoral studies gave her the skills to understand and write on health care–related topics. She lost this job when the company was downsized, but she was soon hired as an information specialist for Resources for Seniors, in nearby Raleigh, a job in which she can combine editing skills and her experience as a psychologist.

Schafale's interests go beyond the creative and production process of making pottery, and selling it through traditional retail outlets. By agreements

Schafale wanted to find a job that would permit her to spend the maximum time in developing her craft and not be physically taxing.

with several local nonprofits, she provides pottery on consignment for their special events, such as fairs or holiday sales, and the charities keep one-third of the profit on the sale without making an investment in inventory. "I have a strong desire to contribute my work to help others. Pottery permits me to donate a percentage of my proceeds to public-interest groups who support hunger and economic-justice issues."

Schafale is also committed to environmental safety, avoiding the use of toxic materials and testing glazes to assure that they will hold up environmentally under regular use. (In their raw state, some materials, said Schafale, might be nontoxic to end users though hazardous to potters, while other harmful glazes used in dishes can leach into food or the water system.)

An avid computer user, Schafale participates in a worldwide Internet discussion and exchange group of about 2,000 potters. She plans to add e-commerce features to her Web site, www.lightonecandle.com, and perhaps telecommute to her outside job.

NO MORE DISTRESSED BRIDES AND THEIR MOTHERS

Laura Boyes
A DRESS DESIGNER TURNS TO OLD–TIME FILMS

Laura Boyes, now in her late 40s, was aptly named after the principal character in the 1944 noire murder mystery, *Laura*. Her first name glorifies one of her passions, old movies, and provided a hint at the direction her career change would someday take.

Born in Cleveland, she graduated in the mid 1970s as a fine-arts major from the University of Cincinnati. "At college, I studied fashion design. I got very little career guidance when I graduated, so I had a series of unrelated jobs." While living in Cincinnati, she met Will, who was completing his doctorate at the university, and they were married in 1979.

"We moved to Raleigh, N.C., when Will went to work for the Environmental Protection Agency, and two years later we moved to Durham. I started to design wedding dresses and gowns. When Adrienne was born in 1989, dress making provided a way to stay home and work."

Boyes developed a specialty in restoring heirloom wedding dresses, some of which had been worn by several generations of women in the same family.

"I called my business Ruby Design, the name I had given my 1970 car at college; it was also named after my grandmother, who taught me how to sew when I was a young girl. As a teenager I designed and made my own high school clothes.

"Designing wedding dresses and party gowns is peak-and-valley work— no work for a while and suddenly three jobs. It seemed I was working all the time. Some of the job had little to do with design. About one-half of my time was spent counseling distraught mothers and their daughters."

Recognizing her unusual combination of skills and interest in fashions and films, Duke and several local museums offered Boyes paid and volunteer jobs.

Throughout this period, Boyes and her husband continued to be ardent movie fans.

"We've taken Adrienne to the movies since she was ten weeks old; Will and I still go to the movies nearly every Tuesday night. Movies are in my blood. When my own parents married in 1948, they took a film course. My brother, David, and I were taken as kids to films at the Cleveland Art Museum. Now, we found we were doing the same thing with Adrienne."

Fashion and movies began to come together in her life. As a volunteer, Boyes helped the North Carolina History Museum assemble its clothing and costume collection; at the same time she started meeting people socially who were interested in films. Recognizing that Boyes had an unusual combination of skills and interest in fashion and films, Duke and several local museums offered her paid and volunteer jobs.

The North Carolina Museum of Art in Raleigh asked Boyes to help it beef up its winter film series. "At college, I was chairman for two years of the film society, and I would write movie reviews for Cincinnati's independent newspapers. If I had had career counseling back then, I might have become a film critic." Boyes personally favors films produced from the 1940s through the early 1960s, as well as silent movies. This background served her well in structuring a film series as a feature of the museum's winter schedule.

By now, Boyes had become unhappy in her work as a wedding-dress designer. She found some of her work maddening.

"Customers would call me day and night, and on Sundays. When I wanted to charge a certain price, a customer might say, as a way to cut my fee, 'Oh, it's just a simple little dress.' Finally in the middle of 1999 when I was complaining about one customer, Will said, 'Why not go on sabbatical?' and that's what I did, starting the next day."

Boyes was free to pursue her passion for films. For the past several winters, she has conducted an 11-week film festival that has included such old-timers as

Cover Girl, Lady in the Dark, or a silent film, *Peter Pan,* for which her brother, a musician in Chicago, provided the piano accompaniment.

Her museum assignment, along with the title of film curator, spawned additional paid assignments. Barnes & Noble, the sponsor of the film series, contracts with Boyes to talk about films at its North Carolina stores. Then the cable TV channel American Movie Classics retained her to coordinate its Preservation Tours featuring "older" films

She discovered that the Web provided very little content on films that predate the Web. To fill the gap, she designed her own Web site.

when it appeared in Durham.

Before each movie showing, Boyes introduces the film with a 15-minute explanation of the film and the events of the period when it was produced. Each talk is based on research that she does at the Duke library and on the Internet; the audience of up to 300 people ranges in age from college students to senior citizens.

In researching her talks, she discovered that the Web provided very little content on films that predate the Web. To fill the gap, she designed her own Web site, www.moviediva.com, using a how-to book, *Web Pages that*

Suck: Learn Good Design by Looking at Bad Design (Michael Willis, 1998). More than an informational Web site, it is already a commercial venture with film distributors paying her in accordance with sales they receive through her site. In one feature of her Web site, "Moviediva, Jr.," Boyes talks about films from a youngster's point of view, which is based to some extent on the opinions of middle-school students like her daughter.

"Dress designing provided a chance to meet lots of interesting people, but it was never a big income producer. Will paid the big bills, and my work paid for vacations, luxuries and some good dinners. As a result of my new work, we see a lot more films."

ENJOYS WORKING WITH HIS CUSTOMERS

Jeffrey Walker
COOKING BEATS COMMERCIAL BANKING

As a music and business major at Elon College, in North Carolina, Jeffrey Walker, now in his early 40s, considered a career in music or business. Walker picked business and took a job after graduation with Nationsbank (now the Bank of America). He started as a teller, but was soon doing commercial banking. Music became a sideline; he sang tenor in church choirs.

Walker has an entrepreneurial temperament, hardly the spirit appropriate to a highly structured bank setting, where corporate teamwork is critical.

"I met a woman who was opening a family-style restaurant in Greensboro. She needed someone with business skills to help her operate the restaurant. I liked to cook, but up to then, I had never worked in a restaurant. The job lasted about a year.

"Next I went out on my own as a subcontractor for Sherwin-Williams, installing carpets in apartment complexes being built in Durham. Over the next 18 months, I cleared about $500 a week working about three to four days a week."

Though hard, the work permitted him to save some money, but not be tied down to a full-time job.

His next career change began at a most unexpected place. While playing goalie in a soccer game, he met George Bakatschias, an entrepreneur who had been opening trendy restaurants in the Durham area. They talked. Bakatschias was attracted by Walker's business and restaurant experience, and hired him as one of his chefs at Café Georgio. "George taught me some important lessons: buy only quality food, charge

"I learned how to cook Greek food by doing it: I've never taken a cooking course."

fair prices, and give good service so that people come back regularly."

A few years later, Walker went to work for Tavernos Nikos, another restaurant owned by Bakatschias, which was soon sold to another restaurateur.

"I learned how to cook Greek food by doing it: I've never taken a cooking course. The Tavernos kitchen staff is small—myself, a sous chef and a salad chef, and two dishwashers. It's a 12-hour workday from 10 to 10 for five and sometimes six days a week."

An African American, Walker likens some aspects of Greek cuisine to black food. "Both use lots of veggies; Greeks use oregano and rosemary, and blacks like thyme."

Walker had learned an important

lesson as a banker that served him well in the restaurant business. When he had taken banking customers to lunch, he had found that it took too long for the restaurant to put the meal on the table. Customers wanted to get back to work. At Tavernos, he made a point of getting food to the tables promptly.

Wanting some time off, Walker left Tavernos in 1992, moved to Japan, where his sister lived, and learned martial arts. After returning to Durham, he took up Greek cooking again at Tavernos for the next seven years.

"I was the executive chef. I won't tell you what I made, but let me say that the sous chef made $38,000 a year, and I made considerably more than that. Unless one is a celebrity chef, the salary is not that spectacular, considering the long and demanding hours."

Walker left Tavernos in May 2000. "I wanted to work more regular hours, have more time off and, anyway, ten years is much too long to work for one restaurant. It's a field where you easily burn out. That's one reason I took a break in 1992."

Walker's current plans include catering and owning a restaurant, eventually fusing them into new ventures. "Whatever I do, I want to get back to working directly with customers, something I missed as a chef." Walker has taken the first step as an entrepreneur with J. D. Catering, which initially is specializing in corporate and private parties.

FROM THE KITCHEN TO MANAGEMENT CONSULTING

Lydia Gabor
AN INTERPRETOR FOR THE DEAF, BAKER AND RESTAURANT MANAGER

As a high school student in Rye, N.Y., Lydia Gabor, now in her 30s, had a deaf friend. Impressed with the friend's ability to sign and cope with life's problems, Gabor was inspired to want to work with the deaf. At the same time, she and her older brother, Michael, catered parties when they were in high school, and she cooked at a New England ski lodge to pay her weekend and vacation skiing expenses.

She went to Michigan State University intending to be a teacher. "My grades were not high enough to transfer to the school of education, so I graduated as a sociology major. There were few job openings for people with a college degree in sociology, so I worked as a legal secretary in a Washington law firm."

Two years later, Gabor returned to school for a two-year sign-language interpreting program at the Rochester Institute of Technology, in New York. There, for the next two years, she interpreted for deaf students attending Rochester. As a result of the repetitive movement necessary in sign language, however, Gabor injured her right hand.

"I adored interpreting," says Gabor. "Except for my injury, I would still be in it. My other passion was cooking, particularly baking. My father's mother, who is Hungarian, was a superb baker, and I learned from her."

"When I was growing up, food was a big thing in our house. My parents love to try new and different things. To my father, food is a big social event. He feels a meal should last at least two hours."

When Gabor looked around for a new career, she found that the hand and arm motions used in cooking and baking

"I enjoyed food and beverage management. It permitted me to work in a restaurant, yet not deal directly with the preparation of food."

differ from the hand muscles needed to sign, so her previous injury wasn't an issue. Rejected for insufficient work experience on her first try for admission to the Culinary Institute of America, Gabor was accepted in the cooking program at Johnson & Wales University (www.jwu.edu), which has its main campus in Providence, R.I., and satellite campuses in Charleston, S.C., Vail, Colo., Miami, Fla., and Norfolk, Va.

Her preference was its Vail, Colo., campus, so that she could go to school and ski, but enrollment there was closed. With a partial scholarship, she spent one year at Johnson & Wales' campus in Miami, Fla. Afterward. she tried the Culinary Institute again, was accepted as a baking and pastry student and attended for a year. Her real interest is baking. "I'm an okay cook, but a great baker."

Her first baking job was at the Greenbrier, a luxury resort hotel in West Virginia. Gabor found the Greenbrier to have a rather structured work environment that did not suit her independent temperament. Even though she describes herself as a passionate baker, she wanted to do something more with her career in food service than bake.

The next year, one of the Greenbrier's executive chefs asked her to join him on the staff of Eli's Tavern, a soon-to-be-opened restaurant at a West Virginia ski resort. As general manager, Gabor had responsibilities for purchasing, hiring, handling the payroll, and training the staff in the use of computerized point-of-sale equipment. "I was making $40,000 a year at Eli's. It sounds like good pay, but it wasn't so great considering that I was putting in ten- to 12-hour days. Compare this with the wait staff, who made about $60,000, including tips, and had no other responsibilities.

"I now realized that I no longer wanted to be a baker, chef, or caterer working on the cooking line in a kitchen. At Eli's I enjoyed food and beverage management. It permitted me to work in a restaurant, yet not deal directly with the preparation of food on a daily basis. This does not mean that I no longer wanted to bake."

As a result of some ownership problems beyond her control, Eli's didn't make it past the first year and once again Gabor was back on the job market. After months of job searching, she introduced herself to a prospective employer by sending a résumé to a professional Web site (www.pastrywiz.com). Six weeks later she got a response from the owners of the Green River Inn, in western Vermont. After visiting and negotiating, they offered her the position of resident manager.

Green River Inn has 14 bedrooms and a 35-seat restaurant. Gabor worked a split shift. In the morning, she was responsible for breakfast, which satisfied her creative interest in baking and pastry. She had the afternoon off and returned to run the inn and restaurant at night, and helped the chef prepare the dinner pastries. An avid skier, Gabor had anticipated spending her free time skiing, but her hopes weren't fulfilled. After Christmas, the chef resigned and Gabor substituted in the kitchen. Two months later, she left, too, having tired of the chaotic seven-day-a-week work schedule at the Inn and her previous kitchen jobs.

In April 2001, she was hired by Opus 2 (www.opus2.com), a management consulting and software firm in Portsmouth, N.H., that specializes in the restaurant, hotel, and leisure and entertainment industries. Although she spends two weeks each month visiting with clients, Gabor says that she is excited to use her culinary know-how without having to work weekends and holidays.

HER BUSINESS SKILLS ARE RELEVANT

Linda Besse
FROM GEOLOGIST TO REALTOR TO WILDLIFE ARTIST

Wildlife artist Linda Besse, now in her early 40s, strives for realism in her paintings. She starts by observing and taking photos of animals in their natural habitat, whether it is Africa, Central America, Iceland, or Yellowstone National Park. The spirit of adventure reflected in her work is a far cry from her youth in East Providence, R.I., where her father was an Episcopal minister and her mother a lab technician. But Besse did relish vivid stories her great uncle told of his exploring and hunting animals in Africa.

As a student at Colgate University, Besse enrolled in a geology course to meet the school's science requirement, but got hooked. She majored in geology, and went on to graduate school at the University of Eastern Washington to prepare for a career as a hard-rock geologist, finding and helping to develop sources of such minerals as gold, silver, copper, lead, zinc and titanium.

"By the time I had my master's degree in 1985, the price of gold had plunged from its high of $800 an ounce, and so had job opportunities for hard-rock geologists."

Meanwhile, in 1984 she married James Olson, also a geologist whom she met at a mining conference. Geologists rarely have a sedentary life. They work onsite, often for months at a time. "My husband was on assignment in Alaska.

I flew up to see him. We sat on the side of a mountain and talked about what I could do. If we both worked as geologists, we would be so far apart that we'd never see each other."

With few jobs in her field, Besse made a 180-degree career change. She decided to be a real estate broker in

"I'm a self-taught artist who relies on field sketches and photographs to create my paintings."

Spokane, where the couple already had a home.

"I knew nothing about real estate. I had always lived in rectories; my parents did not own their own home. I liked the flexibility in real estate sales of not having to work a 9-to-5 day. If I wanted to take time off when Jim was home or spend time with him on locations I could do it." What's more, real estate sales represented a challenge, a career that Besse had never considered.

Besse took a few real estate courses and was licensed in the mid 1980s. Until she left real estate in 1999, she worked for the same Spokane firm as a commissioned broker. Meanwhile, Olson continued to travel extensively, but by 1992, he, too, tired of a peripatetic life, and went to work as a self-employed general building contractor. By then, he and Besse had designed and built themselves a 4,000-square-foot home in Mead, a small town a few miles north of Spokane. "This experience helped me as a broker," said Besse. "Unlike most brokers, I knew intimate details about home construction that helped in dealing with customers."

In 1996, when the couple were on vacation in Hawaii, Besse saw an artist at work in a small town. "And for some reason he caught my attention. I had never had any previous interest in painting nor did I ever have a hobby other than singing in church choirs or chorales. The closest I had ever got to drawing was in high school biology, when the teacher asked us to draw a fetal pig or starfish. I'd create elaborate drawings and every part was a different color."

Returning home, Besse bought art supplies and set out to teach herself oil painting. Besse took six, two-hour lessons in Spokane, the only instruction she has had. After that, she decided to learn by trial and error. "I'm a self-taught artist who relies on field sketches and photographs to create my paintings."

"At first, I did two or three paintings a year, and I didn't see much real development. I would go to wildlife art shows in Seattle, and see what other artists were doing and how they were doing it. I found the artists very helpful. They were willing to share their professional experiences with me."

Over the next two years, Besse developed a technique of drawing on untempered, gessoed hardboard, sealing it with a turpentine wash, and painting directly on the board.

"I was fortunate to meet Gamini Ratnavira, originally from Sri Lanka, an incredible naturalist, who now lives in California. I bought one of his paintings at a wildlife art show. He offered to look at photos of my work. I sent pictures of my paintings that he critiqued. Gamini was instrumental in my technical development and in suggesting where I should show my work."

"If I was going to switch careers, I wanted to do it before I was 40. I also knew that I did not want to be selling homes forever."

By 1998, painting was more than a casual pursuit. She worked 60 hours a week in real estate and other another 40 hours at her painting, but she had decided that art was her passion. It was time to make a career choice. "If I was going to switch careers, I wanted to do it before I was 40. I also knew that I did not want to be selling homes forever."

Besse left real estate in mid 1999, but she still maintains ties in the field and makes a few thousand dollars a year in commissions by passing along referrals to brokers from previous customers who want to buy or sell a home. At the time she left, she was making between

$60,000 and $70,000 a year, considered a good income from real estate commissions in Spokane, where home values are not overly inflated.

"When I announced that I was leaving the business, I was the number-one sales performer in the office. The other brokers in the office were surprised at my decision. Everyone who leaves the industry seems to do so because they aren't doing any business."

It has been two years since Besse became a full-time artist. She expects within the next few years, according to her business plan, to equal what she earned as a Realtor. To launch her new career, she had few capital expenses other than the cost of the 700-square-foot studio with a 14-foot ceiling and skylight, which her husband built for her. Most of her operating expenses consist of purchasing art supplies, going on trips to photograph wild animals, advertising in art magazines, and attending art shows, which cost up to $1,500 a show.

"I don't have an agent; I'm my own business manager. Unlike a lot of artists who are horrible at marketing themselves, I like it. I handle my own public relations. Many of the things I do to promote my art, I used in the real estate business. I mail a full-color newsletter at least four times a year to about 800 people, some of whom were past real estate customers."

Besse created her own Web site (www.besseart.com), but she has a Webmaster to maintain and update the site every three weeks.

Besse finds that it's hard to draw an anatomically correct animal from memory, and she prefers to observe animals in their natural habitat. The animals in a zoo, she says, are less aggressive and heavier than animals in the wild, and zoo animals "carry themselves differently." In the past two years she has traveled to South Africa, Guatemala, Belize, and Iceland. On each trip, she uses a field camera and zoom lens, and shoots about 30 rolls of film of animals and the terrain.

Besse is her own business manager, and she spends one day each week on business-related chores.

Field trips provide excitement as well as some danger; she has dodged armed skirmishes among the locals and has tracked leopards. In Zimbabwe she learned that hippos kill more people in Africa than any other animals.

Her paintings range in size from 6 by 9 inches, priced at $500, to 2 feet by 3 feet, costing about $6,500. Besse also sells up to 75 signed and numbered copies of her work, reproduced by a printing process that is equivalent in printing quality to lithographs. This "giclee" printing process uses digital imaging to make the prints. Prints are priced at 10% of what an original painting would cost.

Besse works six days a week. Unlike some artists, she works on only one painting at a time. It takes her about one week to do a large painting, and she creates about 40 paintings a year. One day each week is spent on business-related chores—going to framers, buying supplies, preparing her newsletter and advertisements, getting ready for art shows or negotiating with studios to display her paintings.

Using Your Skills in Nonprofits

WANT MORE OUT OF JOB THAN A PAYCHECK." "I'D LIKE TO make better use of my talents working for an organization that is mission-driven." "I'm burned out and I'm bored." These are some of the comments that Jane Kendall hears from job seekers and career changers. As president of the North Carolina Center for Nonprofits (www.ncnonprofits.org), she routinely fields questions from managers and professionals who want to switch from corporate America to the nonprofit field. Their central theme, also often heard by outplacement consultants and career coaches, is that they want more *meaningful* employment.

A similar message appears in *The Street Lawyer*, John Grisham's fictional account of the migration of Michael Brock, a 32-year-old antitrust lawyer, from a large Washington law firm where he was making $120,000 to a $30,000 job in a three-person legal clinic helping the homeless.

The nonprofit sector operates under a number of different names: the not-for-profit sector, the third sector, the independent sector, the philanthropic sector, the voluntary sector, or the social sector. According to the National Center for Nonprofit Boards (www.ncnb.org), the nonprofit sector grows steadily at an annual rate of 4% to 6%.

Approximately 1.1 million nonprofits—hospitals, colleges and universities, museums, public radio and television stations, and social-welfare agencies classified by the Internal Revenue Service as eligible to receive tax-deductible charitable contribu-tions—employ more than ten million Americans, or 7% of the workforce. Nonprofits exclude churches and synagogues, which do not file with the IRS, as well as countless organi-zations that are too small to be officially required to file for tax-exempt status.

A Demanding Career Path

Employment opportunities in the nonprofit field are as varied as those in the private sector, and hiring practices differ by agency. A large metropolitan hospital employs teams of budget managers, publicists, and systems analysts, whereas administrative work at small nonprofit agencies is handled by the director alone or by the director and a handful of workers.

Life in a nonprofit agency is hardly a serene refuge from the hubbub and demands of the business world. Nonprofits endure continual money problems. According to the National Center for Nonprofit Boards, about 40% of the nonprofit sector's revenues are from dues and fees, about 30% from government grants and stipends, and the remainder from private contributions and miscellaneous sources. A legislative budget cut or a change in the types of projects a foundation will support sends shivers through the nonprofit community. As a result, non-profits can face continual budget shortfalls, which in practical terms means personnel cutbacks, leaner fringe benefits, smaller annual pay raises or salary freezes, inadequate facilities, and outdated equipment.

An Impressive Job Market With a Lower Pay Scale

Nonprofits need accountants, lawyers, publicists, marketers, and computer programmers, among other workers, but the pay isn't great for most nonprofit employees. According to a salary study by the North Carolina Center for Nonprofits, the typical college graduate who goes to work full-time for a North Carolina nonprofit earns $29,000 a year, 34% below the national average wage in business, 15% below the average government salary, and 8% below the average nonprofit salary nationally.

The national salary average for nonprofit directors hovers around $75,000. The Community Resource Exchange (www .crenyc.org), which provides management assistance to nonprofits, found that the executive director of a small to medium-size group in New York City earns on average $62,000; the fund-raiser, $59,000; the controller, $58,000; and the information-systems manager, $43,000. According to the 2000 salary survey of *The Chronicle of Philanthropy* (http:// philanthropy.com), these findings contrast sharply with the median pay of $225,000 paid to the CEOs at the nation's 240 largest nonprofits.

An Easy Transition From the For-Profit Sector

The transition from the private to the nonprofit sector is not difficult, as long as a job applicant follows a few guidelines. In the private sector, marketers often get promoted to top corporate jobs up to and including that of chief executive officer. Similarly, in the nonprofit sector, directors need to demonstrate a proven fund-raising record, which is a form of marketing. Just read the job descriptions for the heads of colleges and universities, social-service agencies, and even public libraries. To be sure, scholars become university presidents, but it is their fund-raising abilities that usually pluck them from the academic ranks. No wonder social-service workers and educators who aim for promotion learn early in their careers how to raise money. While there's no official rite of passage, up-and-comers in higher education with an eye toward jobs in college administration show their stuff as faculty members by repeatedly obtaining grants and endowments for their academic programs.

Managers and professionals require little special training. Other than having a familiarity with the laws that govern nonprofits, a corporate lawyer needs little additional schooling to qualify for a nonprofit legal position. It's even simpler for a computer-systems analyst or Webmaster, where the skills are more portable. Similar ground rules apply to financial managers, publicists, and fund-raisers.

Entry-level caseworkers in a nonprofit social-service agency usually qualify for employment with an undergraduate degree in social work. Museums hire college fine-arts majors, but promotion to a prestigious job as a curator normally requires a graduate degree. Libraries often seek employees with a master's in library science.

Want to become a fund-raiser? One approach to take while you're still working in corporate America is to become a nonprofit board member.

Want to become a fund-raiser? One approach to take while you're still working in corporate America is to become a nonprofit board member, a route taken by Richard Schneyer, who is profiled in this chapter.

For a practical look at the qualifications needed to land a nonprofit job, read the ten to 12 pages of employment advertisements in *The Chronicle of Philanthropy.*

Careers in fund-raising are spelled out via the Association of Fundraising Professionals (www.nsfre.org), formerly the National Society of Fund Raising Executives.

For specific information on social work, visit these Web sites:
- **the National Association of Social Workers** (www.naswdc.org)
- **the Council on Social Work Education** (www.cswe.org)
- **the Association of Social Works Boards** (www.aswb.org) for information on state licensing.

Learn the Basics

There are some surefire ways to get your foot in the door of the nonprofit world. As is true of so many other fields, it's best to start as a volunteer, where you'll have a chance to learn the ropes and be disabused of any romantic notions. It's an opportunity to see firsthand how nonprofits operate, and how the jobs differ from comparable ones in the private sector. Eventually, you might become a trustee or a committee member of a small to midsize nonprofit, most of which have trouble attracting volunteers.

If you want more hands-on experience, volunteer for a job essential to the agency's mission—say, as a driver for Meals on Wheels or a reader to the blind. Whatever the assignment, it's a chance to test the waters without making a commitment.

The Nonprofit Information Center (www.ncnonprofits .org/infocenter.html) provides insight into some tactics for productive volunteering:

- **Research the areas of interest** that parallel your interests.
- **Consider the skills you have to offer.** If you enjoy outdoor work, have a knack for teaching, or like to interact with people, seek volunteer work that incorporates these interests into an assignment.
- **Want to learn some new skills?** Perhaps your goal is to switch from corporate sales to nonprofit publicity and communications. As a starter, volunteer to edit the newsletter or write news releases.
- **Don't get overcommitted.** A manager with a heavy travel schedule should avoid volunteer assignments that conflict with weekday workplace demands. Good intentions backfire when a volunteer fails to show up for work. A sound alternative is the weekend volunteer.

Susan Ellis runs Energize, Inc. (www.energizeinc.com), a Philadelphia-based consulting firm that specializes in training volunteers. Ellis has some suggestions for wannabe career changers:

- **Decide whether you want to be a cog in a large organization** or a key player in a smaller agency.
- **Volunteer with several organizations** as a way to judge how comfortable you are with the work in each. If you are personally uncomfortable dealing with homeless or mentally retarded people, it makes no sense to work for an agency that deals with such clients.
- **Don't limit your volunteer search to large institutions,** such as hospitals, libraries, and churches. It makes more sense to volunteer in a smaller agency where it is easier to be elected to the board, do hands-on work, and become familiar with the agency's operations. Many newspapers publish weekly listings of agencies that need volunteers, such as day care centers,

community theaters, civil-rights agencies, drug rehabilitation or mental-health centers, soup kitchens, prisons, shelters for battered women and children, public schools, recreational centers, historical restoration, or retirement centers.

Volunteer experience gives career changers the opportunity to include such activities on their résumé. A career changer who has been a board member or a volunteer newsletter editor or a financial adviser offers any other nonprofit organization practical experience and job-related credentials. Moreover, trustees and staff members are possible job references.

There is even a virtual way to become a volunteer. The Virtual Volunteering Project (www.serviceleader.org/vv/), located on the University of Texas campus in Austin, has developed a program that allows people to volunteer via their home or office computer. This is one way to build up volunteer credits and experience prior to making the plunge. Virtual volunteers are shut-ins, college students, and professionals and managers who may be too busy to take a break from workplace duties. Their assignments range from researching and writing articles for brochures, newsletters, and Web sites; providing online mentoring to schoolchildren; or supervising a non-profit's online chatroom.

A word of caution: Do not volunteer with the idea that the agency will be a future employer. The idea is to obtain non-

---

POINTS TO REMEMBER

- **Supporting** an organiza-tion's mission is the point.
- **The nonprofit sector** produces annual revenues in excess of $650 billion.
- **The pay in a nonprofit** is considerably lower than that in the private sector.
- **Volunteering** is a good way to learn the ropes.

It can even be done online.
- **Learn about nonprofits** at workshops and in contin-uing education courses.
- **Nonprofits need man-agers** and professionals with strong business skills.
- **Corporate and profes-sional skills** are transfer-able to the nonprofit sector.

profit experience, not to audition for a new job. Even so, a board member is occasionally recruited as an agency's new director or a volunteer publicist may be recruited as the staff communications manager.

Nonprofit Management Courses

Experts advise career changers to take courses in nonprofit management. Fifteen years ago there was little to nothing available in this area, but the growth in nonprofits has spurred the development of continuing-education programs for nonprofit managers. Start by searching continuing-education Web sites at larger universities. The menu at New York University's Center for Philanthropy and Fundraising (www.scps.nyu.edu /dyncon/phil), for example, consists of courses in nonprofit accounting, marketing, fund-raising, law, and Web-site development that can be taken individually or packaged into a certificate program. A typical NYU course, which costs between $400 and $600, meets six to ten evenings in sessions of two hours or longer.

Duke University (www.learnmore.duke.edu) takes its nonprofit courses on the road, presenting workshops in 12 of North Carolina's largest metropolitan centers. A typical workshop consists of a single three- to four-hour session costing $36 to $72. Duke's curriculum features courses on how to write grants, work with the Spanish-speaking community, lobby, direct an agency, and manage a database. Students who pass approximately 8 to 10 qualifying courses receive certificates in nonprofit management.

Some People Who Made the Change

The career changers who are profiled in this chapter were propelled into nonprofit work by a desire to have jobs where their contributions would make a difference in other people's lives. It was this altruism that they couldn't satisfy in their previous careers. I hesitate to call them idealists, because that word is sometimes taken to mean a lack of practicality, but they do convey an idealistic spirit in their attitude toward their work. They know that they could use their skills to make more money, but they feel that what they now do "at the office" makes nonprofit work worthwhile. In addition, they tap the skills they have learned in previous careers for their nonprofit assignments.

MAKING AFFORDABLE HOMES

Bob Calhoun
BUILDING FOR PROFIT AND BUILDING FOR PASSION

From 1980 to 1992, Bob Calhoun, now in his late 40s, ran a small construction company in Chapel Hill, N.C., but despite his success, Calhoun was not completely satisfied with the direction that his work was taking him. His goal was a career that would let him blend his spiritual needs with his skills in construction. He found the answer at Habitat for Humanity.

Calhoun's company, Design & Construction, worked for high-end, upscale housing consumers. "I was becoming increasingly dissatisfied with the social and environmental realities in my construction work. Furthermore, the religious and spiritual principles I desired to follow were inconsistent with my work. What drew me to volunteer with Habitat for Humanity gave me the strength for the leap of faith into a new field."

Calhoun started in construction as a carpentry subcontractor while he was a student at Florida State University. After graduation, he had a brief stint working for an architect-builder in Durham, N.C., and spent two years studying architecture at the University of Florida before he realized that he was more interested in construction than design.

Calhoun and his wife, Pauletta, returned to Durham, and started Design & Construction, which specialized in building mid- to high-priced homes and an occasional commercial facility. At its peak, the company employed about 25 craft workers.

In the mid 1980s, Calhoun's social consciousness came to the fore. "I get my social conscience from my mother, a social worker, and my interest in building from my father." To have a change of

"What drew me to volunteer with Habitat for Humanity gave me the strength for the leap of faith into a new field."

pace and to put his convictions to the test, he volunteered with a Habitat for Humanity operation.

By the early 1990s, Calhoun decided to take a paid job as construction manager with the Durham Habitat affiliate. "At the time, Habitat had a three-person staff. I didn't know how I would like working as a full-time Habitat employee, so I decided to test the waters for a year. I officially closed my own firm, but legally it existed on paper for a year or so more."

Making the transition from commercial to nonprofit work would mean a cut in income, so some hard decisions had to be made. "Pauletta and I consulted with our two children (at the time, ages 10 and 14). I told them that my new job meant that they could no longer go to Carolina Friends School and that we would be selling our vacation home in Florida." Family income would further decline, when Pauletta, a nurse, became ill and had to leave her job.

To supplement his salary, Calhoun continued to do some consulting and design work. Two years later his Habitat duties increased, requiring all his time. A staged salary increase was arranged so that he could continue as a full-time Habitat staffer.

When Habitat's director resigned in 1994, Calhoun was named as his successor.

"By then, I had discovered that I brought a number of related skills to Habitat. I already knew how to work with customers and suppliers. And, no different from my home-construction days, Habitat runs three different companies that do land development, construction, and finance. We have to conform to the same codes and regulations as any other builder, even though we seem to operate on what I like to call 'biblical economics,' that is, our ability to turn a little into a lot."

There are some differences in how Calhoun now manages. No longer an independent builder, Calhoun reports to a board of directors, but he feels that his experience has bearing. "I knew how nonprofit boards operate, since I had served on a number of them." In this capacity, he also learned some of the basics of fund-raising. His Habitat

workday, however, is divided between managing an agency with a several-million-dollar budget, and raising funds to support the operation.

Since its founding in 1985, Habitat in Durham has built more than 100 homes, and it is committed to build another 40 to 50 homes over the next few years. It now has a $2-million budget; within the Habitat family of 1,500 affiliates in the U.S., only 15 other groups have constructed more homes.

The entire staff has changed since

"We seem to operate on what I like to call 'biblical economics,' that is, our ability to turn a little into a lot."

1994. Turnover at times can be rampant, because staff members have skills that are in demand, and industry and sometimes even other nonprofits can afford to pay more for those skills. Calhoun seeks staff members like himself who have worked in construction or in corporate America but prefer to work in a nonprofit environment where they can support the organization's mission.

"When we have a job opening, we advertise and receive a huge number of résumés from people who want to switch into the nonprofit field. Since Habitat is well known, we also attract many curiosity seekers." Calhoun looks for applicants who have related work skills and have been volunteers either with Habitat or other nonprofits. That experience gives them insight into the difference between a nonprofit's mission, where there is no motive to make a profit, and the private sector, where profit dictates nearly all management decisions.

In recent years, Calhoun has found his answer in people like Mary Brown, who worked for 20 years in General Motors Acceptance Corp.'s mortgage operations. When GM closed its local office, Brown was job hunting, and her skills made her suited to head Habitat's mortgage section. Prior to joining Habitat as its new projects director, Gene Cook worked at Disneyworld, in Orlando, as a maintenance and construction electrician, for Orange County, Fla., in construction administration, and as a volunteer for Habitat. Brenda Fennell previously worked in Washington, D.C.,

as a volunteer coordinator, using the same skills to supervise a pool of more than 5,000 Habitat volunteers.

Bill Wissmer retired from the Navy as a supply officer, then worked as a financial consultant before he became Habitat's fiscal officer. "He knew about fiscal controls, but I had to teach him how to apply them to home construction."

Even with Habitat's excellent reputation, it isn't easy for Calhoun to recruit volunteers. He finds that people with strong design or construction skills often view working for Habitat as a form of busman's holiday. Thus the agency has to recruit, educate, and train nonskilled and do-it-yourself amateurs to be volunteers.

Calhoun is often asked by business and professional people how they can get into nonprofit work. "When I wear a Habitat T-shirt on vacation, I advertise what I do for a living."

PROTECTING WOMEN

Margaret Barrett

BEING A LAWYER WAS NEVER ENOUGH

A few years back, Margaret Barrett, now in her mid 30s, attended a workshop for university women educators and administrators in which the participants were rquired to write a personal mission statement. Her statement shows what motivates her and points to the direction her career would take.

"I want to motivate others to achieve their dreams, while working with them to reach our common goals. I want to take time to reflect about what I'm doing, and to nurture relationships that are more important to me. I want to simplify complex issues for people and to help them get through times of difficulty, while dealing with them in an honest and straightforward manner."

Barrett is a native North Carolinian, reared in Buies Creek, a small town between Raleigh and Fayetteville. After graduating from the University of North Carolina in 1987, she went to Europe. "I had never been abroad before. I got a work permit, a job bartending in London, and I traveled. It was a chance to get ready for the next part of my career."

As a UNC political science major, Barrett had taken a number of courses in women's issues and was a campus activist. Going to law school seemed like a natural step, but she wasn't particularly sure that she wanted to be a practicing attorney. Nonetheless, law school won

out in her personal debate. At UNC's School of Law, Barrett wasn't especially interested in business or corporate law. She focused on courses in child custody, immigration issues, and divorce and family law. She organized campus seminars and conferences on "women in the law." And she volunteered with

"I want to simplify complex issues for people and to help them get through times of difficulty, while dealing with them in an honest and straightforward manner."

Helpline, an organization serving a number of local agencies, including the local Rape Crisis Center, which provided invaluable on-the-job training for the future. Law school taught her how to keep an open mind on issues, and how to deal effectively with people, critical skills in her future jobs.

As is customary with law students, Barrett spent her summers as an intern, and although this work failed to give her specific career direction, she found that she was interested in working in higher education with students or in a job related to public issues.

When Barrett graduated in 1991 from UNC Law, she took a job with the Charlottesville Group, in Charlottesville, Va., which employed 80 lawyers to conduct research and write legal memorandums for other lawyers throughout the U.S. But she found that the job ultimately ran counter to her earlier career ambitions.

By then, she had married Craig Carlson, a social-studies teacher, and after 18 months in Virginia, they were eager to return to Chapel Hill.

"I applied for four jobs in higher education. It took me five months to get a job at UNC. I was hired as assistant dean of students and a judicial-programs officer. My boss, Fred Schroeder, felt that my legal training would be an ideal asset, since many of the issues I'd be dealing with had legal or semilegal aspects."

Eighteen months into the job, Schroeder retired as dean and Barrett was named acting dean. Her legal training helped her to come to grips with student-related issues. "I was not called upon to be a decision-maker, but to be an adviser to decision-makers. Being a lawyer, I challenged students to look at their different options, and to arrive at their own decisions, which, of course, is a key part of the Socratic method that lawyers use."

Barrett knew that she would not be named permanent dean at UNC, and neither she nor her husband wanted to relocate so that she could get a similar job at another college. Taking that direction would mean constant moving, a treadmill that she wanted to avoid. Also, she was tiring of the bureaucracy in a university with 24,000 undergraduate, graduate, and professional students.

Barrett decided to stay at UNC one more year while searching for a job in the nonprofit sector. Meanwhile, she reasoned that it would be wise to learn something more about nonprofits and how they operate. "Before I had the chance to take a single course in non-profit management, I called the Orange County Rape Crisis Center to see

Barrett had to learn new skills in managing finance, raising funds, managing volunteers, and directing a six-person staff.

whether I could do an internship with them. I was told that the director was leaving, and they were looking for a new director. I researched the job and found that it was a perfect match for me." The center's board concurred, and Barrett became director in September 1999.

Barrett had to learn new skills in managing finance, raising funds, managing volunteers, and directing a six-person staff, which operates centers in Chapel Hill and nearby Hillsborough.

Her salary is about the same as it was at UNC, but Barrett no longer receives a benefits package comparable to the one at her former job. "Compared with my UNC workday, where I was all over the board, I am now more focused, because the Rape Crisis Center has a single mission. I continue to use the Socratic method with my staff. I challenge them to produce the answers." At the Rape Crisis Center, Barrett is a key decision-maker, in contrast to her UNC days, when she was a cog in a large organization.

SIMPLY SIMULTALENTED

Murray Decock
HOCKEY PROFESSIONAL, PIANIST AND FUND-RAISER

Murray Decock, a Canadian from Winnipeg, Manitoba, who is now in his early 40s, started playing the piano when he was 11—late for anyone with ambitions to be a serious concert musician. "I performed piano recitals between age 12 and 17, and entered competitions in Winnipeg. Most of the time I finished second to some fellow who would eventually go to Juilliard. Hockey was my *real* interest." Decock was a good enough hockey player to receive an athletic scholarship to Colgate University, in Hamilton, N.Y. Until then, Decock had thought little about a college education.

In his first year at Colgate, Decock played hockey and practiced the piano an hour a day just to unwind.

"By January of my freshman year, a piano teacher who heard me play offered me independent-study credit for the spring semester if I would give a recital in May. I probably worked harder for that recital than for any course I took that spring. Lodged in the back of my mind was the thought of a music major and a possible musical career. During my first year, I learned how to balance hockey and piano."

Hockey, however, never took a back seat. Besides majoring in music and English literature, Decock played varsity hockey for four years and in 1980 was drafted and signed as a free agent by the Winnipeg Jets. Over the next two seasons, Decock played with several minor league teams in Tulsa and Fort Wayne, Ind.

Decock began to realize that his professional hockey career would be brief and that he'd never play for a

"I had to look at different options if we were to continue living in an area we both liked."

National Hockey League team. He was hired by the Trinity-Pawling Preparatory School, a boarding school in upstate New York, to coach hockey, teach Shakespeare, and direct the school's musical. He might have stayed at Trinity-Pawling longer, but he married a Colgate classmate, Sally Campbell, and was then accepted into Indiana University's graduate music program.

Decock was hired as an associate instructor at Indiana, so that his tuition was paid along with a stipend, a critical factor since both Decocks were attending graduate school. After earning his master's degree, he entered the University of Maryland's doctoral program in music. "While working for my doctorate, I also taught piano, tended bar in

Gettysburg, and picked cherries to pay the bills." Sally found work as a college administrator at Beaver College in southern Pennsylvania.

Sally left Beaver in the mid 1980s and went to Colgate as the dean of freshmen students. Decock commuted from Maryland to upstate New York while completing the doctoral course-work. He received his doctorate degree in the mid 1990s.

By now, Decock had become skilled at pursuing dual careers in music and coaching hockey. Relocating to Colgate to join Sally, he coached the Hamilton Central High School hockey team to several league championships, taught piano at Colgate, and served as a concert soloist, assistant conductor, and accompanist with the university's orchestra.

"When I was escorting the Colgate orchestra on a 1992 European concert trip, our first gig in Rome was a late-afternoon mass in St. Peter's Basilica. One of the monsignors who saw me sitting at the organ asked me to play the processional and recessional music on the organ for the cardinals and the Pope. The monsignor helped me with the all of the registrations on the organ, since I was essentially a pianist, and he made me sound like a pro. It was one of the most amazing moments of my musical life. He couldn't speak English and I couldn't speak Italian. We did all of this by body language. At the end of the concert, he gave me the traditional three-cheek kiss of congratulations."

By the mid 1990s, Decock's career took another turn. Up to then, his wife's salary had been the prime source of income, but Sally was burned out from job counseling and advising students, and she wanted to stay home with the couple's two children, Sam, then five, and Lucy, three (Charlie was born in 1996). "What was I going to do? Colgate had a rather small career track for a musician, so I had to look at different options if we were to continue living in an area we both liked."

"The technical side of fund-raising is easy to learn. My ability to talk athletics, arts, and literature gave me credibility with the alumni and faculty."

To be on the safe side, Decock investigated other job opportunities. "Most were at mediocre schools that combined six or seven different jobs. I got one job offer at a prep school, but it required that we live as a family in a dorm for seven years. No way!"

When an opening occurred in Colgate's development office, Decock took it, even though he knew little about fund-raising. "It had less to do with raising money, and more to do with selling Colgate. I found Colgate an easy concept to sell. The technical side of fund-raising is easy to learn. My ability to talk athletics, arts, and literature gave me credibility with the alumni and faculty. Truthfully, I'm not sure I would have been out off the block so fast at a different college. Now I feel I can do this work anywhere."

Decock was promoted to director of Colgate's Annual Fund with a salary that equaled his wife's former pay. "Sally had been making $15,000 more a year than I made in my first fund-raising job." Three years later he was promoted to director of development.

Decock finds certain similarities among classical music, hockey, and fund-raising: "Music and hockey both require daily workouts, and all three require the ability to set goals. From music, I learned to pay attention to detail, and the ability to start with something that is brand new, in the form of a musical piece, learn it and perfect it, and to complete the task by a specific date. Similar skills are necessary in fund-raising."

But there are differences. A hockey player and a musician get use to an audience's ovation for a job well done. "One doesn't get the same recognition and approval in a staff position, where you do the work in the name of others."

BRINGING COMPUTERS TO THE CLASSROOM

Bonnie Moore
FROM THE NEWSROOM TO A NICHE NONPROFIT AGENCY

Bonnie Moore, now in her early 50s, believes that in the darkest moments of despair, one can find inspiration. For Moore such an event took place in the early 1980s following her divorce. She was determined to get a job, and, as a single mother raising her two young sons, she could have found a "safe" job using her training as a special education teacher, but she wanted more of a challenge.

Moore, a native of St. Mary, W.Va., is a graduate of Marshall University, with majors in special education and speech and communications. She taught school in West Virginia for several years while putting her husband through dental school. They moved to Durham, where he would work.

When she was divorced, Moore decided she wanted to "be a TV babe. I'd even work for nothing to get started. I told employers to give me a shot and let me learn the business. I just wanted in." Her first interview was at WTVD in Durham, owned at the time by Capital Cities Broadcasting and subsequently, as a result of two acquisitions, by ABC and Disney.

Impressed with Moore's tenacity, a good work habit in news-gathering organizations, "WTVD gave me a job and a chance to learn the news business. When I left the first day for work, my older son said that he was happy for me, but wondered why I wanted to go to work when other mothers stay home."

Starting in the mid 1980s, Moore spent the next 15 years in the newsroom and eventually was put in charge of all newsroom assignments for a 65-person team of photographers, reporters, and a helicopter crew.

"Is this what life is all about? I wanted a job where I could feel some soul."

"Although I was a newcomer to TV news, I learned to be cool. I became a good peacemaker, and I was able to get people to do things they did not want to do.

"It was tough at first. Some of the people in the newsroom treated me as a cross between a Junior Leaguer and a Betty Crocker type from the suburbs. Fortunately, I found a mentor, Lynn Wilson, who taught me how to read a news report, showed me the ropes by taking me to police headquarters, and taught me how to 'work the telephone' to set up interviews and get information from news sources."

By the late 1990s, Moore started to feel that she wanted to leave TV news.

A blizzard on January 25, 2000, that produced a 24-inch snowfall unheard of in central North Carolina clinched her decision. Moore went to work at 1:30 A.M., and she was still in the newsroom 18 hours later. "Is this what life is all about? I wanted a job where I could feel some soul. I wanted to use my know-how to help others meet their challenges in life. By then, I felt the huge burnout factor of my newsroom work. It was time to move on and try something different."

Moore started her job search by networking with people who she had met over the past 15 years in TV. Less than a month later, ExplorNet, a Raleigh-based nonprofit, offered her a job that was based on her newsroom experience but that paid less than television. Explor-Net (www.explornet.org) was started by a former WTVD reporter, along with several others from the same TV station,

with a goal of equipping schools with computers, and providing computer training for students and teachers. It planned to recycle older equipment, but after working for several months on a trial run of a project that failed to get funding, Moore was named to direct an ExplorNet program that trains teachers in North Carolina to incorporate computers into their lesson plans.

"In my new job, I no longer boss 65 people, but I found that many of my newsroom skills were transferable. I know how to get others to do work that they don't want to do, and I'm skilled in instant problem solving. TV also taught me how to open doors to set up news interviews—that is, to learn how to reach people, interest them in an inter-view and get it done—but it also made me impatient. I still get annoyed when people don't return my calls."

PART OF A UNIVERSITY TEAM

Richard Schneyer

BANKING GAVE HIM A LEG UP IN NONPROFITS

Richard Schneyer, who is now in his late 40s, graduated from the State University of New York in New Paltz in 1973 and began his banking career began with a 21-month training program at Chase Manhattan Bank, which was followed by another four years in branch banking. "In 1977, New York City was going through some rough financial times. Chase, which built up a network of branch banks and had been preaching the importance of decentralization, decided to reverse its strategy and move toward centralization. I saw my opportunities diminishing; it was time to move on."

Schneyer sent out résumés to banks in Houston and Denver, which were cities where he wanted to live. The Houston "vibes" were better and he was hired as a credit analyst with Southern National Bank. He spent the next 11 years there as a commercial-banking specialist. "Compared with Chase, which was huge, I could get my hands around my work at Southern National. I could make things happen."

In the late 1980s, the economy once again went sour, and Schneyer found himself laying off staff members, fore-closing on small family-owned businesses, and doing a lot of unpleasant work. "Industry mergers proved to be personally unsettling and counter-productive."

On evenings and weekends, Schneyer was a volunteer at Covenant House, the Houston branch of an organization of the same name that was started in New York City to help runaway kids. He helped these teenagers learn to write résumés and showed them how to prepare for the job market.

"I had the inside track on the job. I had been a volunteer and worker in Houston. I knew the organization, and what it did."

As a single man with manageable expenses, Schneyer began to consider new career alternatives. After discussing his ideas with friends, he decided to leave banking.

"Some people at Covenant House suggested that Spanish would be helpful if I was considering full-time work for nonprofits in Texas. I had taken Spanish in high school and college but my skills were rusty. After looking at my bank account, I decided I had enough money to quit my job. I thought about it over the weekend, and on Monday I gave notice. I had always seen the need to have a 'go to hell' fund, which gives you the freedom to walk away from a job. Tuesday was my last day on the job; Thursday I left for Guatemala for one month, a way to immerse myself in Spanish. I spent one month living with a family of very modest means. They had few possessions and yet they got by. Back in Texas, my friends and I were surrounded by material things."

When he returned to Houston, Schneyer needed a paying job, and he talked to some people at Covenant House. The development director asked him to do some research for a modest fee. "I had enough money to get by for the next six months, even though I would soon discover that it would take another six months to get a full-time job."

His Covenant House relationship increased to two full days a week and then to four days a week. The pay was poor, so Schneyer also worked four hours a day with a résumé service to pay his bills. To increase his scant knowledge of fund-raising techniques, he took courses conducted by the Houston chapter of the Association of Fund-raising Professionals.

Schneyer continued to look for full-time work. "In 1989, when I was reading the Sunday *New York Times*, I saw that Covenant House in New York wanted to hire a corporate and foundation development officer. The job sounded interesting, but I was ambivalent about returning to New York. But I had the inside track on the job. I had been a volunteer and worker in Houston. I knew the organization, and what it did."

A few months after Schneyer went to work in New York, scandal broke. Covenant House's finances and the role that its founder, Father Bruce Ritter, had played were suspect. By the following spring, the organization had dire financial troubles and Schneyer left.

Once again, he turned to the Association of Fundraising Professionals. "I was asked to run the job bank and résumé service for its upcoming convention in New York. As an insider, I read the notebook containing job openings. One was

He took courses conducted by the Houston chapter of the Association of Fundraising Professionals.

for the director of major gifts and planned giving for the Lighthouse for the Blind." Schneyer applied, was interviewed, and got the job raising funds to support the Lighthouse's education and self-help program for the blind.

In this and future jobs, Schneyer found that his past banking skills—motivating people, budgeting, talking to people about their financial assets, and knowing about the business—enabled him to speak with confidence to lawyers and accountants who advise their clients on charitable donations.

Going from banking to nonprofits initially meant a 60% pay cut. His income, however, has increased with each job.

He spent six years at the Lighthouse. "I would still be there if my immediate boss had not left, but he did and I had bad chemistry with his successor. This forced my hand to look for another job."

By this time, Schneyer had become a board member of the Association of Fundraising Professionals, and he heard that Columbia University's Graduate School of Journalism had a job opening. He applied, and became senior development officer, responsible for raising major financial donations from the school's 7,500 alumni.

Schneyer's fund-raising jobs, past and present, have some similarities and differences. The Lighthouse often required a gentler, more emotional approach, while Columbia's appeal to journalists and communications companies stressed the need for journalism education and Columbia's program in an enthusiastic, but no-nonsense style.

"I had to adjust my style to interest alumni who work in journalism or mass communications. It is somewhat intimida-ting to write a letter to an alumnus who won a Pulitzer prize, even if it is prepared for the dean's signature. You know the letter is being read with an editing pencil in hand."

After four years at the Journalism School, in September 2000, Schneyer was named the Law School's develop-

"When I first left banking, a friend said that I would 'soon be clawing my way to the top in a new career.' I am, and loving every day of it."

ment director, a job that offered him the opportunity to advance his career while remaining on the Columbia campus. "In accepting this position, I reflected on the comment of a close friend when I first left banking for nonprofit work that I would 'soon be clawing my way to the top in a new career.' I am, and loving every day of it."

Index